ISLAM, IRAN, and WORLD STABILITY

Also edited by Hamid Zangeneh

Modern Capitalism and Islamic Ideology in Iran
(with Cyrus Bina)

ISLAM, IRAN, and WORLD STABILITY

Edited by
Hamid Zangeneh

ST. MARTIN'S PRESS
NEW YORK

First published in the United States of America 1994

Printed in the United States of America

ISBN 0-312-12118-0

Library of Congress Cataloging-in-Publication Data

Islam, Iran, and world stability / edited by Hamid Zangeneh.
   p. cm.
  ISBN 0-312-12118-0
  1. Iran—Politics and government—1979– 2. Iran—Economic
conditions—1979– 3. Islam and world politics. I. Zangeneh,
Hamid.
DS318.825.I85 1994
955.05'4—dc20   94-6695
                         CIP

C·O·N·T·E·N·T·S

A·C·K·N·O·W·L·E·D·G·M·E·N·T·S

This book offers an empirical and theoretical discussion of Islam, Iran, and the world. Its intention is to open a dialogue among the interested parties. Even though each individual author discusses a topic in theory, the volume maintains a practical outlook for the seekers of peace, prosperity, and human dignity. While the seemingly festering domestic as well as international relations of the Islamic Republic are being examined, their regional and international implications are considered and analyzed. That is, while internal battles among different ruling factions of the Islamic Republic are being discussed, their ramifications for the economic and security interests of the United States, Europe, littoral states of the Persian Gulf, Egypt, Israel, and other countries are taken into account as well.

A work of this caliber could not have been accomplished without the help and assistance of many able scholars and friends. Among those who contributed to this endeavor, in one way or another, are Hossein Akhavi-Pour; Abbas Alnasrawi; Hooshang Amirahmadi; Sohrab Behdad; Cyrus Bina; Mehrzad Boroujerdi; Mohammad Derakhshesh and *Mehrgan* journal; Joseph DiAngelo, Jr.; Manoucher Dorraj; Nader Entessar; Rafat Fazeli; Reza Fazeli; Joseph P. Fuhr; Hamid Hosseini; Robert Looney; Ali Madani; Akbar Mahdi; Janice Moore; R. Niknam; Manoucher Parvin; Bernard J. Reily; Siamack Shojaei; Abdol Soofi; and Charles Waldauer.

I would like to thank the Economics Department and the School of Management of Widener University for their moral and material support. The support staff of my department provided invaluable assistance. I would like to thank, Cecilia Hrubovcak, Andrea M. Huchinson, Kay Veacock, and Ann Marie Kasarsky for their assistance. Kishore Tamidela's research assistance was appreciated. I was fortunate to have received the assistance of Frances E. Gray.

A special thank-you to Simon Winder, Senior Editor of the Scholarly and Reference Division at St. Martin's Press for his professionalism and efficiency. Also, Laura Heymann, Assistant Editor of the Scholarly and Reference Division at St. Martin's Press, provided guidance that was appreciated.

On a personal level, thanks to my wife, Janice, and my children Zacharia John and Parisa Marie for their support and patience.

N·O·T·E·S O·N C·O·N·T·R·I·B·U·T·O·R·S

EDITOR:
Hamid Zangeneh is Associate Professor of Economics at Widener University, Chester, Pennsylvania. He holds a Ph.D. in economics from the University of Missouri-Columbia. He served as the treasurer and as the executive director of the Center for Iranian Research and Analysis (CIRA). He is currently a treasurer and a board of director member of the Middle East Economic Association (MEEA). He has published on monetary economics, finance, Islamic banking, and the political economy of Iran in scholarly journals such as *Applied Economics, Quarterly Journal of Business and Economics, Journal of Economic Education, Journal of Research in Islamic Economics, Journal of Comparative Studies, The Journal of Economics and International Relations,* among others. He is the co-editor (with Cyrus Bina) of *Modern Capitalism and Islamic Ideology in Iran* (New York: St. Martin's Press, 1992).

OTHER CONTRIBUTORS:
Hossein Akhavi-Pour is Professor of International Economics in the Department of Management and Economics at Hamline University in St. Paul, Minnesota. He received his Ph.D. from Kansas State University in 1981. Akhavi-Pour is a member of the editorial board of the journal *Critique,* and currently is the director of the Center for Critical Studies of Iran and the Middle East. His areas of specialization include political economy, regional economics, development, and international trade.

Hooshang Amirahmadi holds a Ph.D. in regional planning and economic development from Cornell University and is a professor in the Department of Urban Planning and Policy Development at Rutgers, the State University of New Jersey. He is chair and graduate director of the department and director of the university's Middle Eastern Studies program. Amirahmadi is the author of the *Revolution and Economic Transition: The Iranian Experience* (Albany, N.Y.: State University of New York Press, 1990). His other publications include five co-edited books. He has also published numerous journal papers, book chapters, and review articles. He has held several fellowships and has been a recipient of several grants from NEW, SSRC, NJDHE, NJCH, U.S. Outreach Fund, and the National Council on U.S.-Arab Relations, among others.

Cyrus Bina is a scholar at the Harvard Center for Middle Eastern Studies, where he has been working since 1990. He holds a Ph.D. in economics from the American University in Washington, D.C., and has completed postdoctorate studies at Harvard University. Bina has published extensively on such topics as OPEC and the international oil market, global transformation, and Islamic political economy in such scholarly journals as *Energy Economics, American Journal of Economics and Sociology, Arab Studies Quarterly,* and *Harvard Middle Eastern and Islamic Review.* He is the author of *The Economics of the Oil Crisis* (New York: St. Martin's Press, 1985) and co-editor (with Hamid Zangeneh) of *Modern Capitalism and Islamic Ideology in Iran* (New York: St. Martin's Press, 1992). As a leading authority on the present global transformation, he was nominated for the 1991 Grawemyer World Order Award.

Manochehr Dorraj is Associate Professor of Political Science at Texas Christian University. He has published a number of books and articles in the areas of Comparative Politics and International Relations. His most recent articles have been published in the *Third World Studies Journal, the Journal of Developing Societies, International Journal of Comparative Religion,* and *Arab Studies Quarterly.* He is the author of *From Zarathuster to Khomeini* (Boulder, Colo.: Lynne Rienner, 1990). He is also co-author of a book entitled *Political Culture in the Middle East* (London: Routledge, forthcoming).

Nader Entessar is Professor of Political Science and Chair of the Social Science Division at Spring Hill College in Mobile, Alabama. He was formerly a research fellow at the Institute for International Political and Economic Studies in Tehran. Entessar's most recent books include *Kurdish Ethnonationalism* (Boulder, Colo.: Lynne Rienner, 1992), and with H. Amirahmadi, *Reconstruction and Regional Diplomacy in the Persian Gulf* (London: Routledge, 1992), and *Iran and the Arab World* (New York: St. Martin's Press, 1993). He is the author of several book chapters and articles, which have appeared in such journals as *Third World Quarterly, Journal of Third World Studies, Conflict, Journal of South Asian and Middle Eastern Studies, Conflict Quarterly,* and *Boston College Third World Law Journal.*

Hamid Hosseini is Professor and Chairman of the Economics Department at Kings College. From January 1, 1994, until August, 1994, he was a visiting scholar at Harvard University. He was a visiting scholar at the

University of Chicago in 1984. Prior to coming to Kings College, Dr. Hosseini taught at the University of Oregon, Wayne State, and Jundi Shapur University in Iran, where he also chaired the economics department. Dr. Hosseini has written and published extensively on various aspects of economic theory, international economics, economics of the Middle East, the Iranian economy, and Islamic economics.

Akbar Mahdi is an Assistant Professor of Sociology at Ohio Wesleyan University. His publications include *Sociology in Iran* (co-authored), *Sociology of the Iranian Family, Resources for Teaching Sociology of Development and Women in International Development,* and numerous articles and reviews on topics ranging from sociology of knowledge to the political economy of Iran and Islam in *Feminist Forum, Contemporary Sociology, the Review of Iranian Political-Economy and History, the International Social Science Review, the Resources for Feminist Research, Michigan Sociological Review, the Social Science Journal, and Teaching Sociology.* He is currently serving as the executive director of the Center for Iranian Research and Analysis (CIRA) and is the editor of the *Michigan Sociological Review.* He is also serving as the liaison coordinator for the Middle East American Sociological Association.

Janice M. Moore holds a Ph.D. in political science from the University of Missouri-Columbia. She is currently an executive of the Transitional Residence Independence Service (TRIS), in Stratford, New Jersey. She is responsible for the institution's research and quality assurance/utilization review. She taught at the University of Missouri-Columbia and Central Michigan University. She has published several book chapters and journal articles on Iran and in the area of managed health care.

Siamack Shojai is an Associate Professor of Economics and Finance and the Chairman of Economics and Finance at Manhattan College. He holds a Ph.D. in economics from Fordham University. He has held teaching positions with Fordham University and Lafayette College. His articles have appeared in the *Journal of Energy and Development* and the *Journal of Economics Development,* among others. He a co-editor of the *Oil Market in the 1980s: A Decade of Decline* (New York: Praeger Publishers, 1992). His next book, *Global Oil Markets,* is forthcoming in 1994.

ISLAM, IRAN, and WORLD STABILITY

I·N·T·R·O·D·U·C·T·I·O·N

Hamid Zangeneh

As the cold war of the superpowers has passed into history we find ourselves fortunate to be in a position to contemplate the future without the prospect of complete annihilation of the human race. However, as we enter new, uncharted waters, we witness the emergence of other problems to which our attention must be turned. Even though the bipolar world has clearly disappeared, what has come about in its stead is, as yet, ambiguous. It all depends on the issue that is considered.

On the military front, there is no doubt that there is no other country with the massive capabilities of the United States. The show of force in the Persian Gulf against the Iraqi aggression is a good indicator of the United States' military ability and of her willingness to use it in similar situations. This point was made clear by former President George Bush, who made a statement to the effect that "this war put the Vietnam syndrome out of our minds." With this relatively new state of affairs, however, comes the question of whether this militarily unipolar world will produce political stability across the earth. The answer would probably be both yes and no. The existence of stability in any particular country or region of the world will depend, to a considerable extent, upon the United States' "national interest" and how it is perceived and defined.

There is no reason to doubt that in those areas where the U.S. "national interest" is being threatened the U.S. government will actively seek to restore stability. This active involvement in the politics of other political entities will occur regardless of which party and/or persons occupy positions of power in the U.S. government, as the case of Kuwait has vividly demonstrated. On the other hand, if the United States does not feel that its "national interest" is directly threatened, there is a good possibility that it will pursue a policy of benign neglect, as has been the case in Bosnia-Herzegovina. The United States, according to Secretary of State Warren Christopher in an interview on ABC television's "Nightline," will provide some humanitarian aid and, if the international community mandates, will provide some air support for an internationally sanctioned military engagement. In other words, the United States will not take the leadership role, as she did in the case of Kuwait, where the U.S. "national interest" was directly threatened.

On the economic front, a different environment exists. By now, almost all scholars agree that U.S. economic leadership has been decreasing since the late 1960s. Many reasons, both international and domestic, could be used to account for this decline. In the international arena the "rising sun" of Japan, the rapid growth of the Pacific Rim countries, and the creation of the United States of Europe, when taken together, could explain a great deal of the diminished leadership of the United States. Domestically one could point to the substandard educational system within the United States, which produces graduates whose skills cannot compare to those of their cohorts abroad.

In any case, however, since the late 1960s the prominence of American manufacturing has been on the decline. Major manufacturing plants, where automobiles, steel, and clothing were once produced, have been closed. The number of manufacturing jobs within the United States have diminished, while lesser-paying jobs in the service industry have flourished. This has meant a lower standard of living for the average U.S. citizen.

The political abilities and/or constraints of the United States result directly from her military and economic status vis-à-vis the rest of the developed and underdeveloped world. The degree to which the United States occupies a leadership position in the world is not the same as it was during the cold war when all countries, developed and underdeveloped, had to choose, to a large extent, between the two ideological poles, i.e., the United States or the Soviet Union. At that time, pro-Western countries in Europe or other parts of the world allowed the United States a high degree of latitude in defining a proper course of action against the Soviet bloc. Today, however, with the dissolution of the Soviet Union and the ratification of the Maastricht Treaty (which will ultimately lead to a United States of Europe) there is no reason for the Europeans and the Japanese to acquiesce to the demands of the United States as they once did. These countries are now pursuing their own economic/political goals and objectives, which may challenge rather than correspond with those of the United States. One case in point is the zigzag or flip-flop in policy decisions made by the U.S. and European countries with regard to Bosnia-Herzegovina. In this situation, the Europeans did not acquiesce to the military intervention advocated by the Clinton administration. It would, however, be a grave mistake to discount the influence that the United States continues to wield. Even though the leadership role occupied by the United States has lessened, either due to domestic political decisions or due to the creation of new economic pillars in Europe and the Far East, this does not mean that Third World countries such as Iran are in a position to challenge her with impunity. These countries must carefully strategize ways in which they can advance and pursue their own "national interests" and yet avoid any direct collision with the United States, which, as the Iraqis have learned, could be quite costly.

Manochehr Dorraj sets the stage for the discussion and understanding of the history and evolution of the current "New World Order." He reminds us that the concept is not new. It has always meant the imposition of "rules of the game" by the more powerful countries on the less powerful nations. As long as the Communist bloc was functioning and the bipolar military world existed, it was improbable, if not impossible, for the United States to proclaim a new world order. But the inefficiencies and corrupt bureaucratic system of the Eastern bloc gave birth to the government of the activist reformer Mikhail Gorbachev, who initiated the historic programs of *perestroika* and *glasnost* that led to the dismantling of the Eastern bloc and the end of the cold war. The Iraqi aggression against Kuwait, which resulted in a show of force by the U.S. (allied forces), along with the dissolution of the Soviet Union, gave the United States a good opportunity to show the Europeans, Japanese, "and other allies that they were still dependent on American military protection to safeguard their economic interest." But the show of force and possession of military might may not necessarily lead to unquestioned political leadership for the United States. Most likely, the United States must share this leadership role with the united states of Europe and Japan. As for the Third World countries, it is probable that the rise of an economic multipolar world would lead to "cooperation among advanced industrial states, accommodation and cooperation of the former Soviet Union and Eastern Europe, and domination of and confrontation with the Third World . . . unless the nature of North-South relations changes from one dictated by a politics of greed and domination to a mutual accommodation and cooperation, only increasing environmental degradation, poverty, and conflict lie ahead for the Third World."

As was discussed before, the bipolar world passed into history without the annihilation of a nuclear exchange. But whether or not we have entered a unipolar or multipolar world system depends on the context under discussion. In our world as it has evolved, we find it necessary to distinguish between military, economic, and political superpowers. The United States of America is not the sole superpower, except for her military strength. Possession of unquestionable military might no longer automatically implies political preeminence. In today's world, economic power could very well supersede military power in positioning a country on the totem pole.

This rearrangement of hierarchy among nations could have serious implications for world peace and stability. Cyrus Bina argues that a combination of U.S. economic decline and the rise of Japan and Europe has resulted in self-doubt and insecurity for the United States. This sense of loss of economic and political power and prestige is what led to the "military intervention" in Iraq. This, Bina argues, "symbolizes the United States' doubt about its future role in the new world order." Military intervention, in other words, is "not a sign of strength," but, it is due to "political despair." This contrasts sharply with the U.S. military interventions "which were conducted out of U.S. strength." According to Bina, it is imperative to understand that the economic decline of the United States is a direct result of "transnationalization of the global economy, beyond the boundaries of nation-states." Therefore, he argues, the Islamic order, which is presented as an alternative, cannot succeed as an independent entity and will have to become a part of the greater global system. An analysis of the post-Khomeini economic and political policies of the Islamic Republic indicates that this has been recognized by the recent leaders of the Islamic Republic. If so, then, what would be the future for Iran, the Islamic world, and the world at large? "[I]n the absence of economic and political hegemony, the United States tends to resort to military confrontations" such as "the invasion of Panama" and the "military expedition against Saddam Hussein in Iraq. [T]he United States is unwilling to accept the reality of its modified role in the emerging world. Thus we have no choice but to bear the risk of violent transition and political upheaval, such as what we have seen so far, at least for the remaining part of the 1990s."

During the initial post-revolution period, Iran attempted to present Islam, at least in the immediate region, as a legitimate mode of governance and an alternative to the "corrupt servants" of both "East" and "West." However, there has been no evidence that the residents of those targeted countries, or, for that matter, of any other countries, paid serious consideration to Iran's suggestions. This disregard has occurred for many reasons. At least up until now, the Islamic alternative has not yet gained even universal acknowledgment or understanding. It has never been taken seriously as an alternative mode of government, or as one that could compete with liberal capitalism and its variations. So, according to Akbar Mahdi, in the absence of a serious challenge from the

Islamic ideology, "the new world order is the same as the old world order only without the Soviet Union as a contending superpower. From a world system perspective, the changes are merely political and the world system economically remains the same, that is, a capitalist world economy that demands increasing integration and uniformity."

However, Mahdi asserts that the political changes are not insignificant and should not be ignored. The United States will try to redefine the new world system as a system in which economic power is subservient to military and political might. According to this scenario, Mahdi maintains, "the choice of a military solution of the crisis in the Persian Gulf was another example of 'imperial temptation' for the military might without taking responsibility for its ruins." As for the future of the Middle East, U.S. foreign policy is not very different from what it was before. During the cold war, the U.S. foreign policy was centered around four objectives: "containing Soviet expansion . . . ; securing an uninterrupted flow of oil . . . ; insuring stability of region's markets for American goods and capital; protecting the state of Israel." The disappearance of the Soviet Union, combined with the pending turn of events toward resolution of the Palestinian problem and achievement of an Arab-Israeli peace agreement leaves only fundamental economic objectives that would be essential in any period.

But does Islam remain a threat, big enough to be used by the "military-industrial" establishment as "the enemy of the Western" interest and ideology in place of the Soviet Union? "The answer to this question is certainly 'no.' No matter how much Islamic militants might wish the answer to be yes, and no matter how much ideologues of the military-industrial complex in the Western countries attempt to give the appearance that the answer is yes, neither the Islamic military nor Islam as a religion represents a *real threat* to the West." Islamic movements that have transpired in Iran, Egypt, Algeria, and other countries are not against "the West." Rather, they are against the corrupt undemocratic governments that failed them. This "would certainly pose a challenge to the Western world" and their economic interest. "But such a challenge is far from a threat." The United States, Mahdi suggests, "should abandon the policy of isolating and suppressing these [Islamic] activists. Instead, it should look for policies and options that encourage participation by these Muslims in their national politics, improve their economic situations, and provide them with a sense of control over their lives."

Since the revolution of 1979, Iran has been changing and reshaping her priorities and policies to position herself in a more secure environment and to achieve a prosperous economy. These transformations have taken place on several fronts. Initially, the Iranian leaders embraced policies that were, as Hooshang Amirahmadi points out, ideologically based and confrontational in nature. They found, however, that they were vulnerable on many fronts. Iran's desire to be considered an independent sovereign nation led to a foreign policy of "Neither East, Nor West" in her relations vis-à-vis the superpowers. Instead, Islam was presented as an alternative paradigm. However, due to the international reaction, the policy of "Neither East, Nor West" has now been replaced with a policy of "both East and West." The change of heart, Amirahmadi points out, is not confined to Iran's relationships with the superpowers. It is evident in Iran's reorientation of policies toward the Persian Gulf littoral states as well as other countries. However, even though there is a change in policy and orientation, there is a keen awareness of Iran's position and vulnerabilities within and without the country. For countries with a multiethnic population such as Iran, the newly reawakened nationalism emerging around the world and the greater emphasis on "self-determination" and "self-rule" is a potentially dangerous and explosive notion. These forces and movements could lead to bloodshed if their energies and desires are not channeled toward unity and coexistence. Border and territorial bickering and disputes, oil policy, the arms buildup in Saudi Arabia and Kuwait, the Islamic movement, and collective security issues among the Persian Gulf littoral states are among the points of contention that could ignite the fire between Iran and her neighbors or outside powers any time. Hooshang Amirahmadi's chapter sets the stage for the discussion and understanding of the history and evolution of current Iranian policies toward countries of the region as well as toward other countries that have a vested interest in the region. He concludes that "Iran seems to have little realistic alternative but to work out its difficulties with the United States by focusing on issues that divide them. In the long run, however, Iran must have its eyes on the emerging economic and technological forerunners in the world."

As previously discussed, there has been a significant change in the way Iranian government has treated the littoral states of the Persian Gulf since the revolution of 1979. From the time of Ayatollah Khomeini's ascension to power and until the time of his death, Iran considered herself to be one of the true and legitimate leaders of the Third World and of the Islamic community. This manifested itself in hard-line rhetoric regarding the oil and foreign policies of pro-Western littoral states in the Persian Gulf, and of other countries such as Egypt, Jordan, Turkey, and so on. This pleased neither the leaders of these countries nor those of the Western countries whose interests were being challenged. As a result, despite her legitimate right to participate in the affairs and decisions that affected the countries within the region, Iran was isolated and marginalized by the regional and international communities. This did not trouble the late Ayatollah Khomeini; therefore, there was no change in the policies. In actuality, these regional and international relationships were seen as evidence in support of Iran's anti-Western policies. The policies of Iran were based on confrontation with the West and its allies; the obvious material and other support of Iraq, occurring on the part of almost all Arab and Western countries, resulted in destruction of much of Iran's infrastructure during the long and deadly Iran-Iraq War. This was interpreted as a sign of the legitimacy of Iranian policy and reinforced the nation's resolve to fight the war until victory. However, after eight years of destruction on both sides, the cease-fire was accepted with much humility and in a disheartening fashion. After the cease-fire, a period of indecision and infighting among different factions of the Iranian political establishment took place, and have since been dubbed as the radical/pragmatist view of domestic and foreign policies. The pragmatists, led by President Rafsanjani, were able to overcome the resistance of the radicals. Iran then initiated a policy of re-appointment, helped with the release of Western hostages in Lebanon, and made other overtures to the West. As yet, these gestures have been unfruitful. Even so, the Iranian foreign policy has shifted toward what Nader Entessar calls the process of "de-Khomeinization of Iranian foreign policy and its evolving realignment with the policies with the pro-Western Arab states in the region."

Nader Entessar explains the course of foreign policy changes that have taken place in the post-Khomeini era. He discusses the impact that the allied war against the Iraqi aggression in Kuwait had upon Iran, and her change of policies toward the United States, the Persian Gulf states, and other countries of the region. He argues that the more cooperative and accommodative policies of Iran have been rebuffed and ignored by Washington. Rather than ceasing the moment and establishing a more businesslike and friendly relationship, American strategists have instead appeared to adopt a plan "invoking the specter of the so-called fundamentalist Islam," and, accordingly, have embarked upon what appears to be a concerted effort to confront Iran. The term "containment" has been increasingly used in the same fashion as it had been during the heyday of the U.S.-Soviet cold war, with the "Communist menace" giving way to an equally perceived menace—"fundamentalist Islam."

The reconfiguration of the Soviet Union and Germany, the collapse of Marxism as it was practiced in the Eastern bloc countries, the rise of Islamic movements, U.S. assertiveness in the Middle East, the end to the bloody and savage war between Iran and Iraq, and the passing of Ayatollah Khomeini from the political scene, have all contributed to a change in the thought processes of a majority of the leaders throughout the world. These changes in the political arena led to the much discussed and celebrated statement by former President George Bush that we are entering a "new world order" where the rule of law, peace, and prosperity rather than individual tyranny and violence transcend the globe. Of course, the "new world order" would be based on the principles of market economy and liberal democracy. Siamack Shojai suggests that countries of the world have an option of choosing either to join the "global order," in which all countries share the bounties of economic growth and development, or, to create a regional order, in which North America, Europe, and the Pacific Rim countries replace the old bipolar world order. The latter case, he argues, "would provoke trade wars with fierce competition over access to strategic commodities like oil." Whether or not Iran would be successful in joining the international economic order depends on the course of action that is pursued by the leadership of the Republic. Iran could prosper along with other nations if she chooses a realistic plan that will allow "full participation of all indigenous forces . . . based on freedom of economic activity" and will promote democracy by creating "democratic institutions capable of adapting to the Iranian and Islamic culture. . . . The political deadlock . . . is due mainly to unwillingness of some to do away with authoritarian tendencies disguised under Islamic rules or secular aspirations. The existing political institutions are too rigid and exclusive . . . for the creation of an inclusive, modern, progressive political system."

The metamorphosis of the Islamic Republic's economic policy in the post-Khomeini era, evolving from an ideological dogma to a more realistic view, is obvious. There are serious and concerted efforts to depart from what was considered irrelevant to something that will determine the survival and legitimacy of the Islamic Republic, domestically and internationally. This is true especially since the Islamic Republic has maintained that Islamic economics reflect a different paradigm, separate and distinct, from capitalism and socialism. Hamid Hosseini argues that "the economic structure that emerged after the 1979 revolution, although given an Islamic pretense, resulted from a process of improvisation rooted in the expediency of Iranian Islamic leaders and their deep desire to create an Islamic society/government at any price." This, along with the cultural and historical propensities of Iran in general, resulted in a larger bureaucratic nightmare. Hosseini provides several reasons for the change of heart by the Iranian government. These include recent trends in the process of privatization throughout the world along with pressure from the World Bank and the International Monetary Fund, among others. These changes have translated themselves into different industrial policies, as well as different approaches to foreign direct investment, foreign exchange control, and import and export of non-oil commodities in Iran. The government has changed its hard-line position against direct foreign investment in Iran. This investment is now advocated and solicited, against the explicit principles of the Iranian Constitution. As these new directions have emerged, the question arises as to whether or not they are diverging from what was and is considered Islamic, or has there been a change in the interpretation of Islam. In other words, have the governmental and religious leaders of Iran found that the Islamic system is not a different paradigm, but rather, is a version of capitalism albeit with greater social responsibility. Hamid Hosseini argues that the new decisions have no contradiction with Islam, that is, the "new developments are in every respect Islamic. They are, in particular, more Islamic than the practices of the Islamic regime in the first few months of its existence."

Immediately after the revolution of 1979, the Iranian political, social, and economic landscape began to reflect a higher degree of social responsibility and sensitivity toward the less-privileged sector of the society. This led to a massive reorganization of national priorities as compared to those of the late deposed Shah's period. Economic welfare of the deprived was given top priority. Issues of social responsibility were stated within the Constitution as the "rights of the people." For example Articles 30 and 31 of the Islamic Republic's Constitution stipulates that "the government must provide all citizens with free education. . . . To own a dwelling commensurate with one's needs is the right of every individual and family in Iran. The government must make land available for the implementation of this principle." Also, Article 44 of the Constitution explicitly stipulates that "large-scale and major industries, foreign trade, major mineral resources, banking, insurance, energy, dams and large-scale irrigation networks, radio and television, post, telegraph and telephone services, aviation, shipping, roads, railroads, and the like; all these will be publicly owned and administered by the state."

To fulfill the ambitions of Articles 30 and 31 and the mandate of Article 44, the government embarked on a massive nationalization and confiscation of private property that was presumed to be vital to industry or that was illegitimately acquired during the previous regime. However, the government found itself unable to manage and maintain these enterprises due to a shortage of capital and due to the lack of a managerial level work force (depleted due to deportation and emigration occurring before, during, and long after the revolution). As a result, the policies of the first post-revolution decade were reversed. The government is now pursuing economic revitalization by, among other methods, what the officials call privatization. This is the subject of Hossein Akhavi-Pour's chapter. He discusses several dimensions of privatization and reasons for its failure in Iran. He maintains that Iran opted to privatize the State-owned Economic Enterprises (SEEs) through selling stocks of these companies to the public. However, this endeavor has not been successful for several reasons. Among other things, neither the public nor the stock market managers have been very familiar with the nuances of the stock market's functioning. Also, no clear goals have been presented by the government to justify privatization. "As a result, there is no overall strategy to guide the process." Akhavi-Pour concludes that a bottom-up rather than a top-down approach to privatization is necessary if it is to be successful in improving the economic condition of the country.

Whether or not the Islamic Republic could push the concept of privatization to its potential depends on its ability to confront the roots of economic stagnation and social discontent. That is, the leadership of the Islamic Republic must address the causes of economic, political, and social unrest first, before embarking upon a new direction. In the last chapter of this book, Hamid Zangeneh and Janice Moore maintain that some of the basic problems of the Islamic Republic are of the republic's own creation and are self-inflicted. They argue that the Islamic Republic, in order to maintain government control, dismantled and eliminated many key political and religious groups during the post-revolution era. In the process, a great number of management-level technocrats and businessmen who were, to a large extent, apolitical, were deported or forced to leave through intimidation and harassment. In addition to the personal and financial insecurity that is inherent in the system, this lack of managerial knowledge and expertise has made it very difficult for potential entrepreneurs to engage in private enterprise in Iran. These are problems that could be remedied rather easily if the government could bring itself to pursue a less dogmatic course and, instead, could become more in tune with the needs of its citizens. "Whether or not an ideologically based government such as the Islamic Republic of Iran is able to compromise or ignore some of its ideology, nationalism, religion, and other similar dogmas for the sake of the collective well-being of the country remains to be seen."

All in all, the different viewpoints contained within this book provide a set of perspectives that are destined to enhance the discussion about "Iran, Islam, and World Stability." These chapters provide analyses of present-day Iran from the perspective of a historical understanding, as well as from the perspective of current reality and future expectations. From these analyses have emerged a number of recommendations, pragmatic in nature, which should be attended to by concerned individuals, groups, and governments who have a stake in peace, prosperity, security, justice, social justice, and preservation of human dignity and values around the region and the world. It is hoped that these recommendations will, in a positive way, illuminate the path for all involved.

THE NEW WORLD ORDER: PROSPECTS FOR THE THIRD WORLD

Manochehr Dorraj

There is nothing more difficult to carry out,
nor more doubtful of success, nor more dangerous to handle,
than to initiate a new order of things.
—MACHIAVELLI

The fateful decade of the 1980s ushered in one of the most dramatic and remarkable sequences of events that the world has witnessed since the Second World War. These portentous changes were inconceivable even a few years prior to 1985. In the early 1980s the Soviet bureaucracy seemed well-entrenched and immutable under Brezhnev, creeping along the well-trodden path laid out by Stalin. The Soviet Union was engaged in a costly arms race with the United States, and their conflict over the Third World had further intensified tensions between the two superpowers. The 1979 Soviet invasion of Afghanistan brought the dawn of the "the second cold war," further escalating the nuclear arms race. The Soviets also showed no sign of giving up their tight control over Eastern Europe, and Eastern European Stalinist regimes, with the exception of Poland, displayed no major signs of vulnerability.

Considered against this background, what has transpired since 1985 is indeed epoch-making and will have a profound impact on the future of international order. The avalanche of change in Eastern Europe and the

Soviet Union has had a far-reaching impact not only on European and East-West relations, but also on the Third World, thus introducing the inception of a "new world order," again.

In what follows the contending perceptions of the new world order are assayed and the ramifications of the new world order for the Third World are analyzed.

GEORGE BUSH AND THE AMERICAN PERSPECTIVE

The idea of a new world order is not new. Its roots can be traced to the League of Nations, created by the Treaty of Versailles in 1919. The basic principle of the League of Nations was for a voluntary cooperation of equals brought together for a common purpose. This early call for an international coalition was echoed in President Bush's State of the Union address after the victory over Iraq early in 1991. Bush called upon the world "to fulfill the long-held promise of a new world order—where military brutality will go unrewarded and aggression will meet collective resistance."[1] He further described a world in which "the principles of justice and fair play would protect the weak from the strong and in which, the United Nations, freed from the cold war, could fulfill its historic duty."[2] For the most part, the policies of the Bush administration in the post–cold war era, however, negated this lofty image of the new world order. The U.S. invasion of Panama and the American-led coalition's military emasculation of Iraq in which, depending on the source, tens or hundreds of thousands of Iraqi soldiers and civilians reportedly died, were much closer to the examples of the old world order of imperialism and power politics than anything new. For the Bush administration, however, the American-led coalition against Iraq constituted the essence of the new world order. The Persian Gulf War would have been a risk that the United States could have ill-afforded a decade earlier.

Released from the constraints of a deterring Soviet power, in 1991 the United States was in a position to act with much less restraint to protect her interests and punish one of her former allies who had stepped out of line. In other words, "the victory over Iraq was made possible above all by the far greater victory over the Soviet Union that preceded it."[3] But the Persian Gulf War was also fought to "kick the Vietnam syndrome, once and for all." The U.S. defeat in Vietnam, followed by the Iranian and Nicaraguan revolutions, signaled the erosion of American power, thus evoking a nationalist resurgence and the conservative backlash of the Reagan era. Many argued that Vietnam and its liberal cultural baggage represented a detour in American history. By 1980 America had returned to the main characteristic of its history. The legacy of the Vietnam War, the first war that was fought live on television, graphically capturing the horrors of death and destruction, evoked a pacifist sentiment in the public, especially among the educated middle class. When President Ford contemplated sending American troops to Angola against the Soviet-backed MPLA (Popular Movement for the Liberation of Angola), the Congress and the public overwhelmingly rebuffed the idea. By 1980, as far as the Washington policymakers were concerned, the lessons of Vietnam had been learned: America must engage in military conflicts only where swift victory was possible and public resistance to the war minimal. Reagan's invasion of Granada and Bush's wars against Panama and Iraq are good examples of that mental framework. Another lesson of the Vietnam War was that American unilateralism of the past had to be replaced by American-led coalition-building to provide a pretext of consensus and thus legitimize U.S. policy. Hence, if in Vietnam a relatively youthful empire still in its economic prime could afford to pay the cost of war single-handedly for more than a decade, by 1990 a graying America on the verge of economic decline could ill-afford such a draining endeavor. Nixon's doctrine of Vietnamization of war, "we pay and you fight," took a 180-degree turn during the Persian Gulf War and became "you pay and we fight."[4] Saudi Arabia, Kuwait, Japan, and Germany paid the major bulk of the cost of the Persian Gulf War, and the United States provided the half-million soldiers, which was by far the largest contingent of the coalition. The emphasis on a swift victory was instigated as much by the need to reduce the financial cost of the war as by the possibility of waning public support.

The end of the cold war provided a glimmer of hope that, with the fading of the "Soviet threat," a more benign and humane mission could be found for American troops. In 1990 some Democrats in Congress (Senators Al Gore and Sam Nunn) even envisioned the possibility that the new mission of Pentagon laboratories and American soldiers could be primarily directed toward cleaning up the environment.[5] But the war with Iraq put a swift end to such optimism. The Emperor appeared in his comfortable old clothes, assuming the role of the enforcer once again.

Psychologically, the Persian Gulf victory provided a moment of euphoria for a nation suffering the painful consequences of economic decline, allowing it to forget her troubles at home. Politically, it gave the Bush administration an opportunity to demonstrate to the world, as well as to those who wished to trim the defense budget drastically, that there was still a need for a global policeman. More specifically, Bush hoped that it would prove to Japan, Germany, and other allies that they were still dependent on American military protection to safeguard their economic interests. The bombing of Iraq to the "preindustrial age" and the extent of devastation wrought on the country's infrastructure were also designed to warn Third World nations of the consequences of attacking Western interests. Secretary of Defense Dick Cheney's statement in this regard is revealing: "By winning the war as fast as possible, America will appear stronger in the eyes of the entire world, and she will have proved that she has the resources to institute a new world order."[6] As Jerry Sanders, Academic Coordinator of Peace and Conflict Studies at the University of California at Berkeley, aptly notes, you cannot achieve this goal either through sanctions or multilateral negotiations using the United Nations' Security Council. You must demonstrate that you have unipolar power by being willing to use it.[7]

A declining economy and the inward-looking vision that marks Clinton's administration so far may not guarantee a noninterventionist course in U.S. foreign policy in 1990s. On the contrary, this may intensify the imperial temptation. As political scientists Robert Tucker and David Hendrickson observe, "A nation resentful of its declining economic performance, which finds that its status as the world's only superpower rests above all on its military strength, may find itself tempted to demonstrate that its own peculiar asset, built up in the course of a rivalry that is no more, still has a continuing relevance in world politics."[8] They argue that universalization of American security frontiers and the excessive use of force and interventionism pose a danger not so much to America's "purse" as to America's "soul." To pursue its imperial ambitions, the United States increasingly has to betray its democratic ideals.[9]

Perhaps even more dangerously, as the war with Iraq graphically demonstrated, future wars driven by "smart bombs" and other sophisticated weaponry, which insulates the combatants from the actual horrors of war, may desensitize the public to the use of force abroad. For television viewers, the Persian Gulf War at times must have seemed like a video game in which a computer-guided missile launched from a ship hundreds of miles away hits its target with an impersonal accuracy. The increasing automation of modern electronic warfare, combined with an escalating manipulation and control of the media and the press, has created a certain surrealistic aura that further helps desensitize the soldiers and the public. Keeping the press at bay and feeding them selective Pentagon-controlled "pool reports" during the invasions of

Granada and Panama are clear examples of forging reality and pacifying the public resistance to war. Seen in light of the global trend toward democratization, this is indeed an ominous development in the heartland of democracy. In fact, this tendency has evoked a bewildering sense of irony among some of the more sensitive observers of the American political scene: "The irony of the present moment is that, while our own maxims are in danger of changing from liberty to force, free institutions have captured the imagination of peoples throughout the world."[10] In a broader perspective, the major irony of the end of the cold war is that whereas, since 1985, the former Soviet Union has taken major concrete steps to dismantle the apparatus and abandon the policies that nurtured and sustained the cold war, in the United States the institutions and the apparatus of "the military-industrial complex" for the most part have remained intact. Although the Soviet Union disengaged from such areas of bilateral conflict as Eastern Europe and Afghanistan and even withdrew support from its former allies such as Nicaragua and Cuba, the United States maintained the overwhelming majority of its forces in Western Europe and insisted upon the addition of Eastern Germany to NATO. The United States also invaded Panama and spearheaded the war with Iraq. While the raison d'être of the American military-industrial complex—the Soviet threat—has faded, the complex itself has not. In fact it is being trimmed and modernized to function more efficiently.

The inevitable question is then, What is new about the new world order from the American perspective? If one looks beyond the facade and puts the words in the context of political realities that animate them, then the answer would be "not much." As Steve Weber aptly notes, "World order, through the history of the state system, has basically meant attempts by great powers to impose their preference on lesser powers."[11] If so, nothing has changed except the collapse of one of the superpowers in the former bipolar system. Former Secretary of State James Baker envisioned the implementation of the new world order in the postwar Middle East, for example, to entail five points: first, to create a new regional security arrangement; second, to reduce the arms race; third, to narrow the gap between the rich and the poor nations in the Arab world through creation of a regional bank for reconstruction; fourth, to resolve the Israeli-Palestinian conflict; and fifth, to reduce American dependence on Middle Eastern oil drastically.[12] The new regional security arrangement has not materialized; instead the arms race in the region has escalated. No steps have been taken to reduce the immense gap between the rich and the poor in the Arab world. The U.S.

dependence on Middle Eastern oil has not diminished. In fact, U.S. import of Middle Eastern oil has increased since the war and it is projected to increase even more in the near future.[13] The Palestinian-Israeli peace settlement, although tenuous, is the only positive development in the region in the postwar era.

The resolve and rigor that the Bush administration displayed in organizing and executing the Persian Gulf War, allegedly against Saddam Hussein's abuse of human rights in Kuwait, were in stark contrast to its passivity and inaction toward atrocities of the Bosnian Serbs against Muslims in the former Yugoslavia. By all accounts, Saddam Hussein's abuses in Kuwait, repulsive as they were, seem minuscule compared to the crimes committed by the Serbs in Bosnia-Herzegovina. Systematic ethnic cleansing, mass genocide of innocent civilians, concentration camps for men and rape camps for women—the viciousness and barbarity displayed by the Serbs are matched only by the Nazis' crimes during the Second World War. Yet for two years there was a disturbing reticence on the part of the Western allies to use force against the Serbs. NATO, groomed for decades to prevent war and aggression in Europe, suddenly became a helpless giant. Moreover, the Western allies voted for a United Nations' imposed arms embargo, which practically barred the Bosnian Muslims from receiving any heavy weapons to defend themselves. Serbs have inherited the arsenal of the former Yugoslav army and they have been resupplied by the Belgrade and the Russian governments. Unfortunately, the Bosnian Muslims do not have oil; therefore, they are dispensable. When Iraq violated the U.N. resolutions in January of 1993 it was bombed repeatedly, when the Serbs did the same they were appeased.

The double standard of the Bush administration shattered any illusions that the new world order would be based on a new moral foundation. The only hopeful sign in this otherwise bleak picture was President Bush's troop deployment in Somalia to help feed the hungry that under the Clinton administration degenerated into a campaign against General Adeed and his supporters.

MIKHAIL GORBACHEV AND THE SOVIET PERSPECTIVE

Much of what is dubbed the new world order would have been unthinkable without the reforms initiated by Mikhail Gorbachev in the former Soviet Union. He introduced new policies of *perestroika* (restructuring) and *glasnost* (openness), drastically reduced the arms race, de-ideologized

Soviet foreign policy, and unilaterally withdrew from the East-West conflict, most notably in Afghanistan and Eastern Europe.

Gorbachev argued that in the age of nuclear weapons, with the survival of the human race at stake, the idea of class struggle had become obsolete. He emphasized peaceful resolution as the only acceptable solution to conflict among nations. He asserted that the Soviet Union so far had been bogged down in the periphery of the world (Third World conflict such as Afghanistan and Cuba), while the central issue of world politics in the nuclear age is the improvement of superpower relations.[14] Gorbachev, more than any other leader of the twentieth century, is responsible for putting a halt to the cold war. Therefore, the causes and the nature of his reforms deserve a closer scrutiny.

The genesis of Gorbachev's reforms was embedded in the reality of Russian history and Soviet social developments since 1917. The lethargic czarist autocracy and Stalin's murderous reign of terror flourished in a backward peasant society burdened by the weight of the past and the military interventions of Russia's more-developed neighbors; by the time Khrushchev began his attempt to reform the system the Soviet Union had changed from an agrarian to an urban society. By the 1960s, the Soviet Union was an urban, educated, and diverse nation with an expanded and sophisticated military system, a relatively cultured intelligentsia, and a labor force whose ranks had considerably increased.[15] The decrepit conservative bureaucracy no longer offered viable channels for expressions of consciousness, sophisticated cultural tastes and the rising political expectations of the urban groups and classes. This profound chasm between economic, social, and cultural developments on the one hand and the political underdevelopment of the system on the other constituted the basic contradiction that triggered Gorbachev's reforms.

Urbanization and modernization gave rise to the notion of the autonomous individual and forcefully introduced the rights of this individual to the public consciousness. With the expansion of communication and the emergence of the Soviet Union as a superpower, it was no longer possible to shield Soviet citizens from the rest of the world as previous leaders had attempted to do. By the 1970s, there was an increasingly well-informed public opinion in the making that the state had to recognize. For the most part, this public opinion no longer believed the official statements and became increasingly cynical and apathetic toward politics. It is ironic that one of the most politicized countries in the world had produced the most apathetic citizens.[16] Gradually, a profound contradiction emerged between an increasingly diverse and educated populace and the straightjacket of the Communist Party, which demanded their passive obedience and deprived them of their democratic rights.

On the economic front, the globalization of the Soviet economy, a process that began under Stalin, had come to fruition under Brezhnev. Brezhnev expanded Soviet economic relations with the outside world, and the Soviet Union maintained active trade relations with the Communist bloc and many Third World, as well as Western, nations. The Soviet industrial capacity also enlarged, yet its industry remained primitive; by the 1980s it was patently clear that the Soviet Union was lagging behind in modernizing its industrial goods, industries, and the related technological capacity. The fact that even today the majority of Soviet exports are still raw materials (oil and gas) puts the Soviets on par with many Third World countries.[17] The gap between the professed ideology—that the Soviet Union under socialism will "catch up with and outstrip" the most advanced Western society (the United States)—and the stark reality of dismal Soviet economic performance could no longer be concealed by official pronouncements about progress and advancement. According to Gorbachev, in the last twenty years, the Soviet national income did not progress in real terms except in the production of alcohol.[8]

The "third industrial revolution" (the revolution in high technology and computers) in the West and Japan, which beginning in the early 1960s had revolutionized their industries and technologies, by and large bypassed the lethargic Soviet economy altogether.[19] Given the pace of these colossal technological breakthroughs, the ramifications for comparative Soviet stagnation in the modernization of its technological base became fully apparent only by the late 1970s. Gorbachev's reference to the Brezhnev period as "the era of stagnation" partially reflected this realization. Hence, the remarkable resurgence of Japanese and German industries and their reemergence as new economic hegemonic powers made it increasingly clear that the new era of global dominance and supremacy may not depend so much on military superiority as it does on economic might. In light of these developments, Gorbachev began a complete reassessment of the costly, wasteful, and dangerous policy of the nuclear arms race.

"The new thinking" departed from the premise that the revitalization of the Soviet economy was the key to transforming the society. This revitalization, however, requires democratization of the political system, its leadership, and the Party, as well as a flourishing art and culture. The new leadership hoped this would release the innovative energies of the people, entice them politically, and mobilize them to actively participate in the process of reform and self-government. Fearing their removal from power, old bureaucrats and politicians refused to accommodate these newly energized groups. The Gorbachev leadership, in contrast, encouraged their political involvement. For only mass participation, argued many reformers, would guarantee that the old Stalinist "vampire" would not rise again.[20]

The staggering increase in the intelligentsia in the past four decades and their emergence in key positions of economic, social, and cultural life also had an impact on the pattern of elite recruitment and circulation. A number of these individuals found their way to the top leadership of the Party and cautiously began advocating reform. As their numbers swelled, their social weight increased and their leadership position within the Party and civil society solidified. The intelligentsia—whose ranks had been decimated during the civil war under Lenin, virtually perished under Stalin's reign of terror, and kept silent during Brezhnev—found the long awaited opening to assert themselves.[21]

As the old institutions, structures, and policies proved incapable of giving expression to these energized and resurgent political groups, the most perceptive and astute members of the Communist Party began a dialogue on the necessity of social transformation and reform. Andropov, Kulakov, and Gorbachev were among some of the better-known representatives of this new thinking. After his ascendence to power, Gorbachev increased the number of intelligentsia in the Party, and they became the most ardent supporters of his reforms. The real test of *perestroika*'s success, however, depended upon the critical support of the working class, which under Gorbachev remained lukewarm and suspicious.

Gorbachev's historic attempt to change the political structure marked by "statism"—the preeminence of an overbearing bureaucratic state and the corporatist domination of its subjects—was a formidable task indeed. The list of his accomplishments on the political and cultural fronts remains impressive. He began reforming a system that many thought to be "monolithic," "totalitarian," and unreformable. The criticism against government policy, which was punishable as anti-Soviet activity only a few years previously, became part of the mainstream. Gorbachev and his co-reformers introduced a new outlook on the role of citizenry that genuinely respected personal dignity and human rights. There was a sincere attempt on the part of the new leadership to break away from the traditional paternalistic and patriarchal Russian political culture that treated the citizenry as mere subjects. The arbitrary rule, lawlessness, and the cult of personality rendered moot the individual rights and civil liberties guaranteed to Soviet citizens through their constitution. Gorbachev was genuinely committed to a decisive change, if not the destruction of, the Stalinist political heritage and a break with the Russian autocratic and authoritarian political culture.[22] The very spontaneity of the movement and the fluidity of the system, however, bears the seeds of tremendous potential for progressive transformation as well as the possibility of sudden collapse and disintegration. If the second scenario materializes, this may in turn engender a resurgence of Russian nationalism to replace the collapse of Communism. In this case, nervous initiatives on the part of a desperate former superpower that still possesses formidable destructive capabilities cannot be ruled out. In a country with a deep-seated tradition of an authoritarian political culture, autocratic rule, and a well-entrenched bureaucracy, building a democratic society is a formidable task indeed. After all, recent Soviet history provides a precedent. Khrushchev's attempt at democratization of the system was halted by Brezhnev and in the final analysis, Khrushchev's initiatives did not alter the nature of the system. Why should we suppose Gorbachev and Yeltsin will fare any better? The answer lies in the dynamic process of reform itself.

What has transpired politically in the Soviet Union since 1985 can be characterized as a dual dialectical process of unwinding and unbecoming of the old system on the one hand and an intellectual rebirth and resurgence on the other. Whereas the former indicates the unraveling of the Stalinist system of repression, the latter signifies a tremendous potential and opportunity to restructure Soviet society on a new and democratic basis with profound ramifications for global politics in general and East-West relations in particular. However, there are as many perils lurking in the unfolding dynamics of the social forces that have been unleashed by Gorbachev and his successor Yeltsin as there are promises and potentials. The unraveling of the old system is occurring at a much faster pace than the capability of the Soviet regime to build new and cohesive institutions capable of replacing it. Since the new institutions that can command the public trust and confidence are not yet in place and neither Gorbachev nor his successor, Yeltsin, were able to deliver on their promise of economic prosperity, what we witness is a profound political vacuum and a crisis of legitimacy.

Watching their economic status deteriorating under Yeltsin, many people have become disillusioned with democracy. To transform itself from a political ideal to a political reality, the nascent Russian democracy must successfully navigate the untested waters of transition from a planned economy to a market-oriented economy, yet utilize Western capital without adopting an unbridled form of capitalism that may engender millions unemployed and impoverished. If *perestroika* fails to deliver in the economic realm, then the potential for civil war, ethnic and national strife, or protracted regional conflicts would also become enormous. For a centralized command administrative system, Gorbachev introduced such massive changes that it is doubtful if the system is going to cohere. Just as the Civil War defined the new character and the identity of the American nation, it may well be that it will require severe internal strife to define the new Russia and its mission in the world.

While a retreat is quite possible, a complete reversion to the old Stalinist type of leadership is improbable. The Soviet Union and the world have been drastically transformed since 1985. The far-reaching impact of Gorbachev's reforms and their unintended consequences have touched the far corners of the globe. He has changed the political map of the world without resorting to military force or intimidation. Having experienced a political awakening in the past eight years, the Russian people cannot be cowed to submission easily again. If Russian leadership proves incapable of delivering on its promises of economic prosperity and political freedom, over the long haul it may find itself overwhelmed by the very forces it has unleashed. The failure of the old guard to stage a successful coup d'état and oust Gorbachev from power in August of 1991 and the replacement of Gorbachev by Yeltsin are indicative of the volatility and spontaneity of the political process.

What has been done cannot be undone. Gorbachev unleashed forces that no longer could be controlled. The unfolding process of change that his initiatives helped to put in motion had a life and dynamism of their own. Gorbachev was like a pilot who knew he had to take off but had no idea where he would land. Like Lincoln at the end of the American Civil War, Gorbachev had to concede that at the end of his battle to democratize Soviet society, he was led by events rather than leading them. Gorbachev seemed to be aware of this. He hoped that the cultural and intellectual revival engulfing the country would create enough enthusiasm, creativity, and energy to produce a new generation of leaders capable of dreaming of even bolder visions than his own and providing a better leadership than his team.

Gorbachev's Foreign Policy Agenda

In the area of foreign policy, the new Russian thinking departed from the old dogmatic Stalinist ideological approach to the world and was much more flexible and innovative in its assessment of global politics. Peaceful resolution of conflict, constructive alliance with the "class enemy," non-ideological and nonconfrontational relations with all nation-states were declared as the major themes in the new thinking on foreign policy.[23] The new thinking began with a critique of the past: Prior to 1985 the Soviet Union was involved in a costly conflict with the West over the Third World; Afghanistan and Nicaragua being the most recent examples. The Soviet Union was bogged down in the periphery of world politics. The key to the resolution of global conflicts, however, lies in the improvement of the superpowers' relations.

The tremendous resurgence of Japanese and German industrial capacity since the Second World War revealed to the Soviets that their tardy economic development was, to a large extent, due to their preoccupation with costly military expenditure and presence. The Soviets realized that they were involved in a wasteful arms race that took financial resources away from investment in consumer-oriented technologies to satisfy domestic needs, as well as generating hard currencies. The new approach was intended to broaden the basis of Soviet international alliances and partners.

The new Soviet thinking on foreign policy included a commitment to the United Nations.[24] Referring to the United Nations as an effective world parliament, the Soviets abandoned their delinquent behavior toward the UN and paid all of their past membership dues. Another cornerstone of the new Soviet foreign policy was a conviction that in the nuclear age there is too much at stake (the destruction of the human race) to risk an East-West nuclear confrontation. Instead of emphasizing the primacy of class struggle, the Gorbachev leadership spoke of supremacy of common human values, safeguarding the survival of the planet and the well-being of the people in it. Hence, "democratization of international relations" and decreasing regional and global conflict constituted parts of this new thinking.[25]

The main objectives of Soviet foreign and domestic policy became directly linked. The Soviets aspired to halt the arms race and disengage themselves from regional conflict as well as reduce the costly financial burden associated with such commitments. In the Soviets' new thinking, the achievement of these goals would improve East-West relations, the key to revitalizing the Soviet economy. The economic modernization of the Soviet Union was the ultimate goal of *perestroika,* and Soviet foreign policy under Gorbachev was designed to serve this paramount concern.

On the economic level, the Soviets decentralized foreign trade, and the state enterprises were authorized to take part in foreign markets and joint ventures. Foreign companies were also allowed to invest in the Soviet Union.

Gorbachev spoke of a "Common European Home." He intended to integrate the Soviet Union into the European Community and create an economic zone that stretched from the Atlantic to the Urals. It is naive to think that Gorbachev's abandoning of Eastern Europe was instigated by altruistic or humanitarian considerations. While those factors might have played a minor role, the overarching reason was a realization that the Soviets had overextended themselves and their global commitments were disproportionate to their meager resources. Such commitments were also shifting valuable resources away from the domestic economy. Overburdened financially and militarily, the Soviets decided to unleash an impoverished Eastern Europe on its rich Western neighbors and let them carry the burden of financing and subsidizing its former satellites.

Because of the centrality of a revitalized economy and improvement of Soviet technological competitiveness to Gorbachev's domestic reforms, the political significance of Eastern Europe assumed a secondary position in the overall scheme of Gorbachev's "new thinking." Hence, abandoning Eastern Europe, a costly dependency on the Russian economy, was a calculated yet bold tactical initiative with unforeseen short- and long-term political and strategic repercussions.

Seen in this context, the new Russian foreign and economic policy toward the Third World is consistent with their overall strategy. The new leadership has chosen to avoid conflict with the United States and its allies over the Third World. The new thinking also questions the wisdom of creating financially costly dependencies such as Afghanistan, Cuba, and Nicaragua. The Soviets subsequently withdrew from Afghanistan and substantially cut their aid to Cuba and Nicaragua. Instead, Moscow has sought to establish relations with its former adversaries (for example, Israel and Saudi Arabia) or improve relations with countries where such relations were tenuous and shaky (as in the Philippines and Chile).

Russian economic policy toward the Third World is a reflection of domestic *perestroika.* As the former Soviet Union changes to a domestic economy based on market prices and individual or enterprise-oriented incentives and expands its private sector, its economic relations with the Third World are evolving along the same lines; that is, they are assuming a more market-oriented character.[26] Russians are experimenting with a wide array of economic cooperation schemes, including production sharing, turnkey industrial contracts, joint ventures, and tripatriate industrial cooperation between the Russians and the Third World, as well as the industrialized nations of the West. In their economic relations with the Third World, they are expanding trade with more-developed countries, such as South Korea, Brazil, and India, that are capable of producing consumer goods that the Russians can use. With the less-developed countries of the Third World, Russians are primarily interested in their raw material and agricultural products. For example, to stabilize their export earnings since the plummeting of oil prices in 1986, the Russians buy oil from Third World countries and resell it to the West.[27]

With the disintegration of the former Soviet Union, as Russia turns inward and tends to her ailing economy, struggling to find a way out of her chronic economic crisis, it is less likely that she will be as actively engaged in global affairs as she was during the cold war. She possesses neither the ideology, nor the will or the resources to do so. The cold war propaganda and the concomitant Western preoccupation with the Communist threat inflated Soviet power beyond all proportions. With the cold war over, Russia is revealed for what she has been all along: a Third World economy with a First World military capability. Therefore, Russia's involvement in the Third World is likely to be low-key, selective, and determined primarily by the dictates of her economic interests.

THE NEW WORLD ORDER: CONTENDING VISIONS

Besides the U.S., the Soviet, and the post-Soviet perspectives, there are also several prevalent theories among intellectuals and academics on the broader meaning and implications of the new world order. A brief account of these theories follows.

The first and perhaps the most controversial is the "End of History" triumphalism of strategist Francis Fukuyama. Fukuyama argues that with the end of ideological competition between East and West and the collapse of Communism, the West can now celebrate the global victory of liberal ideology and "the common marketization" of the world. More specifically, the political changes in the former Soviet Union and Eastern Europe are perceived as harbingers of a universal triumph of Western capitalism, the free enterprise system, and consumerism. These changes, contends Fukuyama, will in turn generate democratization. Since democracies do not fight wars against each other, what lies ahead is the possibility for an unprecedented era of international cooperation and peace. Thus, according to Fukuyama, universalization and eternalization of liberal democracy signals "the end of history."[28]

On the other end of the political spectrum is the political scientist John Mearsheimer's pessimistic and sobering analysis, which depicts the end of the cold war as the collapse of a balance-of-power system that restrained the destructive forces of ethnic and national conflicts that engulfed Europe in major wars between 1648 and 1945. To Mearsheimer's credit, in August 1990, amidst the pervasive optimism and euphoria that marked the aftermath of a democratic revolution in Eastern Europe, he proclaimed that with the receding of the cold war into history, the possibility of war and conflict in Europe, especially in the Balkan states, had increased.[29] Less than a year later, the bloody civil war in Yugoslavia put a damper on the sanguine views of the triumphalists, lending a new urgency to Mearsheimer's warnings. Mearsheimer contends that the post-1945 peace in Europe was based on three factors: the bipolarity of the power structure and superpowers' ability to keep their client states in check; a relative military power parity between the two superpowers; and the deterring impact of the large stock of nuclear arms on both sides. The emergence of multipolar world and power asymmetries has drastically altered these conditions, giving birth to nation-states with competing and often conflicting national interests.[30] He sees the post–cold war as an era fraught with great dangers. The end of the cold war has created a new era of disorder and the potential for violence is far greater in the near future. Hence, nuclear proliferation, which was well contained during the cold war, is more likely to spread in the decades ahead as smaller nations race to obtain nuclear arms, thus increasing the chances of a nuclear war.[31]

The renowned historian Paul Kennedy perceives "imperial overreach," specifically U.S. and Soviet involvement in bilateral conflicts in the Third World, a costly arms race, and the imperial policing of the world, as the main catalysts responsible for their domestic, economic, and social decline.[32]

While Kennedy draws attention to the limitations of a declining American empire to chart the future of the world, the journalist Charles Krauthammer declares that the collapse of Communism in the former Soviet Union and Eastern Europe has ushered in a new historical juncture: this is a "unipolar moment." The United States is the single remaining superpower, unmatched in its political and military strength. He sees American military success in the war against Iraq as vindication of his thesis. He discards the declinist perspective and argues that in the absence of American intervention only anarchy can exist. America is the only power with the necessary reach and resources capable of establishing order in a chaotic world.[33]

Finally, Richard Gardner sees in the new world order the dawn of practical internationalism marked by the reinvigoration of international law and the United Nations. Given the ever-increasing extent of global interdependence and cooperation and the recent active political participation of the UN to end many regional conflicts in the past decade, if the dominant Western powers approve, then it is possible that the UN could use Article 43 of its charter to create a permanent rapid deployment force to become further empowered to carry out its missions.[34]

An examination of these contending theories calls for a reassessment of the new world order. While the power politics of the past may not have changed, something in our world has changed profoundly. Many reflective minds speak of the end of modernity, the end of history, or the end of philosophy. The pervasiveness of the apocalyptic language in postmodern art and literature marks the closing of one historical era and the beginning of a new one. This new order of the world deserves a closer look.

THE NEW WORLD ORDER: A REASSESSMENT

To understand the essence of the new world order, the broader and deeper context of the postmodern society in which the changes of the past decade have unfolded must be grasped. Two predominant contradictory forces propel modern society: forces of integration and forces of fragmentation.

The forces of integration are instigated by the need to secure freedom from want, that is, satisfying economic needs. Economic needs promote interdependence, international cooperation, and free trade. The global invasion of "fungible" commodities and consumer goods attest to this fact. This overriding logic of forces of global integration may explain why the Soviet attempt to break away from the pervasive pattern of economic integration failed. This same logic may also explain why the ideological and confrontationist path of the past among the remaining communist nations has been replaced by an accommodationist and a "pragmatist" one.[35]

Human needs are not confined to the economic realm alone. Psychological needs must also be satisfied. The foremost among them is freedom from fear. The process to secure freedom from fear, however, is a heterogenous one. Whereas in some parts of the world it may end in establishing democracies, in other parts of the world it may be found in pursuit of nationalism, revolution, or religious revivalism led by charismatic authoritarian leaders.

Whereas the forces of global integration are universal, the forces of global fragmentation are culture-specific and particular. There is an inherent tension between the search for freedom from want and the achievement of freedom from fear. Whereas freedom from want requires integration and increased collaboration, freedom from fear involves breaking up large and potentially oppressive political structures such as multinational empires or states that have been held together by force.[36] This is not a new phenomenon. The industrial revolution of the late eighteenth and early nineteenth centuries was a byproduct of an integrative and cross-national process. But this period also witnessed the rise of nationalism, which led to the breakup of the Austro-Hungarian, Russian, and Ottoman empires and destroyed their common markets. Hence, the imperialism of the late nineteenth and early twentieth century linked the remote corners of the world to the heartland of European capitalism and its colonial domination. But in doing so it gave rise to national liberation movements that created some 170 separate modern nation-states today.[37] The challenge of modern history has been to strike a balance between these two forces of integration and fragmentation, globalization and nationalism.

Politically, there is also a dual development: The emergence of suprastate regional trading blocs and their governmental associations combined with a resurgence of autonomous substate nationalism. Although international law recognizes the sovereignty of suprastate entities such as the European Community, it denies them to substate entities (national and ethnic minorities). The entire international system of the twentieth century is based on the sovereignty of states. Other groups that did not possess a state (ethnic and national minorities) were deprived of sovereignty. Since international law did not recognize nonstate entities as sovereign, these minorities could get recognition and thus autonomy only by seizing state power. This is yet another explanation for the revival of ethnic and nationalist militancy.

With the decline and disintegration of the empires—the Soviet empire being the last one—and the rise of global democratization, hitherto suppressed ethnic and national minorities have found an opportunity to assert their right to self-determination. This could be considered as the second wave of anti-colonialism, the first one being the anti-colonialism that swept Latin America, the Middle East, and Africa in the late nineteenth and early twentieth centuries. Hence, the theoretical basis of classical liberalism—allowing political rights exclusively to individuals—has been shattered. Both classical liberalism and Marxism have failed to incorporate individual and group rights simultaneously within a single authority structure. Therefore, both Marxist and liberal states are being challenged by minority groups. The emerging state of the twenty-first century may well have to incorporate non-state forms of sovereignty.[38]

On the supra-state level, three trading blocs are emerging: a mark-dominated bloc led by Germany (EC), a dollar-dominated bloc led by the United States (NAFTA), and a yen-dominated bloc led by Japan (ASEAN). The strongest economic bloc in the world is no longer the United States but the European Community, within which Germany has become the strongest nation. Perhaps fear of resurgent German domination motivated Mitterrand and Thatcher to plead with Gorbachev against German reunification. The creation of a joint French-German security force and a joint Italian-British military force also indicates that Europeans intend to be less dependent on an American military umbrella and the political cost associated with it.

Since 1985 the Japanese have invested more than $25 billion in the economies of Southeast Asia in an attempt to create a sphere of "co-prosperity" throughout the Pacific. Japan has also opted for a more independent course in its foreign policy. For example, Japan and the United States are pursuing different policies in regard to China since the crackdown on the democracy movement in Tiananmen Square. While the United States maintains its distance from China, Japan has been much more accommodating. Japanese military power is growing rapidly and it possesses the sixth-strongest military in the world. If this trend continues, Japan will also be much less dependent on U.S. military might in the future.

The Americas bloc ("the debtor bloc") may not fare too well in face of the astronomical increase of the U.S. budget deficit. As her economic power declines, the United States cannot maintain military superiority for long. Conscious of this fact, the American free trade zone (NAFTA) is supposed to provide the American economy with a sufficiently large market and supply of resources to maintain its economic competitiveness and viability.

A clear international division of labor is emerging. The developing nations of Africa, the Middle East, and parts of Latin America have become the producers of primary commodities (raw materials and mineral resources), the newly industrializing countries of Southeast Asia (Taiwan, South Korea, Hong Kong, and Singapore) are engaged in a bustling manufacturing business, and the industrial world (the United States, Western Europe, and Japan) are leading the technological and information-based service economies. In the United States alone, for example, currently 75 percent of the population is employed in service industries. Facing increasing environmental regulation, higher taxes, and labor costs, much heavy industry is also moving from the First World to the newly industrializing countries.

Despite the wishes of Gorbachev and Yeltsin to the contrary, the former Soviet Union has been left out of her "common European home"—the European Community—in this emergence of regional blocs and international division of labor. Indeed, as they become deeply mired in debt and exceedingly dependent on Western capital, loans, and expertise, much of the former Soviet Union and Eastern Europe may undergo some kind of "Latin Americanization." The future for these regions may not hold economic prosperity and democracy. Rather, it may well usher in a new era of fragmentation, ethnic strife, and rising violence induced by increasing economic inequality and the disappearance of a social safety network for the poor. In the unfolding fragmentation of the former Eastern bloc, such countries as Hungary, Poland, and the Czech Republic may ultimately become integrated in the European Community, while less-developed countries, such as Romania, Bulgaria, Slovakia, and the former Yugoslavia, may increasingly assume the characteristics of Third World economies. The same holds true for Russia, Ukraine, and the Balkan states, which hold a better promise of development than the less-developed Central Asian republics and the Caucasus of the former Soviet Union.

Prospects for the Third World

With the collapse of Communism in the Soviet Union and Eastern Europe, an alluring model of self-sufficiency and economic equality lost its luster for many Third World societies. From Ethiopia to Angola and Algeria, many former command economies began experimenting with privatization and a free enterprise system. Hence, since the Soviet support of Third World nationalism that to some extent deterred Western domination has disappeared, we may witness a new era of Pax Americana. This, however, is only one side of the story. Now that the restrictions of the cold war alliances have been lifted, the possibility of Third World

maneuverability and independent action has also increased. Such possibilities are always circumscribed by the pervasive poverty, economic
dependence, and political vulnerabilities of Third World societies.
Nevertheless, as long as they do not seriously threaten Western "interests," the semi-independent actions of Third World leaders may be more
tolerated by the United States and its allies. In the absence of "the communist threat," the future methods of control are more likely to be economic ones rather than military ones. The IMF and the World
Bank–sponsored privatization programs, the removal of impediments to
free trade and free enterprise systems, and further integration of the
Third World into the world capitalist economic system are among the
major Western policies to control the Third World. Where economic
pressures are not effective, the United States has not hesitated to use
military power to subdue its Third World opponents. A leak from the
Bush administration indicated that "much weaker enemies" must be
defeated "decisively and rapidly." Any other outcome could be "embar-
rassing" and might "undercut political support."[39]

The era of prolonged conflicts, such as the ones witnessed in Korea
and Vietnam, is over. It is more likely that in future military confrontations, heavy deployment of air power and surgical strikes may become
the dominant modus operandi. As the United States loses its competitive edge vis-à-vis Japan and Germany, some suggest that, as the only
remaining military superpower, the United States must sell its "monopoly power in the security market." In other words, the United States
must charge its wealthy allies a "war premium to protect their interest."[40]

While the end of the cold war has diminished the possibility of major
war and military conflict among great powers, the possibility of North-
South conflict has escalated, as the invasion of Panama and the Persian
Gulf War demonstrate.

Having observed the devastating power of the high-technology
weapons of the allied coalition during the Persian Gulf War and being
aware of the increasing likelihood of regional conflicts, many Third
World nations concluded that to safeguard their sovereignty, they must
acquire high-technology weapons. This has induced a new arms race in
the Third World. In the Middle East, for example, the United States
alone sold $18 billion in arms to its allies—namely Saudi Arabia, Kuwait,
Egypt, and Israel—in 1992. Russia and the former republics of the Soviet
Union, desperate for cash, are also engaged in the burgeoning business
of arms sales in the Third World. The acquisition of modern weapons by
some Third World nations has provided a new pretext for the continued

existence of the military-industrial complex and its never-ceasing quest for more sophisticated weaponry and self-aggrandizement.[41]

The "Soviet threat" having disappeared, now the Pentagon is in pursuit of new enemies. Topping the list of the new foes are the stereotypes of the Middle Eastern "Muslim fundamentalist-terrorist" and the Latin American "drug trafficker." This has given the American defense establishment a new mission. As political scientist Bruce Cummings puts it, "[T]he cold war consisted of two systems: the containment project, providing security against both the enemy and the ally; and the hegemonic project, providing for American leverage over the necessary resources of our industrial rivals. Both the hegemonic and the allied-containment system have survived."[42] While the cold war might be over, its two projects are not. Hence, "the shadow conflict of the cold war" obscured two salient facts. First, the Soviet power was inflated out of proportion. Second, it distorted the real purpose of the cold war for America—intervention in the Third World from Korea to Iran, Guatemala, the Dominican Republic, Cuba, Chile, and Vietnam. The cold war provided a convenient pretext for projecting American hegemony into the Third World.

As of 1991, the Bush administration was engaged in four proxy wars in the Third World to overthrow "Communist" or "unfriendly" governments. In Cambodia the administration supported a coalition dominated by the genocidal Khmer Rouge, which sought to overthrow the Vietnam-backed Hun Sen government. In Angola, it backed the right-wing National Union for the Total Independence of Angola (UNITA) against the Moscow-backed government of MPLA. In Afghanistan, it continued to support seven Muslim conservative groups against the pro-Soviet Njibullah regime. In El Salvador, it supported the right-wing Republican National Alliance (ARENA) against the Marxist Farabundo Marti Liberation Front (FMLN).[43] Despite Castro's conciliatory overtures, the siege of Cuba continues to the present day. These events indicate that the hegemonic project continues despite the end of the cold war. Although the cold war between the United States and the Soviet Union may have ended, it unmistakably continues between the United States and the Third World.

The end of the cold war and the reduced superpower competition, combined with an inward-looking vision of the Clinton administration, may tempt some of the Third World hegemonic powers to step in to fill the vacuum. The Iraqi invasion of Kuwait, for example, can be partially explained as an attempt by Saddam Hussein to establish himself as the new regional power in the face of receding Soviet presence. However, these regional power struggles and rivalries could lead to new wars and conflicts. The vanishing of a bipolar world also connotes that the raison d'être for the nonaligned movement, which for three decades served as the banner of Third World unity and solidarity, no longer exists. This, in turn, leads to fragmentation of alliances and the escalation of regional competition.

So far as the Third World is concerned, one possible outcome of the rise of a multipolar world could be trilateralism and cooperation among advanced industrial states, accommodation and cooptation of the former Soviet Union and Eastern Europe, and domination of and confrontation with the Third World.[44]

More alarming is perhaps the deterioration of conditions within the Third World. Statistics indicate that the developing countries suffered a decline in per capita income during 1980–89. The World Bank estimates that "as many as 950 million of the world's 5.2 billion people are chronically malnourished—more than twice as many as a decade ago. In Africa, per capita food production has declined every year for the past thirty years."[45] Moreover, the average income in most of Latin America in the 1980s fell by 10 percent—and by more than 20 percent in Sub-Saharan Africa. In some urban areas, real minimum wages declined by as much as 50 percent.[46]

The end of the cold war may not be a harbinger of prosperity and freedom in the Third World. Those who point to the successful example of the newly industrializing countries of Taiwan, Singapore, Hong Kong, and South Korea forget that the conditions that made their growth possible are, for the most part, absent in many parts of the Third World. The newly industrializing nations of Southeast Asia developed in an era when protectionism and competition were much less in the world market. Due to an inadequate infrastructure and educational system, the development of high technology is also problematic in many Third World countries. The declining cost of raw materials and the escalating cost of industrial goods deepen the already rampant poverty of the Third World and further impede its economic development. As the former Soviet republics and the Eastern European countries compete vigorously with the Third World to attract capital, investment and loans, the post–cold war period may be an era of diminishing resources for the Third World.

Nor can democracy remedy the problems of underdevelopment and poverty in the Third World. The recent wave of global democratization has had some gains, especially in Latin America. However, in so far as democratization is not accompanied with equitable division of wealth, it is bound to remain short-lived and unstable.[47] Hence, other correlates of democracy, such as a high level of literacy, the absence of internal strife and ethnic conflicts, and cultural norms supportive of democratic rule, are missing in much of the Third World.[48]

With a population doubling every 25 years—one of the fastest rates of population growth anywhere in the world—[49] and the least capability to remedy the pressure of their burgeoning population on their deteriorating environment and meager resources, many parts of the Third World face bleak prospects for economic development. Such poor economic conditions are bound to take their toll on fragile social institutions, thus increasing the possibility of arbitrary rule and authoritarianism, if not chaos. The complete breakdown of political and social institutions and norms in Somalia, and to a lesser extent in Afghanistan and Sudan, provides poignant and tragic recent examples. Such developments may in turn lead to internal strife or extraterritorial wars.

Significant transformations over the past 40 years have also diminished the strategic value of the Third World. The nuclear revolution, the emergence of information and service-oriented production in the industrial economies, and the decline of Soviet power have all contributed to the strategic decline of the Third World.[50]

The massive nuclear arsenals have devalued conquered territory, including Third World territory, in the projection of power. With the ascendence of high-technology and information-based industries, as well as the strengthening of the environmental movement, it is likely that the reliance on raw materials (with the exception of oil) will diminish considerably in the near future. If the "second cold war" was fought over the control of the Third World, the decline of the Soviet Union also renders the Third World strategically less significant.[51] Many Third World countries that had confrontations with the United States (for example, Cuba, Nicaragua, Angola, Ethiopia, Vietnam, and Cambodia) were also the recipients of Soviet aid and arms; without Soviet assistance, they have opted for more accommodationist policies toward the United States and Western Europe. Whether the United States and its allies will take this gesture as an opportunity to rebuild North-South relations on a new and more humane basis remains to be seen.

CONCLUSION

Although the economic and cultural contexts of global politics have changed dramatically and the cold war has come to an end, much of the old power politics has persisted as the order of the day. The colossal changes since 1985 pose exciting challenges and opportunities for re-creating the world. Yet the obstacles are formidable and daunting. The tenuous coexistence of integration and fragmentation forces that induce both economic interdependence and cultural particularism have given rise to a global village on the one hand, and the resurgence of primordial loyalties and atavism on the other. The rise of virulent ethnic, religious, and national conflicts threaten to break asunder the fiber of many nation-states. The old superpower rivalry and East-West confrontations are being replaced by regionalism and regional conflicts. As the old empires disintegrate, the process of unwinding is outstripping the capacity to create new institutions and viable social and economic policies to rebuild the newly independent nations. Thus, incoherence and fragmentation are emerging as the norm of the postmodern and post–cold war era.

The prospects for the Third World in the new world order are less than promising. While the trend toward democratization in some parts of the Third World is encouraging, the challenge of economic development in face of an increasing population, limited resources, and the cycle of dependency and poverty is formidable indeed. Unless there are funda-mental changes in the global economic and power structure, or new policies emerge to address Third World endemic poverty, the North-South conflict will replace the East-West conflict.

The proliferation of the arms race within the Third World and the pre-eminence of regional conflicts, increasing economic competition, and the rise of primordial loyalties render the meager achievements of democ-ratization negligible in promoting development. Unless the nature of North-South relations changes from one dictated by a politics of greed and domination to a mutual accommodation and cooperation, only increasing environmental degradation, poverty, and conflict lie ahead for the Third World.

NOTES TO CHAPTER 1

1. William Safire, "The New World Order," *The New York Times Magazine,* 17 February 1991, 14.

2. Richard K. Herrmann, "The Middle East and the New Order," *International Security,* vol. 16, no. 2 (1991), 43.

3. Robert W. Tucker and David C. Hendrickson, *The Imperial Temptation: The New World Order and America's Purpose* (New York: Council on Foreign Relations Press, 1992), 2.

4. *Middle East Report,* vol. 20, no. 6 (November–December 1990), 2.

5. *The Christian Science Monitor,* 23 July 1990, 8; 25 July 1990, 18.

6. As cited by Jerry Sanders, "History and World Order: Framing the Past to Shape the Future," in *Confrontation in The Gulf,* Harry Kreisler, ed. (Berkeley, Calif.: Institute on International Studies, University of California, 1992), 164.

7. Ibid., 165.

8. Tucker and Hendrickson, op. cit., 16.

9. Ibid., 16–17.

10. Ibid., 210–11

11. Steve Weber, "American Foreign Policy and The New World Order," In Kreisler, ed., op. cit., 50.

12. Jerry Sanders, op. cit., 157–58.

13. Peter Kemp, "Oil Tide Turns in OPEC's Favor," *Middle East Economic Digest,* vol. 37, no. 8 (26 February 1993), 2–3.

14. See Mikhail Gorbachev, *A Time For Peace* (New York: Richardson and Steirman, 1986); and *Perestroika: New Thinking For Our Country and the World* (New York: Harper & Row, 1987).

15. Moshe Lewin, *The Gorbachev Phenomenon: A Historical Interpretation* (Berkeley, Calif.: University of California Press, 1988), 44–46.

16. Ibid., 45–57; 145–53.

17. Thomas H. Naylor, *The Gorbachev Strategy: Opening the Closed Society* (Lexington, Ky.: Lexington Books, 1988), 121–24.

18. Severyn Bailer, "Domestic and International Factors in the Formation of Gorbachev's Reforms," *Journal of International Affairs,* vol. 42, no. 2 (Spring 1989), 285.

19. Ibid., 288.

20. Stephen F. Cohen and Katrina Vanden Heuvel, *Voices of Glasnost: Interview with Gorbachev's Reformers* (New York: W. W. Norton & Company), 13–32.

21. Lewin, op. cit., 58–82.

22. Cohen and Vanden Heuvel, op. cit., 13–32.

23. Sylvia Woodby, *Gorbachev and the Decline of Ideology in Soviet Foreign Policy* (Boulder, Colo.: Westview Press, 1989), 5–54.

24. Ibid.

25. Ibid.

26. Giovanni Graziani, *Gorbachev's Economic Strategy in the Third World* (New York: Praeger Publishers, 1990), 1–15.

27. Ibid., 30–71; 83–109.

28. Francis Fukuyama, "The End of History?" *The National Interest* (Summer 1989), 3–18. This thesis is further developed in his book *The End of History and The Last Man* (New York: The Free Press, 1992).

29. John J. Mearsheimer, "Why We Will Soon Miss the Cold War," *The Atlantic Monthly* (August 1990), 35–50.

30. Ibid., 36.

31. John J. Mearsheimer, "Disorder Restored," in *Rethinking America's Security: Beyond Cold War to New World Order,* Graham Allison and Gregory F. Treverton, eds. (New York: W. W. Norton & Company, 1992), 224–25.

32. Paul Kennedy, *The Rise and Fall of Great Powers: Economic Change and Military Conflict from 1500 to 2000* (New York: Random House, 1987). For the opposite

perspective, see Henry R. Nau, *The Myth of American Decline: Leading the World Economy into the 1990s* (New York: Oxford University Press, 1990).

33. Charles Krauthammer, "The Unipolar Moment," in Allison and Treverton, eds., op. cit., 293–306.

34. Richard N. Gardner, "Practical Internationalism," in Allison and Treverton, eds., op. cit., 267–78.

35. John Lewis Gaddis, "The Cold War, the Long Peace, and the Future," in *The End of the Cold War: Its Meaning and Implications,* Michael Hogan, ed. (New York: Cambridge University Press, 1992), 32–33.

36. Ibid.

37. Ibid., 43.

38. Guntram Werther, *Self-Determination in Western Democracies* (Westport, Conn.: Greenwood Press, 1992).

39. Noam Chomsky, "A View from Below," in *The End of the Cold War: Its Meaning and Implications,* Michael Hogan, ed. (New York: Cambridge University Press, 1992), 142–43.

40. Ibid., 143.

41. Ibid., 148.

42. Bruce Cummings, "The End of the Seventy-Years' Crisis: Trilateralism and the New World Order," in *Past as Prelude: History in the Making of the New World Order,* (Meredith Woo Cummings and Michael Loriaux, eds. (Boulder, Colo.: Westview Press, 1993), 26.

43. Stephen Van Evera, "The United States and the Third World: When to Intervene?" in *Eagle in a New World,* K. Oye, R. Lieber, and D. Rothchild, eds. (New York: HarperCollins, 1992), 105.

44. Cummings, op. cit., 30–31.

45. Gar Alperovitz and Kai Bird, "The Fading of the Cold War—and the Demystification of Twentieth-Century Issues," in *The End of the Cold War: Its Meaning and Implications,* Michael Hogan, ed. (New York: Cambridge University Press, 1992), 212.

46. Ibid., 213.

47. Zehra Arat, *Democracy and Human Rights in the Developing Countries* (Boulder, Colo.: Lynne Rienner, 1991).

48. Samuel P. Huntington, *The Third Wave: Democratization in the Late Twentieth Century* (Norman, Okla.: University of Oklahoma Press, 1991).

49. Nicholas Eberstadt, "Population Change and National Security," *Foreign Affairs,* vol. 70, no. 3 (Summer 1991): 117–18. According to Eberstadt by the year 2025, about 84 percent of the earth's population will live in the developing world.

50. Van Evera, op. cit., 115.

51. Fred Halliday, *The Making of the Second Cold War* (London: Verso Publishers, 1983).

Farewell to the Pax Americana: Iran, Political Islam, and the Passing of the Old Order

Cyrus Bina

The last decade of the twentieth century is seemingly pregnant with what may become of the twenty-first century, as perhaps the late nineteenth century was, long before the eclipse of Pax Britannica and the succession of Pax Americana. The tensions of unfinished social revolutions were present everywhere during the second half of the nineteenth century in Europe. These tensions were renewed unexpectedly and flourished on a global scale through the Russian Revolution (1917), the Chinese Revolution (1949), and many more revolutionary movements in the Third World during the twentieth century. Finally, despite three centuries of struggle for separation of church and state, the late twentieth century is revealing its latest drama in a series of political surprises in terms of Islamic ideology. I will argue that today's Islam is presenting itself as a *third* ideological alternative to either capitalism or so-called communism.

For despite numerous events of lasting significance, the twentieth century may well be remembered for two events that are now close to their final stages. These are the rise and fall of Soviet "Communism" and the rise and fall of American global hegemony. Islamic ideology, however, has lately been presented as a third alternative to the prevailing East-West models.

The fall of the Soviet Union, which not long ago had been considered inconceivable, is now an established fact. But the fall of U.S. hegemony and its cause, especially since the recent Kuwait crisis and the U.S. (or the so-called allied) military intervention against Iraq, has not yet received wide recognition, particularly in the United States. A typical argument within the established political circles runs as follows: With the fall of the Soviet Union, the United States automatically obtained further dominance over the entire world. Hence, the new world order is but the "unipolar" world of unrivaled America. This assessment is nowadays shared equally by the left, including the radical left, as well as the right within the existing political spectrum almost everywhere in the world.

It is now common to employ the lack of Soviet deterrence in explaining, for instance, the severity and asymmetric nature of the U.S. (allied) encounter against Iraq. But this sort of reasoning relies primarily on the viability of the status quo associated with the postwar international system minus the Soviet bloc, despite evidence to the contrary. This view, which is solely focusing on the Soviet decline as the triumph of capitalism, neglects to consider other factors such as the rise of Japan and the European Community, which point to more fundamental changes that have ravaged the configuration of the post-1945 global economy.

I believe that the Soviet disintegration is not the cause but the catalyst in the recent U.S. military action in the Persian Gulf. The size of the expedition, the flimsiness of the target, the manner of response, the dubitable political objectives, and the lack of concern about the enduring and harmful political consequences on the part of the United States are together an indication of circumscribed hegemony. While it is tempting to be dazzled by the shining armor of U.S. military capability, I wish not to consider such a military victory as a sign of U.S. strength. Rather, this military intervention symbolizes the U.S. doubt about its future role in the *new world order.* And it is a reasonable doubt indeed. In other words, beneath this magnificent and unwavering show of force is a detectable political despair.

The decline of the U.S. global hegemony is also discernible from the breakdown of the postwar client-state system. The imposition of the handpicked authoritarian regimes and subversion of the independent nationalist governments in the Third World have long created reservoirs of indignation and volcanoes of rage against the United States. The fragility of the U.S.-supported regimes and the high degree of political polarization have already crippled the postwar subsystem of client states. In the absence of a strong secular movement in the Islamic world, the crises of the client-state system have manifested themselves in terms of the reaction of Islamic ideology. Islamic revivalism, therefore, can be regarded as a political response to the decline of the client-state system. With the decline of both the Western and Soviet political models, the Islamic political movements are increasingly presenting themselves as alternatives.

This chapter is divided into five sections. Section 1 provides a short introduction to the global system under Pax Americana. Section 2 presents a critical interpretation of the U.S. cold war policy, along with three broad containment objectives. Section 3 will provide the connection between the U.S. hegemonic decline and the globalization of the world economy and polity beyond the nation-state. The rise and fall of the client states in the age of Islamic revival will be studied in Section 4. Here, the peculiarities of the Iranian political structure under the Islamic Republic will be examined. My goal in this section is to show the wider implications of what has happened in Iran for the entire "Muslim world." In Section 5, I attempt to reveal the crisis of the U.S. hegemony through the recent U.S. intervention in the Persian Gulf. The main objective of this chapter is to show the transformation of the world beyond the intentions of the actors involved.

1. THE COMING OF PAX AMERICANA

The basic feature of the present global crisis can be seen in recent U.S. military interventions, especially the most recent one in the Persian Gulf. These interventions are the symptoms of a degenerating status of global order that began in the interwar period (1919–39) and quickly paved the way for American ascendance. This global order acquired a hegemonic structure following World War II, but unlike the preceding order was not essentially dependent upon *outright* colonial conquest.[1] World War I put an end to the European monarchies of old imperial order; with World War II a new form of imperialism emerged.

What can be learned from this history, among others, is that the *essential* mission of the emerging world order, known as Pax Americana, was to achieve hegemony over the global economy, global polity, and the socioideological fabric of the world community as a whole.[2] As this hegemony has been challenged from time to time, the United States has resorted to the rule of force through overt and/or covert military interventions of varying magnitude. Here, besides the inherent fragility of such a hegemonic rule, the option of gunboat diplomacy was a last-resort, contradictory, and premature exercise in search of total obedience of the entire world, the old and the new alike.[3] Nevertheless, the missions of these military interventions were qualitatively different from that of the old order during the ascending decades (1945–75) of Pax Americana.

These military interventions were not for colonial plunder, but rather geared toward something more profound, that is, the establishment and control of institutions that were conducive to the transnational accumulation of wealth. Colonial plunder was no longer feasible and, more important, it was indeed a clumsy way of accumulation in the absence of systematic mechanisms for the production and reproduction of wealth. This attempt at a systematic and universal transformation of the less capitalistically developed world was made along with the twin objectives of the transformation and integration of the Third World within the global economy and the imposition of authoritarian political control over the Third World to keep the status quo within the global polity.

The origin and nature of the U.S. post–World War II hegemony, therefore, cannot be adequately understood by reflecting on U.S. military activities alone. For instance, one wonders why continued U.S. military superiority has not been able to save the United States from its sharp economic and political decline since the mid-1970s. The United States has long been losing its competitive national industrial base, has become the largest debtor nation in the world by accumulating more than $4 trillion in national debt, has urban decay and rural poverty of proportional magnitudes, and most important, has lost, as a nation, its technological edge vis-à-vis Japan and the European Community. What has given the United States the status of a global hegemon, since 1945, is precisely its economic strength, combined with the dominance of its rising political power and the might of its firmly established international political institutions. Thus, contrary to the neoconservative visions, such as "the end of history," and despite the unparalleled popularity of the "unipolar" thesis, U.S. global decline is well underway and does not seem reversible.[4]

Although the international system of nation-states has a long history dating from the industrial revolution, Pax Americana presents its specific form in the postcolonial half of the twentieth century. Early U.S. military interventions were part of the American global ascent. Those interventions were conducted out of U.S. strength, whereas the U.S. military interventions of today are none other than counterproductive reactions against the loss of hegemony due to the process of globalization. Resorting to aggression will only make matters worse in the long run. For the time being, however, the world is inevitably entering into a transitional period of disorder. Today, the question of international security has become a major issue in global politics. It is an issue that has also taken center stage in the United States. But, global security is inseparable from global order. The real issue, therefore, is not the security arrangements themselves but for whom they are made and in whose interest. All global orders come with their own corresponding security arrangements. The present world order is dissipating and so is its arrangement for global security.[5]

2. THE U.S. DOCTRINE OF COLD WAR

From the standpoint of economic hegemony, the post-1945 world order bestowed upon the U.S. dollar the status of *universal* currency. Institutionally, the powerful U.S.-dominated global institutions, such as the International Monetary Fund (IMF) and the World Bank, came to oversee and influence the modus operandi of global development, as the ground was paved for proliferation of U.S. dominion throughout the world. Hence, for instance, the advent of a newly devised international monetary arrangement—known as the Bretton Woods system (1945–1971)—became dominant.[6] This monetary standard—coupled with the Marshall Plan for the postwar reconstruction of Europe and the Agency for International Development (U.S. AID) dealing with the Third World—radically furthered the scope of the IMF, the World Bank, and hence the United States' influence in the global economy.[7]

In the meantime, the restructuring of the entire globe depended upon incorporating the Third World—nearly two-thirds of the world's population—into the global economy. Eventually, the peak of U.S. global hegemony was reached after a careful imposition of an elaborate and nearly uniform system of land reform programs in many Third World client states within the U.S. orbit. In Iran, for instance, subsistence agriculture was eradicated to incorporate its economy into the global marketplace.[8] Such a market-oriented shift encouraged the production of cash crops for export, and increased consumption and importation of foodstuffs from the international market. This, ipso facto, typifies the kernel of the modernization (or, more appropriately, pseudo-modernization) paradigm according to Western development models, which, on a grand scale, was forcefully implemented in many Third World countries during the 1950s, 1960s, and 1970s.

A common characteristic of all these economic and social reforms has been a strong authoritarian tendency, without appropriate political reforms conducive to genuine democratization. Instead these programs were allowed to be carried out almost universally from above, often by the same dictatorial regimes who, as darlings of the Western powers, particularly the United States, have actually crushed all democratic movements at inception, and who have brutally dismantled the budding and fragile institutions of democracy in order to safeguard the last outposts of postwar neocolonial legacies.[9] Rhetoric aside, in the minds of many it is doubtful that Washington has ever been interested in democratization of the Third World, let alone democratization of the Islamic world.[10]

From the standpoint of political hegemony, the United States tried to preserve the global status quo in terms of a broad dual objective of containing the Russians on all possible fronts and containing Third World nationalism under the convenient rubric of anti-Communism.[11] The annunciation of the above twin goals was officially celebrated by the Truman Doctrine (upheld, in principle, by all the U.S. presidents from Harry Truman through George Bush), which set the entire course of the postwar global polity on the offensive of the cold war.[12] Finally, the above *external* containments found their *internal* counterpart in the domestic affairs of U.S. citizens. This containment, however, was born out of the real or imagined references to the external threats. McCarthyism was only one example of such repercussions.

3. BEYOND THE NATION-STATE

I have argued that an important global development since World War II has been the elimination of outright colonialism and the institution of formal independence for the existing colonies associated with the fading global order under Britain and other contending colonial powers of the time. The result has been the recognition of many newly established nation-states in the postwar polity. The postwar economy, however, was the subject of a de facto tripartite division, namely, advanced capitalist countries (the First World), the Soviet bloc (the Second World), and the less-developed and postcolonial countries, known as the Third World.

The postwar development of global capitalism emerged both intra-nationally (within the nation-state boundaries) and internationally (beyond such boundaries). Its complex unity can be demonstrated through the continuing triumph of capitalism over the traditional socioeconomic institutions in the Third World; the continuing development of capitalism in the advanced capitalist countries beyond the nation-state; the eventual disintegration of the Soviet bloc into the market economies of a divergent structure; and the contemporary development of the world as a whole toward a transnationalized socioeconomic order. Today, these interrelated changes are the fundamental basis of the global economy and its corresponding global polity.[13]

The postwar transformation of the Third World, through the stage of "primitive accumulation," is tantamount to the departure from the *colonial* world order, the maintenance of which centered on the politico-military dominance. Under Pax Americana, the raison d'être of global hegemony originated in socioeconomic reproduction. Here, contrary to outright plunder, the motivating factor has been to penetrate into every corner of the globe and to remove every shred of pre-capitalist structure that may stand in the way of global capitalist production, as long as it serves the hegemony of the United States. Historically, the complexity of transformation under the above system has been considerable, especially from the standpoint of challenges that were brought to bear on the very structure of the nation-state. It is also within such a context, for instance, that the significance of the last four decades of import-substitution and export-led development in the Third World can come to light.[14]

The further Pax Americana engaged in a worldwide eradication of traditional social relations, the further it extended the scope of the globalization process. At the same time, the broader the extent of globalization, the narrower the hegemonic sphere of the nation-state, including that of the United States of America. In fact, the key to the decline of Pax Americana lies in this conundrum. The higher the extent of U.S. hegemony, the stronger the potential for the transnationalization of the world. The wider the domain of the transnationalization process, the narrower the confines of U.S. hegemony. This, in part, provides the gist of the present global upheaval in search of a new world order. At the same time, given the globalization of the world economy, the tripartite division of the world has been losing its applicability. Now that the Second World has gone under and the First World, particularly the United States, has similar substantial domestic concerns as the Third World, what is the significance of such a world division anymore? Only for the lack of a better term shall I continue to refer to the less (capitalistically) developed countries as the Third World.[15]

From the standpoint of the global polity, given the disintegration of the Soviet bloc, it is no longer possible to capitalize on the cold war motto of "the Russians are coming." However, the *containment* of the Third World has become even doubly important for the United States.

In the absence of economic and political hegemony, the United States tends to resort to military confrontation and often stops short of achieving its stated objectives. A case in point was the invasion of Panama. If the Panamanian response to the U.S. president during his Panama visit of June 1992 is any indication, the consequence of such interventions has been to deepen the hostilities between the Panamanian people and the U.S. government. Another case is the massive military expedition against Saddam Hussein in Iraq. The long-term political cost of this blunder is heavy and, sooner or later, will be upon the shoulders of the United States. In other words, the cost of the chain reaction motivated by long years of accumulated colonial resentment and, more important, its demonstrated effect on the Third World will be incalculable. What has been paid so far is just the tip of the iceberg.

An important dimension of the U.S. containment of the Third World is the blanket accusation and indeed mischaracterization of the Islamic world. Here, I neither wish to glorify the Islamic ideology, nor to justify the actions of certain Islamic governments, nor to approve of the positions of the various Islamic political groups. Thus, aside from the approval or disapproval of the peculiar political forces in the Islamic world, the racist characterizations of its peoples by the Western world in general and by American society in particular cannot be easily overlooked. This is a significant issue, especially with the arrival of the new right in the center of the political stage in the United States during the Reagan and Bush administrations. Demonizing through such labels as "terrorist nations," "Muslim terrorists," or even the attempt to indict an entire region, such as the Middle East, has been the rule rather than the exception.

In sum, in the absence of economic and political hegemony, given the U.S policy of containment, one may expect that such attacks against Third World tensions will increase during the 1990s.

4. FROM ISLAMIC REVIVAL TO THE ISLAMIC REPUBLIC

The Islamic State Under the Velayat-e Faqih

Islamic ideology would not have received as much attention as it did during the last decade, had it not been for the 1979–80 Khomeini seizure of power in Iran. That is why we consider post-1979 Iran as the precursor of de facto Islamic revival worldwide, even though, in the first place resorting to Islamic discourse was never abandoned in the "Muslim world." Thus, the case of Islamic revival in Iran must be viewed as an illustration par excellence, which has far-reaching implications both for client states and postcolonial states.

"The Islamic Revolution in Iran is the most recent institutional expression of . . . [the transformation of Islam from] a universal religion to a political ideology with universal claims."[16] Hence the term *Islamic ideology,* whose historical roots can be traced to the works of such pioneers as Jamal al-Din Asadabadi Afghani (1838–97), Muhammad Abduh (1849–1905), and Rashid Rida (1865–1935).[17] As for the corpus of the present discourse on Islamic ideology in Iran, it comprises several doctrines of variant tendencies, whose notable exponents are Mahmoud Taleghani (1911–79), Ali Shari'ati (1933–77), and Murteza Motahhari (1919–79).[18] But it was the doctrine of the velayat-e faqih (the guardianship of the religious jurisprudent), by Ruhollah Khomeini (1902–89), that soon after the fall of the Shah came to prominence and became the law of the land.[19]

By the spring of 1979, invoking the dictum of *velayat-e faqih,* and enforcing the regime of the Islamic Republic onto the defunct realm of monarchy, the new state came to existence.[20] The new regime, however, soon embraced the most distinctive characteristic of the Shah's regime, that is, autocracy, despite its revolutionary rhetoric and populist outlook.[21] The *velayat-e faqih* thus must be taken seriously both from the standpoint of theory and in its practice since 1980 in Iran. Moreover, we believe that the contemporary form of state in Iran is living proof of the dialectical relations of both theory and practice of the *velayat-e faqih,* and, as such, it is a typical model that has to be understood on its own, separate from its ritualistic connotation.

"Despite all his diatribes against despot [sic] and his revolutionary language, it is quite clear that the system of government that Khomeini proposes is no more democratic than Maududi's [a Pakistani Muslim thinker] Islamic state. Although it is meant to be government for the people, it is certainly not government by the people."[22] Khomeini himself is explicit on this point when he maintains, "The governance of the *faqih* is a rational and extrinsic matter; it exists only as a type of appointment, like the appointment of a guardian for a minor."[23] In other words, according to Khomeini, the governance of the *umma* under Islamic government follows the guardianship of an appointed *faqih* over a minor (*saghir*) and/or imbecile (*safih*), who, in both cases, are incapable of making decisions according to their own interest and, thereby, are deemed incapable of managing their own affairs. Such a delegation is clearly involuntary and unintended from the standpoint of the subject. It is a kind of representation that obtains legitimacy based upon the *incapacity* of the subject to represent oneself. Here, of course, the guardianship of the minor is limited by the age of the subject, whereas the guardianship of imbecile is a longer proposition, which strives to safeguard the welfare of the subject during the individual's lifetime. The nature of governance under the *velayat-e faqih* is thus analogous to the guardianship under the latter category. Finally, such a governance seems to be leaping, via the *fallacy of composition,* from individual guardianship to the guardianship of the nation as a whole.

Another issue is the anticipation of adequate measures against the probable abuses that may arise from the *faqih's* improper governance once the *velayat-e faqih* becomes the law of the land. In Shi'a Islam, the *faqih's* own personal virtue, combined with a fully developed knowledge of divine law and justice and the inadmissibility of *absolute* ruling by a governing *faqih* over other *foqaha* (plural for *faqih*) are preventive impediments against absolute rule. Khomeini maintained that "the ruler should be foremost in knowledge of the laws and ordinances of Islam and just in their implementation . . . *foqaha* do not have absolute authority in the sense of having authority over all other *foqaha* of their own time, being able to appoint or dismiss them. There is no hierarchy, ranking one *faqih* higher than another or endowing one with more authority than another."[24] "This [latter] principle proved extremely difficult to put into practice after the creation of the Islamic Republic [in Iran]. It is one thing to disagree with a *faqih,* by virtue of the permissibility of difference of opinion on secondary matters, while he is a mere religious dignitary among his peers; *it is quite another to oppose his views when he is acting as [the] head of state.*"[25]

Moreover, given the twofold nature of the *velayat,* he could issue a purely religious order or *al-hukm al-kashif,* having to do with the task of *marja'iyyat,* which would not require Muslims to do anything that had not already been demanded of them. On the other hand, he could issue a custodial order or *al-hukm al-waliyati,* which is given according to the *faqih's* own perception of what is good for the Muslim community.[26] Here, the orders of both kind must be observed by the *umma,* but only the ordinances of custodial type are obligatory for other *foqaha* to follow.[27] The significance of the latter point, however, had already been anticipated by Khomeini in his Arabic version of *Book of Sale (Kitab al-bay),* where he "clearly asserts the superiority of the *faqih* who has acquired the status of political ruler (*hakem*) over the others."[28] "The emerging system is thus an autocracy, which cannot possibly be reconciled with republicanism or democracy as understood in the West."[29]

The Islamic Republic: A Contradiction in Terms

The Islamic republic is a contradictory phenomenon in both theory and practice. It cannot remain a republic anymore in the presence of *velayat-e faqih* and its imposing concept of guardianship as has been explained. For instance, in the constitution of the Islamic Republic of Iran no mention is made of the principle of consultation (*shura*) or democracy except in Article 7 in which the whole process is subsumed under the hegemony of *imamate,* which deals with the question of succession in Shi'a Islam.[30] Secondly, the government of the Islamic Republic in Iran is not Islamic to the extent that the ruling *faqih* affects the lives of the *foqaha* through the mandates of custodial order, a binding rule that may very well diminish the capacity to carry out *independent* religious order. This is nothing except subordination of the task of the *marja'iyyat-e taqlid* to the authority of *velayat* itself. "With the establishment of Islamic government *marja'iyyat,* in practice and officially [*sic*], took the form of the leadership and rule over society; and the *velayat-e faqih* . . . with this revolution reached perfection in practice and occupied its true station."[31] One also has to remember, among others, the early test of this point in connection with the demotion and confinement of Seyyed Kazem Shari'at-Madari, a Grand Ayatollah, in April 1982 in Iran.[32] Under the *velayat-e faqih,* aside from actual practice, there is conceptually a dialectical relation between the religious order (*hokm-e kashef*) and custodial order (*hokm-e velayati*) that cannot be simply overlooked. In other words, there is no a priori guarantee to separate these realms in advance. Given what has transpired in Iran, it potentially poses a contradiction between the *velayat* (in this case *velayat-e motlagh-e*) and the *marja'iyyat* under Shi'a Islam.

The state under the *velayat-e faqih* may be able to dispense with the concept of justice in its manifold variety according to the secular political institutions in the contemporary world. But it can hardly escape the determining pattern of the social formation (and social forces) upon which it has situated itself. "The history of Islam demonstrates one of the best proven and least known laws of history: an appeal to religious, moral, or philosophical principles is necessary, but it is never enough."[33] A vivid example of this can be found in the relative ease of replacing the monarchy by the *velayat-e faqih* in the spring of 1979 and in the insurmountable difficulty, for instance, in running the domestic economy; reconciling the legitimate demands of the rightful political opposition; managing the oil and other sources of national wealth; holding to an independent economic path within the global economy; responding to urban decay and rural poverty; promoting social security and political freedom; adapting a reasonable policy to respond to legitimate demands of national minorities and women; resolving the problem of urban and agricultural land ownership; and finding a fundamental answer to the growing shantytowns, swollen by the destitute, that are now erected as a permanent fixture at the gates of all major cities in Iran.[34]

Despite the apparent delicate differences between the state's ideological and institutional configurations under the Shah and those of the Islamic Republic, there remains one basic theme that has invariably persisted through both state structures. This common denominator is none other than the state's role in the economic, political and ideological reproduction of civil society. Here, the task of economic reproduction is applied to a capitalist economy whose very structure, despite the departure of the *grand* and *comprador bourgeoisie* (the bourgeoisie connected with the transnational capital under Pax Americana), has been dependent upon the state as the main capitalist itself. One may even refer to it as *state capitalism*, a type that would ordinarily characterize many developing economies of the Third World. "Accordingly, there is nothing to indicate, in a compelling way, that the Muslim religion [or the Islamic government] prevented the Muslim world from developing along the road to modern capitalism, any more than there is anything to indicate that Christianity directed the Western European world along that road. [Historically] Islam did not prescribe to or impose upon the people, the civilization, [or] the states that adopted its teaching any specific economic road."[35]

Thus, aside from specific ordinances, speaking of Islamic economics is misleading. Economics as a discipline, to be worthy of the name, would only follow the exigencies of an historically specific *social formation* rather than the specific form of a nation-state.[36] Consequently, describing Khomeini's views as "an Islamic socialism of sorts," without showing compelling evidence from the social structure, would constitute a misreading of his entire corpus and, as such, invitation to further confusion.[37]

As for the role of the state in the political reproduction and ideological renewal, there are certainly many parallels between the Islamic Republic's and the Shah's governments. The most important is centralized control over the realm of political activity and thus exclusion of the entire political spectrum, except for those factions that are intimately connected to the ruling political structure. Similar to the previous regime, even *Nehzat-e Azadi* (the Liberation Movement), an extremely moderate group led by the first prime minister of the Islamic Republic,

Mehdi Bazargan, has long been harassed and forced to give up politics by the Islamic government in Iran. No meaningful (that is, independent or semi-independent) political activity has been allowed in Iran. Again, under the banner of the *velayat-e faqih,* no serious attempt has been made (and, so far, all attempts have been frustrated) to create an adequate political infrastructure for the task of political and ideological mediation. The essential point, once again, lies in the structural incompatibility of the state within a capitalist framework, rather than the willingness (or unwillingness) for change of state functionaries in this case.

Islam and the Challenge of the New World Order

To understand the nature of the Islamic Republic, one needs to examine the historical as well as global context that has led to its ascent. The decline of the international system of nation-states under the Pax Americana and, with it, the fall of the client-state system, must be considered as a precursor to the fall of the Shah. Khomeini's assumption of power in 1979 may seem to have provided a powerful antithesis to the Shah's regime in terms of the *velayat-e faqih.* From the standpoint of political and ideological mediation, however, the basic character of the state under the Islamic Republic has remained unchanged. In other words, despite the apparent differences, the most distinguishing feature of the state in relation to civil society has remained virtually the same.

On the global plane, the decline of the Pax Americana is tantamount to the transnationalization of the world economy and polity. Such a globalization also presents itself as the antithesis of the vanishing client-state system today. The result is the further integration of such states into the global economy and global polity. Thus, simple departure from the status of a client state, in the presence of rapid global integration, is not sufficient for achieving democracy or independence. Moreover, further integration into the world economy is incompatible with the policy of economic independence. As soon as the Islamic movements obtain the control of the state in the declining client states (or the postcolonial states such as Algeria), they will be subject to the pressures of integration into the global system, despite all utterances to the contrary. In other words, the would-be Islamic republics of the future will, by necessity, have to become part and parcel of the global *synthesis.* To the extent that Islamic movements are unable to assume political power, they will remain, covertly or overtly, groups with a critical ideology within their own nation-states, including those with repressive regimes. This is clearly indicative of the *adaptability* of Islamic ideology to the modern global system. It also shows the compatibility of Islam with modern capitalism, in general, and state capitalism and global capitalism, in particular.

For instance, in an international conference, Iran's foreign minister has recently pointed out that "from a global perspective, a new order is gradually superseding in which economic considerations overshadow political priorities." At the same conference, Iran's president, Hashemi Rafsanjani, maintained that "the concluding years of the twentieth century are marked by world events that have replaced the previous bipolar system by a new order. If this order is to persist, cooperation should replace confrontation."[38] Rhetoric aside, here, one will scarcely find any significant irreconcilable discord between modernized Islamic political ideas and the imperatives of the imposing social formation and socio-economic structure. The Islamic Republic of Iran is a case in point, where the social formation and the *essential* features of the state have not been altered. As an example, "Iran has resurrected and amended a foreign investment law from the overthrown monarchy that allows foreign partners a 49 percent stake in joint ventures and full ability to take their profit out of the country."[39] It is widely believed that "Iran's biggest problem today isn't the heralded struggle over ideology between revolutionary hard-liners and pragmatists—President Hashemi Rafsanjani has that battle well under control. It is the struggle over money."[40]

Having said that, one cannot put the two regimes in the same category from the standpoint of *concrete* political and ideological imperatives. My point of reference here is the global order again. A comparison can be made between the two regimes, respectively, from the perspectives of sovereignty, legitimacy, and governance. The sovereignty of the Shah's regime was contingent exclusively upon Pax Americana, whereas the Islamic Republic is exceedingly constrained by the imperatives of global capitalism beyond the nation-state—the antithesis of the global system under the Pax Americana. The legitimacy of the Shah's regime was dependent upon the appeal to past history (of Persian empires: Cyrus the Great and all the rest) and, of course, the cold war rhetoric, whereas the Islamic Republic's appeal is, by and large, to God Almighty himself, and the rhetoric of "neither East, nor West." As for governance, while both regimes are distinctly authoritarian, the Shah's regime, being manifestly isolated from the civil society, was quintessentially bureaucratic and hierarchical. Under the Islamic Republic, on the other hand, the governance has become totalitarian.

Despite its seemingly invariant message, Islamic ideology differs considerably from country to country or from movement to movement. It delineates a wide spectrum of thought, from transparently ultra-conservative to a convolution of eclectic liberal ideas, in attempting to respond to Eurocentrism, particularly its American version. It is thus inappropriate to categorize all these movements as fundamentalist. If applied indiscriminately, the yardstick of fundamentalism runs counter to the very act of reconciliation of Islam with the existing social formations that are, by necessity, transitory and historical. "What is most important in history is [sic] the deep tendencies flowing from economic, political, and social situations, and ideologies must adapt or die."[41]

As has been suggested, the resurgence of Islamic ideology is a *historic reaction* to the inadequacies and failures of the two powerful global ideologies that have shaped the world during the last several decades, namely Pax Americana and its Soviet counterpart. But, it is one thing to pose as a reaction, and quite another to become a new paradigm. "[If history is any guide] the precepts of Islam have nowhere created a social or economic structure that was radically new."[42] This must be a cause for concern for the dispossessed majority in the Third World in general, and those in the Muslim world in particular, where the paradigm of modernization or *market capitalism* à la the United States, and the model of *state capitalism* à la the Soviet Union (now a defunct paradigm), have not been proved entirely successful as a viable alternative to the existing *traditional* way of life globally. It is doubtful that Islam will do better. "Muslim spirituality may exert a beneficial [or, for that matter, a harmful] influence on the style of practical politics adopted by certain leaders. It is dangerous to hope for more."[43]

Today the signs of resurgent Islam are everywhere. In the Sudan, where Hassan al-Turabi's National Islamic Front controls the military government, "the vacuum left by the failures of Western-inspired African socialism and Arab nationalism" has been filled by the Islamic ideology. "Many Sudanese argue [however] that Turabi's vision of an Islamic world held together by religion and economic interdependence could be taken less seriously if it were not for two factors." First, an appeal to those who are both poor and religious. Second, a close link with the Islamic movements in Egypt, Tunisia, and Algeria, including a multimillion trade and assistance program from the Islamic Republic of Iran.[44] Al-Turabi, however, upholds that "Islam is the only force that remains in this part of the world."[45] Here, one has to return to the basic structure of sociopolitical mediation within the now-defunct Sudanese client state in order to unravel the mysteries associated with the crisis of legitimacy and the question of how a remote political entity would become powerful enough to undermine the exiting political order.

In Algeria, the challenge of the Islamic Salvation Front is unmistakable. "Nearly 7,000 members of the front are held in desert camps, many arrested shortly after the Government canceled elections in January [1992] when it became clear the fundamentalists were well on their way to winning control of Parliament."[46] "The military and the police have stepped up arrests of Muslim fundamentalists since the new ruling council vowed to enforce new regulations against political activity in and around mosques."[47] Again, the context of all this rests upon the structure of the state, the capacity of institutional mediation, and the task of political discourse associated with them.

In Saudi Arabia, where the grip of the royal family upon power was seriously undermined by the recent American intervention, there emerged a movement consisting of both liberals and Muslim militants against the ruling monarchy. "[Since the Persian Gulf War] the militant fundamentalists have been building a growing following in the religious institutions and universities that thrive throughout Saudi Arabia. . . . The movement [known as the Islamic Awakening] has fed off the frustrations of hundreds of thousands of university graduates who have been unable to find jobs." These militant Muslims are also displeased with the Women's Renaissance Association, a liberal women's group in Saudi Arabia.[48] "To understand change here, one must first grasp the status quo, no simple task in a nation where there is no recognizable public discourse, where the media offer disquisitions on Yugoslavia and the West Bank but limit national news to lists of brotherly telegrams sent by Fahd and Crown Prince Abdullah."[49] Here, there is no match between the present archaic (that is, tribal) discourse and the constant demand of the masses for participation in the political process in the absence of adequate social reforms and necessary political institutions. In this situation, symptomatic remedies, such as advising the ruling family to provide more freedom to the contending masses, and so on, are limited, often being made contingent upon the maintenance of the status quo. That is why such rescue missions accomplish too little and normally come too late. The house of state is wrecked from the foundation; the client state is simply doomed beyond repair: On the one hand, the rule of the state cannot remain intact without exerting total control over the society, on the other hand, it exasperates the opposition if it relaxes the magnitude of such a control. Consequently, the views that assign the blame of social turbulence to the *pace* of the liberal reforms, introduced by such client states, are missing the most crucial aspect of the client-state system and the nature of political opposition associated with it.[50] Eventually, with or without such reforms, the antagonistic relations of state and society under such regimes guarantee an intense and drastic upheaval. Saudi Arabia is no exception.

Islam has long been playing as a double-edged sword in the hands of the contending political forces in the Muslim world. Afghanistan, for instance, is a typical case in which Pax Americana and Islam (Afghan Mojahedin) have become intimate bedfellows against the "Russian infidels."[51] The Afghan Mojahedin (not to be mistaken for the Iranian Mojahedin), who seized power recently, are militant and, at the same time, exhibit a strong fundamentalist tendency within their ranks. Yet, contrary to the stereotypical rule of thumb, they have never been targeted in the U.S. media as Muslim fanatics. Had there been no gain from the Islamic sword, U.S. policy toward Afghanistan might have been diametrically opposite. The brand of fundamentalism, as real as it may seem, is more of a convenient cover for concealing the real issues. "It is one of those interesting words that have two contradictory meanings. Applied to an opponent, it is abuse; applied to someone you agree with, it is praise."[52]

5. FALLING HEGEMONY AND CRUMBLING CLIENT STATES

In order to illustrate the contradictions embodied in the client-state system and the U.S. hegemony, I have chosen the recent Middle East crisis that is known as the Persian Gulf War. It is now widely recognized that Saddam Hussein of Iraq is a brutal dictator who has now fallen out of favor with the U.S. government.[53] But he is presumably no better or no worse than other dictators in charge of other client states, like King Fahd, Hosni Mubarak, the Kuwaiti emir, and so on, who are still harbored, or even honored, by the United States throughout the Third World. The question is why such a *sudden* displeasure with Saddam Hussein, when the U.S. government knew all along who he was, so far as the question of democracy is concerned, and how he had previously struck his own and other people with weapons of mass destruction.

But the principal U.S. grievance against Saddam Hussein is the fact that he has violated the sacred rules of the household, despite the political maneuver by the United States that he poses a threat to "freedom" in Kuwait. The evidence is now crystal clear in the case of Kuwait: the emir (of Kuwait) is back, the Kuwaitis who courageously stood up and

58   ISLAM, IRAN, AND WORLD STABILITY

fought against the occupation are now displaced, and the U.S. government is no longer interested in democracy in Kuwait.[54] The latter point
is explicable in light of the universal evidence that the U.S. government
has always preferred "stability" to democracy (in the Third World).
Thus, following a long-standing tradition, it had to rely on the rhetoric
of democracy to provide the necessary illusion.

As the record shows, Saddam Hussein is a microcosm of America's
own global policy in the Middle East. Similar, or even worse, client
regimes, namely, Saudi Arabia, Kuwait, Egypt, Morocco, and the tiny
Persian Gulf sheikhdoms, just to name a few, are now enjoying intimate
relations with the U.S. government. Former President George Bush,
nevertheless, continued to pay lip service to the cause of democracy
globally. Meanwhile, the old client-state subsystem is crumbling. The
once enduring vestiges of Pax Americana in many parts of the world are
now beginning to unravel. In addition, these distant ideological symbols
of "the American way of life" are now being vigorously challenged from
within. Unfortunately, far from being the cure, some of these challenges
are worse than the disease itself. The world is literally out of the frying
pan and right into the fire.

Another important factor in the American order is the role of Israel
in the Middle East. Israel is no stranger to the postwar American hegemony and its triad of containments. First, Israel played a decisive role in
assisting the United States in containment of the Soviet Union. In fact,
the containment of the Soviet bloc made Israel an *organic* part of Pax
Americana. Second, Israel has gradually been given a free hand to pursue its own regional interests virtually without limit. In other words, the
containment of the Middle East, from neutralizing Arab nationalism to
disrupting radical political movements in the region, has become synonymous with the existence of Israel. Ironically, this role of Israel has also
been reinforced by the very U.S. client states in the Arab world that
openly have shown animosity toward Israel. Finally, Israel has been given
the privilege of playing a vigorous role in U.S. internal politics. Cases in
point are roles of the Israeli lobby in the U.S. Congress and in the U.S.
presidential elections. Documents suggest that Israel has been the right
hand of U.S. government in the Middle East, being known in foreign policy circles as the strategic asset. As an inseparable part of the now defunct
Pax Americana, aside from the Palestinian question, Israel will have to
adapt to the realities of the emerging world in one way or the other.[55]

The picture becomes more complex if one includes: (1) the reactions
of backward-looking political forces within the client states, including

the Islamic countries, that are both against U.S. domination and hostile to democratic values, and (2) the state of American political consciousness. The first point is of considerable importance, but it falls outside of our main focus in this essay. As for the second point, that is, the ideological peculiarities of the American society, the experience of the Persian Gulf War is a good indication. For instance, the act of hiding behind yellow ribbons during the Persian Gulf War might be explicable in terms of society's own despair in dealing with this suddenly imposed war. Moreover, for many, the lack of interest in the origin of this tragedy may be a sign of resignation and escape from the responsibility of adequate soul-searching. Whatever the case might be, this is the worst kind of nationalism. What is scornful about this national ritual of hypocrisy is the indifference of those who cry easily against a slight impropriety, but do not mind supporting *our troops,* despite the fact that they themselves have seen the slaughter on television, play by play, all day and all night long. The question is: Why should the Iraqis be subjected to such a genocidal ordeal for the crimes of Saddam Hussein? It appears, prima facie, that this punishment was intended for the nation of Iraq for the inability to emancipate itself from the yoke of Saddam Hussein; a dictator whose atrocities have since the mid-1980s become synonymous with American political wisdom. The cheerleaders of this unfortunate drama were not kind enough to realize that they too are the victims of this tragedy. However, the lack of political sophistication is one thing, the absence of compassion is another.

The present crisis, therefore, is as American as it is Middle Eastern. It is as much a crisis of American hegemony as it is the crisis of Saddam Hussein.[56] It is the crisis of the client-state system. Why should the U.S. government be worried about the lack of access to "cheap" Middle Eastern oil—knowing that the globalization of oil has already diminished the regional boundaries and the significance of traditional (physical) control of the oil fields—in the presence of omnipotent rules of the transnational marketplace? Is it the control of oil or the hegemonic decline that prompted the United States to re-open the old and deep neocolonial wounds of yesteryear?

The Pandora's box has already been opened. In the present era of transition, the U.S. threat to peace is not from strength but from weakness. Rhetoric aside, one may ask: What is the idea of being the only superpower in the world and not being able to compete against "lesser powers" in the marketplace? What is the significance of "winning World War III, without firing a shot," where the global order invokes different winning standards through the transnationalization process?[57] It is apparent that at the present historical crossroad there are more questions than answers, but what is certain is the irreversibility of what has already taken place. We are now moving toward a multipolar world of transnational configuration in which U.S. domination will undoubtedly be cut down. This does not mean that there will be a just and nonimperialist world. It does not even mean that, in an immediate sense, there will be a better world. It will only mean that the United States is no longer a global hegemon.

Consistent with this transnational configuration, since (from the mid-1970s on) "cheap" oil and "expensive" oil will no longer differ in the eyes of global market, one begins to wonder about the motivation of attaching a special priority to Middle Eastern oil.[58] Moreover, while the differential cost of the Middle Eastern oil is a sizable sum, it would appear as differential rent embodied in the global price. Speaking of "cheap" oil is but a smokescreen, an illusion.[59]

During the heat of the war with Iraq, the U.S. government was forced to respond to the uproar of "No Blood for Oil" by inventing several reasons for choosing the war option. These included "jobs," "freedom," "democracy," "the naked aggression that will not stand," and "the rule of law." If this analysis is correct, these reasons are all but hollow justifications. Clearly, one may find no consistency between them and the remarks made early on by former president George Bush on the cause of war. He stated explicitly that this conflict was about the preservation of the "American way of life." This objective has been confirmed once again in his 1991 State of the Union address: "We will get on our way to a new record of expansion, and achieve the competitive strength that will carry us into *the next American century.*"[60] My emphasis is on the last four words, whose pointed message is a desire to revive the mastery of the world. In other words, the singular ambition here is to preserve "the American way of life," in the sense of Pax Americana.

One year later, the same theme recurs in George Bush's 1992 State of the Union address. Pageantry aside, his initial intent is unmistakable: "There are those who say that we can turn away from the world, that we have no special role, no special place. But we are the United States of America, the leader of the West that has become the leader of the world. As long as I am president we will continue to lead . . . for the safety and security of our children."[61]

"The American way of life," of course, means different things to different people. In other words, the American way of life, just like beauty, finds meaning in the eyes of the beholder. The American way of the good life for one can be an American way of a miserable life for another. What matters, therefore, is to figure out in whose interest this way of life is branded as American: in the interest of the power elite who benefit from the status quo, or in the interest of the rest of the society. The point is what would George Bush's (American) way of life offer to the majority of American people and how would he guarantee the "security of our children"? One wonders, what the motivation of George Bush was in imposing (and extending) the embargo against starving Iraqi children in the name of the "security of our children"?[62] Imperialist motivation aside, would it be necessary to impose a zero-sum framework to the "security of our children" and "survival of their children"?

On the other hand, one wonders what the American way of life has in common with preservation of the Saudi and Kuwaiti regimes.[63] Buying off and neutralizing the Arabs with their own source of wealth is a "neat" and powerful idea that has long been pursued by the U.S. government for the sole purpose of *preserving* the American hegemony.[64] Here, crying for democracy and preventing it simultaneously has been the rule rather than the exception, as CIA interventions show.[65] This has been the postwar U.S. foreign policy par excellence in the Middle East and throughout the Third World, for as long as one can remember. The irony is that all this has been done in the name of the American people.

It is hard to understand how the appeal to democracy can be reconciled with its continued obstruction. It is indeed a conundrum that, in its modern version under the Pax Americana, has been an important point of global contention. In order to resolve this contradiction, it may be helpful to focus on the position of the client-state subsystem within the overall international system of nation-states since 1945. Here, the postwar era saw the division of the globe into a two-tier system of the client states and (sovereign) nation-states that made the former a political appendage of the latter.

The American global hegemony has taken precedence over the cause of liberty and pursuit of happiness, especially in the client states.[66] The spillover of this peculiar policy has eventually blemished the cause of freedom and democracy in America and the whole system has been riddled with the contradictory notion of democracy and double-talk under Pax Americana.

The decline of U.S. global hegemony is essentially a contradictory and self-inflicted phenomenon. The postwar evolution of the economic institution of Pax Americana has led to the transnationalization of the global

economy beyond the boundaries of nation-states. The further development of transnational corporations superseded the national economies
and national borders in a major way. The United States, as a new hegemon, helped to reconstruct Western Europe and Japan after World War
II. The economic consequence was the enhancement of globalization at
the expense of the U.S. hegemony, that is, the economic hegemony of a
world order that had already embodied the potential of multipolar transformation. The fall of the Soviet Union merely reinforced what had
already been essentially there.

From the standpoint of political hegemony, the nation-state system
under Pax Americana lost its significance. The client-state system has
been challenged by Third World resistance. The Vietnam experience,
particularly, is a classic example that inspired many Third World countries, and that set the stage for an all-encompassing crisis that swept
through the underpinning of the U.S. client-state system. Other challenges have presented themselves in a variety of forms and under divergent manifestations, including Islamic resurgence. The Islamic political
developments in Iran, the Sudan, Algeria, Egypt, Morocco, Tunisia,
Afghanistan, Pakistan, Southeast Asia and, even, the Muslim states of
the former Soviet Union are all reflecting the breakdown of the old
state structure. More generally, the client states are in a state of decom-
position worldwide.[67]

In sum, the current transnationalized world economy and world polity
constitute a corollary of the demise of Pax Americana. Here, the international system under the U.S. hegemony laid the cornerstone of postwar global capitalism, and by doing so provided the conditions of its own
unraveling nearly four decades later. This has been a contradictory aim,
an inescapable development, which was entirely beyond the intention of
the U.S. leadership. The boomerang returned home in a full circle.

The world of the future will be shaped accordingly, despite the
rhetoric advanced by the U.S. elite.[68] The days of the American global
hegemony are numbered, with or without the cold war. The end of the
cold war has been a catalyst that has only magnified the existing symptoms in the global polity. Accordingly, the crisis of the U.S.-sponsored
client-state system is a visible sign of demise within the entire system. All
this points to the decline of American hegemony. At the same time, the
transnationalization of oil has provided a formidable challenge to the
United States since the early 1970s. No amount of conquest, not even the
total military takeover of Saudi Arabia, can alter the decline of U.S.
global hegemony at this stage of global transformation.

Meanwhile, the U.S. reaction to its hegemonic decline, in conjunction with many more disintegrating regions of the world, poses a threat to the world peace. This is a sign of global disorder. The world order under Pax Americana is no more. The new world order has yet to arrive. The present world order is in a state of limbo, depicting a new world disorder. The recent war and the continued U.S. military presence in the Persian Gulf show that the United States is unwilling to accept the reality of its modified role in the emerging world. Farewell to the good old days is not so easy and, above all, is not so voluntary. Thus we have no choice but to bear the risk of violent transition and political upheaval, such as what we have seen so far, at least for the remaining part of the 1990s.

NOTES TO CHAPTER 2

◆

The major points on the issues of U.S. global containment and oil in this essay have been adapted from my "Changing the Old Guard and the New Oil Order," a paper presented at the joint meetings of the Allied Social Science Association (ASSA) and Middle East Economic Association (MEEA) during January 2–5, 1992, held in New Orleans, Louisiana, and my "The Rhetoric of Oil and the Dilemma of War and American Hegemony," *Arab Studies Quarterly* (Summer 1993). I am grateful to my discussant Jim Horner at MEEA for his helpful suggestions and to Jamal Nassar, editor of *ASQ,* for permission to adapt extensive segments for the present chapter. I wish to thank Reza Alavi; Patrice Brodeur; Houchang E. Chehabi; Noam Chomsky; John L. Esposito; Fawaz Gerges; William A. Graham; Gary Gregg; Elaine Hagopian; Paul D. Hanson; Walid Khalidi; Habib Ladjevardi; Richard A. Lobban, Jr.; Zachary Lockman; Roy P. Mottahedeh; Hussin Mutalib; Rina Schimmel; Lawrence E. Sullivan; and Hamid Zangeneh for their invaluable comments on the earlier drafts of this chapter. This chapter also benefited from Babak Bina's technical assistance. The points on the status of U.S. hegemony are drawn from my May 1992 seminar, sponsored by the CMES Committee on Iranian Studies at Harvard University, and my "Towards a New World Order: U.S. Hegemony, Client-States and Islamic Alternative." The usual disclaimer, however, is in order here, as I alone am responsible for the views or the remaining errors. The major part of the manuscript was completed by August 1992.

1. Paul Kennedy, *The Rise and Fall of the Great Powers* (New York: Vintage Books, 1987); Roger W. Louis, *Imperialism at Bay: The United States and the Decolonization of the British Empire, 1941–45* (New York: Oxford University Press, 1978); Richard Krooth, *Arms and Empire: Imperial Patterns Before World War II* (Santa

Barbara, Calif.: Harvest Publishers, 1980); Carlo M. Cipolla, ed., *The Economic Decline of Empires* (London: Methuen, 1970); Raymond Vernon, *Sovereignty at Bay: The Multinational Spread of U.S. Enterprises* (New York: Basic Books, 1971).

2. Ronald Steel, *Pax Americana* (New York, Viking Press 1977); Cyrus Bina and Behzad Yaghmaian, "Post-War Global Accumulation and the Transnationalization of Capital," *Capital and Class*, no. 43 (Spring 1991). For the immediate postwar period see I. F. Stone, *The Truman Era 1945–1952* (Boston: Little, Brown and Company, 1953). In Chapter 16, titled: "Political Scientists at Work and Play: It May Be Political—But Is It Science?" Stone conveys his recollection of the forty-fifth annual meeting of the American Political Science Association (December 30, 1949–January 2, 1950) at the Hotel Roosevelt in New York, where John Foster Dulles delivered the opening address and Lt. General Alfred M. Gruenther, deputy chief of staff of the U.S. Army, was the first luncheon speaker. Nowadays, of course, in addition to this bastion of science and wisdom, there are hundreds of seminars, conferences, symposia, and so on that are held on a daily basis at the major research institutions in this country. This time the troubling issue for all these truth-seekers is how to invent new enemies in order to deal with the problem of peace. But a new George Kennan has yet to be found. See also *Department of State Bulletin*, vol. 10 (May 27, 1944).

3. James Cable, *Gunboat Diplomacy* (New York: Praeger Publishers, 1971).

4. See, for instance, the text of George Bush's State of the Union message where he declared: "Much good can come from the prudent use of power. And much good can come from this: A world once divided into two armed camps now recognizes one *sole and preeminent power, the United States of America,*" *New York Times*, 29 January 1992, A16 (emphasis added); Matthew Wald, "Bush Asserts Need for Foreign Oil," *New York Times*, 21 February 1991, D1; Cyrus Bina, "The Rhetoric of Oil and the Dilemma of War and American Hegemony," *Arab Studies Quarterly* (Summer 1993): 1–20. Cyrus Bina, "Global Oil and Unviability of *Pax Americana,*" *Economic and Political Weekly*, 11 July 1992, 1467–69; Francis Fukuyama, "The End of History," *National Interest* (Summer 1989); as the title of his article suggests, Fukuyama misrepresents and vulgarizes Hegel ad infinitum in order to bring respectability to his racist and colonialist views. He states: "[In] the two world wars in this century—the various provinces of human civilization were brought up to the level of its most advanced outposts—forcing those societies in Europe and North America at the Vanguard of civilization to implement their liberalism more fully" (p. 5). He apparently refers to none other than the two world wars that led to the unprecedented extermination of some eighty million people. This may be somewhat similar to the recent statement by the Pope on the so-called Columbus's *discovery* of America, pointing out that it was not appropriate from the standpoint of the suffering inflicted on the natives but quite a justified act for the spread of Christianity in the New World.

5. Among many good sources, the following books present more explicit analysis: Noam Chomsky and Edward Herman, *The Washington Connection and Third World Fascism* (Boston: South End Press, 1979); Noam Chomsky, *The Culture of Terrorism* (Boston: South End Press, 1988); Noam Chomsky, *Necessary Illusions: Thought Control in Democratic Societies* (Boston: South End Press, 1989); Philip Agee, *CIA Diary* (Baltimore, Md.: Penguin Books, 1975); Daniel Ellsberg's *The Pentagon Papers, New York Times* edition (New York: Bantam, 1971); Thomas Powers, *The Man Who Kept Secrets: Richard Helms and the CIA* (New York: Simon & Schuster, 1979); William A. Williams, "American Century: 1941–1957," *The Nation* (November 2, 1957): 297–300; Fred Halliday, *Arabia Without Sultans* (Harmondsworth: Penguin, 1974).

6. Robert Solomon, *The International Monetary System, 1945–1981* (New York: Harper & Row, 1982); Gerald M. Meier, *Problems of A World Monetary Order* (New York: Oxford University Press, 1974). Following a worldwide monetary crisis, the Bretton Woods system was dismantled officially by the Nixon administration on August 15, 1971. See also David P. Calleo, ed., *Money and the Coming World Order* (New York: New York University Press, 1976); Benjamin M. Rowland, ed., *Balance of Power or Hegemony: The Interwar Monetary System* (New York: New York University Press, 1976). For a systematic treatment and radical critique of the international trade and monetary arrangements, see Anwar Shaikh, "Foreign Trade and the Law of Value," Parts I and II, *Science and Society* (Fall 1979; Spring 1980): 281–302, 27–57.

7. Sidney S. Alexander, *The Marshall Plan* (Washington, D.C.: National Planning Association, 1948). For the notion of Hegemony see Antonio Gramsci, *Prison Notebooks* (New York: International Publishers, 1971), Sec II, Ch. 2; Robert Bocock, *Hegemony* (New York: Tavistock Publishers, 1986); Robert O. Keohane, *After Hegemony* (Princeton, N.J.: Princeton University Press, 1984).

8. Farshad Araghi, "The World Historical Origins of Agrarian Change In Iran: 1870–1970," unpublished Ph.D. dissertation, University of Georgia, 1990. See also a series of original research on the Shah's land-reform programs published in Iran by OIPFG: I. *Dar Bare-ye Eslahat-e Arzi va Natayej-e Mostaghim-e 'An* (On Land Reforms and Their Direct Consequences) (Mordad, 1352 [1972]); II. *Bar-rasi-e Sherkat-hay-e Sahami-e Zera'i* (A Study of the Agricultural Cooperatives) (Aban: 1353 [1974]); III. *Bar-rasi-e Sakht-e Eghtesadi-e Roustahay-e Fars* (A Study of the Rural Economic Structure of Fars Province) (Bahman, 1352 [1973]); and IV. *Bar-rasi-e Sakht-e Eghtesadi-e Roustahay-e Kerman* (A Study of the Rural Economic Structure of Kerman Province) (Khordad, 1353 [1974]).

9. Michael Hudson, *Super Imperialism: The Economic Strategy of American Empire* (New York: Holt, Rinehart and Winston, 1972).

10. For a detailed analysis, see Section 5.

11. Melvyn P. Leffler, "The American Conception of National Security and the Beginnings of the Cold War, 1945–1948," *American Historical Review* 89 (April 1984): 346–81; Stephen L. McFarland, "A Peripheral View of the Origins of the Cold War: The Crisis in Iran, 1941–1947," *Diplomatic History* 4 (Fall 1980): 333–51; David Green, *The Containment of Latin America: A History of the Myths and Realities of the Good Neighbor Policy* (Chicago: Quadrangle Books, 1971); William A. Williams, "The Irony of Containment," *The Nation*, 5 May 1956, 376–379.

12. Harry S. Truman, *Memoirs: Years of Decisions,* vol. I (New York: Doubleday, 1955); Harry S. Truman, *Memoirs: Years of Trial and Hope,* vol. II (New York: Doubleday, 1956); Joseph M. Jones, *The Fifteen Weeks* (New York: Viking, 1955); Walter Lippmann, *The Cold War* (New York: Harper, 1947); George F. Kennan, *Memoirs: 1925-1950* (Boston: Little, Brown and Company, 1967); D. F. Fleming, *The Cold War and Its Origin,* 2 vols. (New York: Doubleday, 1961); Dean Acheson, *Present at the Creation* (New York: W. W. Norton, 1969); I. F. Stone, *The Hidden History of the Korean War* (New York: Monthly Review Press, 1952); Arnold J. Toynbee, *America and the World Revolution* (New York: Oxford University Press, 1961); David Horowitz, *The Free World Colossus: A Critique of American Foreign Policy in the Cold War* (New York: Hill and Wang, 1965); Dwight D. Eisenhower, *The White House Years: Mandate for Change, 1953-1956* (New York: Doubleday, 1963); Dwight D. Eisenhower, *The White House Years: Waging Peace, 1956-1961* (New York: Doubleday, 1965); Otis L. Graham, Jr., *Toward a Planned Society: From Roosevelt to Nixon* (New York: Oxford University Press, 1976); Howard Zinn, *A People's History of the United States* (New York: Harper & Row, 1980); John Lewis Gaddis, *Strategies of Containment: A Critical Appraisal of Postwar American National Security Policy* (New York: Oxford University Press, 1982); Seyom Brown, *The Faces of Power: Constancy and Change in United States Foreign Policy from Truman to Reagan* (New York: Columbia University Press, 1983); Seymour M. Hersh, *The Price of Power: Kissinger in the Nixon White House* (New York: Summit Books, 1983); Richard M. Nixon, *Richard Nixon: The Memoirs of Richard Nixon* (New York: Grosset and Dunlap, 1978); Murray B. Levin, *Political Hysteria in America: The Democratic Capacity for Repression* (New York: Basic Books, 1971); Max Lowenthal, *The Federal Bureau of Investigation* (Washington, D.C.: William Sloane Associates, 1950); D. Caute, *The Great Fear: The Anti-Communist Purge Under Truman and Eisenhower* (London: B. Secker and Warburg, 1978); R. J. Goldstein, *Political Repression in Modern America from 1870 to the Present* (Cambridge, Ma., Schenkman Publishing Co., 1978).

13. Here, my globalization argument is fundamentally different from that of the world-systems variety—originated in I. Wallerstein, *The Modern World-Systems* (New York: Academic Press, 1976) or, its "modified" form, such as the one followed in H. Amirahmadi, *Revolution and Economic Transition, The Iranian Experience* (New York: SUNY Press, 1990). I simply argue that the global capitalism has gone

through the three distinct historic stages, leading to the global economy and polity beyond the nation-state. My approach has nothing to do with the systems analysis or the periodization of the colonial world since the sixteenth century. See Cyrus Bina and Behzad Yaghmaian, "Post-War Global Accumulation" op. cit. See also Sol Picciotto, "The Internationalization of the State," *Capital and Class,* vol. 43 (Spring 1991): 43–64; Ernst B. Haas, *Beyond the Nation-State* (Stanford, Calif.: Stanford University Press, 1964); Hugo Radice, ed., *International Firms and Modern Imperialism* (Harmondsworth: Penguin, 1975); Hugo Radice, "The National Economy: A Keynesian Myth?" *Capital and Class,* vol. 22 (1984).

14. Cyrus Bina and Behzad Yaghmaian, "Import Substitution and Export Promotion Within the Context of the Internationalization of Capital," *Review of Radical Political Economics,* vol. 20, nos. 2 & 3, (1988): 234–40.

15. Cyrus Bina, "A Prelude to the Internationalization of Postwar Economy," *Journal of Economic Democracy,* forthcoming

16. Hamid Dabashi, "Islamic Ideology: The Perils of a Neologism," in *Post-Revolutionary Iran* Amirahmadi and Parvin, eds. (Boulder and London: Westview Press, 1988), 11.

17. Ibid. See also Jamal al-Din al-Afghani, *al-'Urwa al-Wuthqa* (The Firm Tie) (Cairo, 1927); Mirza Asadabadi Lutfullah, *Sharhi Hal wa Athar Jamal al-Din (Afghani)* (The Biography and Works of Jamal al-Din [Afghani]) (Berlin, 1926); Homa (Nategh) Pakdaman, *Djamal-ed-Din Assad Abadi dit Afghani* (Jamal al-Din Asadabadi, Known as Afghani) (Paris, 1969); Nikki R. Keddie, *Sayyed Jamal al-Din "al-Afghani": A Political Biography* (Berkeley and Los Angeles: University of California Press, 1972); Rashid M. Rida, *Tarikh al-Ustadh al-Imam al-Shaykh Muhammad 'Abdu,* 2 vols. (Cairo, 1931).

18. Mahmoud Taleghani, *Eslam va Malekiyyat* (Islam and Ownership), 4th ed. (Tehran: Entesharat Press, 1344 [1965]), originally in Persian; Mahmoud Taleghani, *Society and Economics in Islam,* R. Campbell, trans. (Berkeley, Calif.: Mizan Press, 1982); Ali Shari'ati, *On the Sociology of Islam,* H. Algar, trans. (Berkeley, Calif.: Mizan Press, 1979); Ali Shari'ati *Man and Islam,* F. Marjani, trans. (Houston, Tex.: Free Islamic Literature, 1981); Murtaza Mutahhari, *Fundamentals of Islamic Thought: God, Man and the Universe,* R. Campbell, trans. (Berkeley, Calif.: Mizan Press, 1985); Houchang Chehabi, *Iranian Politics and Religious Modernism: The Liberation Movement of Iran Under the Shah and Khomeini* (Ithaca, N.Y.: Cornell University Press, 1990), 160; see also Roy P. Mottahedeh, *The Mantle of the Prophet* (New York: Simon & Schuster, 1985); Hamid Dabashi, "Taleqani's Qur'anic Exegesis: Elements of a Revolutionary Discourse," in *Modern Capitalism and Islamic Ideology in Iran,* Cyrus Bina and Hamid Zangeneh, eds. (New York: St. Martin's Press, 1992), 51–81.

19. Ruhollah Khomeini, *Velayate-e Faqih: Hukumat-e Eslami* (Tehran: Entesharat-e Amir Kabir, 1358 [1979]), originally published in *Najaf*, 1350 [1971]; Ruhollah Khomeini, *Islam and Revolution*, H. Algar, trans. (Berkeley, Calif.: Mizan Press, 1981).

20. Cyrus Vakili-Zad, "Continuity and Change: The Structure of Power in Iran," in *Modern Capitalism and Islamic Ideology in Iran*, Cyrus Bina and Hamid Zangeneh, eds. (New York: St. Martin's Press, 1992); Shahrough Akhavi, *Religion and Politics in Contemporary Iran* (Albany, N.Y.: SUNY Press, 1980), Ch. 6; Houchang E. Chehabi, "Religion and Politics in Iran: How Theoretic Is the Islamic Republic?" *Daedalus*, (Summer 1991); Shaul Bakhash, *The Reign of the Ayatollahs* (New York: Basic Books, 1984); Ahmad Ashraf and Ali Banuazizi, "State and Class in the Iranian Revolution," *State, Economy and Culture*, vol. 1, no. 3, (1985).

21. Said Amir Arjomand, *The Turban for the Crown* (New York: Oxford University Press, 1988); Hossien Bashiriyeh, *The State and Revolution in Iran* (New York: St. Martin's Press, 1984); Misagh Parsa, *Social Origins of the Iranian Revolution* (New Brunswick and London: Rutgers University Press, 1989). Also see William A. Graham, "Traditionalism in Islam: An Essay in Interpretation," *Journal of Interdisciplinary History*, vol. 23, no. 3 (Winter 1993): 495–522.

22. Hamid Enayat, "Iran: Khomeini's Concept of the Guardianship of the Juristconsult," in *Islam in the Political Process*, James P. Piscatori, ed. (Cambridge: Cambridge University Press, 1983), 172; Abul Ala Maududi [1903–79], *Islamic Law and Constitution*, Khurshid Ahmad, trans., 8th ed. (Lahore: Islamic Publications, 1983).

23. Ruhollah Khomeini, *Islam and Revolution*, part I: Islamic Government, trans. H. Algar (Berkeley: Mizan Press, 1981), 63.

24. Ibid., 61, 64.

25. Enayat, op. cit., 173, emphasis added.

26. Here, a note on transliteration and references is necessary. I could not avoid the mixture of Arabic and Persian concerning the transliteration of original concepts. Where possible, however, I opted for the Persian versions.

27. Enayat, op. cit., 173.

28. Ibid.; see also 180, reference 38.

29. Enayat, op. cit., 174.

30. Amir Arjomand, op. cit., 180.

31. Ibid., Ch. 9, 181: citing 'Adel Haddad in *Ettela'at,* dated second of Shahrivar 1362 [August 1983].

32. Ibid., 180; see also 243, note 22, referring to Ayatollah Golpayegani's criticism leveled against President Khamenei.

33. Maxime Rodinson, *Marxism and the Muslim World,* J. Matthews, trans. (New York: Monthly Review Press, 1981), 143.

34. Cyrus Bina and Hamid Zangeneh, *Modern Capitalism and Islamic Ideology in Iran* (New York: St. Martin's Press, 1992); Cyrus Bina, "The Foreign Exchange Crisis and the Fragility of the Iranian Economy," *Mehregan,* vol. 2, no. 4 (Winter 1994): 117-31 (in Persian with English abstract).

35. Maxime Rodinson, *Islam and Capitalism ,* B. Pearce, trans. (Austin, Tex.: University of Texas Press, 1981), 117.

36. Ibid., 216; for the contrary views see Khurshid Ahmad, ed. *Studies in Islamic Economics,* (Leicester: The Islamic Foundation, 1980); Mohammad-Baqer Sadr, *Iqtisaduna* (Our Economics) (Beirut: 1961), translated into Persian as *Eqtesad-e Ma,* vol. 1, M. K. Musavi, trans. (Tehran: Borhan Press, 1350 [1971]) and vol. 2, A. A. Espahbodi, trans. (Tehran: Borhan Press, 1357 [1978]); Masudul A. Choudhury and Uzir Abdul Malik, *The Foundations of Islamic Political Economy* (New York: St. Martin's Press, 1992). This volume contains a very elaborate mathematical proof of the stated propositions, but it would scarcely go beyond the framework of tautology, particular to modern neoclassical economics.

37. This misconception can be seen, for instance, in Enayat, op. cit., 175.

38. Youssef M. Ibrahim, "Iran's Leaders Ask Wide Cooperation and Ties to West," *New York Times,* 28 May 1991, A11; also "Iran Plans More Oil Output," *New York Times,* 27 May 1991, 35.

39. Elaine Sciolino, "Iran Struggles to Attract Investors," *New York Times,* 30 April 1992, D6.

40. Peter Waldman, "Clergy Capitalism," *Wall Street Journal,* 5 May 1992, A1.

41. Rodinson, *Marxism and the Muslim World,* op. cit., 70; see also John L. Esposito, eds., *Voices of Resurgent Islam* (New York: Oxford University Press, 1983); John O. Vol, *Islam: Continuity and Change in the Modern World* (Boulder, Colo.: Westview Press, 1982); John L. Esposito, eds., *Islam in Asia* (New York: Oxford University Press, 1987); Yvonne Y. Haddad, et al., *The Contemporary Islamic Revival: A Critical Survey and Bibliography* (New York: Greenwood Press, 1991);

Hamid Enayat, *Modern Islamic Political Thought* (London: Macmillan, 1982); Patrick Bannerman, *Islam in Perspective* (London and New York: Routledge, 1988).

42. Rodinson, *Islam and Capitalism*, op. cit., 186. See also Cyrus Bina, "Global Oil and the Oil Policies of the Islamic Republic," in *Modern Capitalism and Islamic Ideology in Iran*, Cyrus Bina and Hamid Zangeneh, eds. (New York: St. Martin's Press, 1992), 121–158.

43. Rodinson, *Marxism and the Muslim World*, op. cit., 304.

44. Jane Perlez, "A Fundamentalist Finds a Fulcrum in Sudan," *New York Times*, 29 January 1992, A3; Chris Hedges, "Sudan Presses Its Campaign to Impose Law on Non-Muslims," *New York Times*, 1 June 1992, A6. See also David Seddon, "Riots and Rebellion in North Africa: Political Responses to Economic Crisis in Tunisia, Morocco, and Sudan," in *Power and Stability in the Middle East*, Berch Berberoglu, ed., (London: Zed Press, 1989), 114–35.

45. Perlez, op. cit.; for Hassan al-Turabi's views see his essay "The Islamic State," in *Voices of Resurgent Islam*, John Esposito, ed. (New York: Oxford University Press, 1983), 241–51. See also Abul A'la Maududi, *A Short History of the Revivalist Movement in Islam*, Al Ash'ari, trans. (Lahore: Islamic Publications, 1972); Mohammad Asghar Khan, ed., *Islam, Politics and the State: The Pakistan Experience*, (London: Zed Press, 1985).

46. Youssef M. Ibrahim, "Two Fundamentalists in Algeria Get Relatively Light Sentences," *New York Times*, 16 July 1992, A5.

47. "Algiers Police Fire Over Crowed of Angry Muslims," *New York Times*, 30 January 1992, A5.

48. Youssef M. Ibrahim, "Saudi King Takes On Islamic Militants," *New York Times*, 30 January 1992, A3. Similarly, concern over the deteriorating economy and high level of unemployment is also at the roots of the current political crisis in Algeria. See, for instance, Youssef M. Ibrahim, "Algeria Descends Into More Chaos," *New York Times*, 29 July 1992, A7. Also see, Rachid Tlemcani, *State and Revolution in Algeria* (London: Zed Books, 1986); Karen Farsoun [Pfeifer], "State Capitalism in Algeria," *MERIP Reports*, no. 35 (February 1975); Ghassan Salamé, "Political Power and the Saudi State," in *Power and Stability in the Middle East*, Berch Berberoglu, ed. (London: Zed Press, 1989); Ahmad N. Azim, "Egypt: The Origin and Development of a Neo-Colonial State," in Berch Berberoglu, ed., op. cit.; Michael Gilsenan, "State and Popular Islam in Egypt," in *State and Ideology in the Middle East and Pakistan*, Fred Halliday and Hamza Alavi, eds. (New York: Monthly Review Press, 1988), 167–90; Hamza Alavi, "Pakistan and Islam: Ethnicity and Ideology," in Halliday and Alavi, eds., op. cit. (New York, Monthly Review Press, 1988), 64–111.

49. Ethan Bronner, "In War's Aftermath, Saudis See Small Changes," *Boston Sunday Globe*, 2 August 1992, 1.

50. This approach is true of many studies on the 1978–79 revolution in Iran. This crucial point has also been missed by those writers who have exclusively made President Carter's so-called human rights policy the centerpiece of their analysis. See, for instance, Robert Looney, *Economic Origins of the Iranian Revolution* (New York: Pergamon Press, 1982), and Marvin Zonis, *The Majestic Failure* (Chicago: University of Chicago Press, 1991), among others.

51. Steve Coll, "The Secret U.S. Role in Afghan War," *Boston Sunday Globe* (Focus), 2 August 1992, 69.

52. George Orwell, *Nineteen Eighty-Four* (New York: New American Library, 1981), 48.

53. For a lucid account of Saddam Hussein's reign of terror see Samir al-Khalil, *Republic of Fear* (New York: Pantheon Books, 1989).

54. Noam Chomsky, "Oppose The War," *Z Magazine* (February 1991); also see his *On Power and Ideology: The Managua Lectures* (Boston: South End Press, 1987). Within the paradigm of the cold war, see Henry Kissinger, "A Postwar Agenda," *Newsweek*, 28 January 1991.

55. Clyde Haberman, "Israelis Worry if World's New Epoch Will Find Them Shunted Aside by U.S.," *New York Times*, 3 August 1992, A8; see also Noam Chomsky, *The Fateful Triangle* (Boston: South End Press, 1983); Maxime Rodinson, *Cult, Ghetto, and State*, J. Rothschild, trans. (London: Al Saqi Books, 1983); Jane Hunter, *Israeli Foreign Policy* (Boston: South End Press, 1987); Teodor Shanin, "The Zionisms of Israel," in *State and Ideology in the Middle East and Pakistan*, Halliday and Alavi, eds., op. cit.; Michael Curtis and Susan A. Gitelson, eds., *Israel in the Third World* (New Brunswick, N.J.: Transaction Books, 1976); Cheryl A. Rubenberg, *Israel and the American National Interest* (Urbana, Ill.: University of Illinois Press, 1986); Edward Tivnan, *The Lobby: Jewish Political Power and American Foreign Policy* (New York: Simon and Schuster, 1987).

56. Cyrus Bina, "War Over Access to Cheap Oil, or the Reassertion of U.S. Hegemony?" in *Mobilizing Democracy: Changing the U.S. Role in the Middle East*, Greg Bates, ed. (Monroe, Maine: Common Courage Press, 1991), 71–8; Murray Waas, "What Washington Gave Saddam for Christmas," in *The Gulf War Reader*, Micah L. Sifry and Christopher Cerf, eds. (New York: Random House, 1991), 85–95; Michael T. Klare, "The Pentagon's New Paradigm," in Sifry and Cerf, eds., op. cit., 466–76; Robert Scheer, "What a Wonderful War," in Sifry and Cerf, eds., op. cit., 492–97; Peter Sluglett and Marion Farouk-Sluglett, *Iraq Since 1958:*

From Revolution to Dictatorship, revised edition (London: I.B. Tauris, 1990); John Barry and Roger Charles, "Sea of Lies," *Newsweek,* 13 July 1992; John Barry, "The Secret War," *Newsweek,* 13 July 1992. The last two sources reveal the U.S. government's deep involvement in the Iran-Iraq War on the side of Saddam Hussein.

57. For the jubilant views on the Gulf War, see the commentaries by J. Muravchilk, "At Last Pax Americana," *New York Times,* 24 January 1991, and C. Krauthammer, "Bless Our Pax Americana" *Washington Post,* 22 March 1991. For a critical view of U.S. potential for war see Raymond Lotta, *America in Decline* (Chicago: Banner Press, 1984).

58. Cyrus Bina, "The Political Economy of Global Oil," *The World and I* (December 1990); Cyrus Bina, "Internationalization of the Oil Industry: Simple Oil Shocks Or Structural Crises?" *Review: Journal of Fernand Braudel Center,* vol. 11, no. 3 (Summer 1988): 329–70; Cyrus Bina, "Limits of OPEC Pricing: OPEC Profits and the Nature of Global Oil Accumulation," *OPEC Review,* vol. 14, no. 1 (Spring 1990): 55–73; Cyrus Bina "The Laws of Economic Rent and Property: Applied to the Oil Industry," *American Journal of Economics and Sociology,* vol. 50, no. 2 (April 1992): 187–203; Simon Bromley, *American Hegemony and World Oil* (University Park, Penn.: Pennsylvania State University Press, 1991), is an excellent work on the subject of oil and the postwar U.S. hegemony, although he ends up with a wrong conclusion. Here, Bromley argues that the American global hegemony, vis-à-vis Japan and the European Community, has remained intact by virtue of the U.S. domination of Middle East oil. My argument is exactly the opposite. I contend that the decline of U.S. global hegemony is the result of the globalization of the world economy and polity, which had remarkably transformed the nature of global oil as well. See Cyrus Bina, "Global Oil and Unviability of *Pax Americana,*" *Economic and Political Weekly* (11 July 1992): 1467–69.

59. For instance, see a commentary by Edward L. Morse, "How to Make OPEC Obsolete," *New York Times,* 1 July 1991, A13, in which he suggests that in the aftermath of the Gulf War the United States must abolish OPEC and hold fast to the Saudi Oil. This view simply fails to understand the post-1973 role of OPEC. See also David R. Henderson, "Do We Need to Go to War for Oil?" CATO Institute Foreign Policy Briefing, October 24, 1990; Keith Scheider, "Bush's Energy Plan Emphasizes Gains in Output Over Efficiency," *New York Times,* 9 February 1991, 1; James E. Akins, "The New Arabia," *Foreign Affairs* (Summer 1991): 36–49. A fairly good historical background can be obtained from S. Muralidharan, "Saddam Hussein, Western Imperialism and Arab Identity," *Economic and Political Weekly,* 22 September 1990.

60. "Text of President Bush's State of the Union Message to Nation," *New York Times,* 30 January 1991, A12.

61. "United States: State of the Union Address," *Keesing's Record of World Events,* volume 38, no. 1 (January 1992): 38711. Reading these official materials in conjunction with documents, such as Ramsey Clark, et al., *War Crimes: A Report on United States War Crimes Against Iraq* (Washington, D.C.: Maisonneuve Press, 1992), is useful.

62. See the Harvard Medical Team report on the immediate effect of war and continued embargo on Iraqi children, Harvard University, June 1991. On the usage of uranium shells against Iraq by the United States, see Eric Hoskins, "Making the Desert Glow," *New York Times,* 21 January 1993, A25. See also "Excerpts from U.N. Report on Need for Humanitarian Assistance in Iraq," *New York Times,* 23 March 1991, 5; and Trevor Rowe, "UN Secretary Troubled by Civilian Casualties in the Gulf," *Boston Globe,* 9 February 1991, 6.

63. Ahmad al-Khatib, "A Military Solution Will Destroy Kuwait," *Middle East Report* (January–February 1991); George J. Church, "An Exquisite Balancing Act," *Time,* 24 September 1990, 45, which is reporting on King Fahd's character. In order to understand the peculiar nature of U.S. foreign policy the existing government documents are excellent sources. For instance, see U.S. Congress, Senate Committee on Foreign Relations, *War in the Persian Gulf: The U.S. Takes Sides* (Washington, D.C.: U.S. Government Printing Office, November 1987), or U.S. Congress, House Committee on Foreign Relations, Hearing before Subcommittee on Europe and the Middle East, *United States–Iraqi Relations* (Washington, D.C.: U.S. Government Printing Office, April 26, 1990).

64. Thomas Friedman and Patrick Tyler, "From the First, U.S. Resolve to Fight," *New York Times,* 3 March 1991, 1. See also Noam Chomsky, "What We Say Goes: The Middle East and the New World Order," *Z Magazine* (May 1991); Chomsky's view on the new U.S. global role is contrary to mine in that he considers "the national state as more a representative of locally-situated capital" rather than as a contradictory entity that would also promote the interest of transnational capital. This assessment is based on our recent correspondence and his kind and encouraging comments on this chapter. See also Patrick Tyler, "U.S. and Bahrain Near Pact on Permanent Military Base," *New York Times,* 25 March 1991, A9, on the U.S. military build-up in the Persian Gulf.

65. To name a few one may recall the U.S. overthrow of Mossadegh (Iran 1953), Arbenz (Guatemala 1954), Goulart (Brazil 1964), Bosch (Dominican Republic 1965), Estenssoro (Bolivia 1964), Sukarno (Indonesia 1965), Lumumba (The Congo [now Zaire] 1960), and Allende (Chile 1973); all to be replaced by the handpicked, U.S.-supported tyrannical regimes. See Thomas Ross and David Wise, *The Invisible Government* (New York, Knopf, 1964); Fred Cook, "The CIA," *The Nation,* 24 June 1961, 529–69; Agee, op. cit.; Bob Woodward, *Veil: The Secret Wars of the CIA, 1981–1987* (New York: Simon and Schuster, 1987); William Blum, *The CIA: A Forgotten History* (London, Zed Press, 1986).

66. G. Kolko, *Confronting the Third World: United States Foreign Policy, 1945–1980* (New York, 1988).

67. Youssef M. Ibrahim, "Tunisia Puts Nearly 300 Muslim Militants on Trial," *New York Times*, 3 August 1992, A8.

68. See, for instance, Peter Grier, "Bush's Vision of U.S. Global Role," *Christian Science Monitor*, 19 November 1991, 6. In order not to fall into the liberal trap of blaming the Republicans for such imperial visions and, more important, to refrain from personalizing the nature of political power in the United States, one has to look at the basic underlying views that are shared with the Democrats. The case in point is the "Cuban Democracy Act of 1992, signed by President Bush in the closing days of the election campaign. It was enthusiastically supported by Governor [now President] Bill Clinton." See Frank J. Prial, "U.N. Votes to urge U.S. to Dismantle Embargo on Cuba," *New York Times*, 25 November 1992, 1.

ISLAM, THE MIDDLE EAST, AND THE NEW WORLD ORDER

Akbar Mahdi

Within four years, the world has experienced dramatic changes that would have been unimaginable only several years ago. While it is too early to predict precisely how events will unfold and what shape the world will take, it is clear that our pre–cold war conceptualization of the world as a bipolar reality has become irrelevant. The most often used phrase describing these changes is the "new world order," which emerged in political discourse in 1990. Unfortunately, such discussions concerned the politics of coercion rather than the politics of persuasion.

The invasion of Kuwait by Iraq, the disappearance of a power known as the Soviet Union, and the collapse of Communist governments in Eastern Europe gave the United States a golden opportunity to reassert its political and military supremacy in world affairs. Moving to the Persian Gulf in order to regain Kuwait from Iraq, former president George Bush brought together a coalition of some Arab and non-Arab countries to support his move against Saddam Hussein in Kuwait. This event marked the beginning of a new political era. In a speech to a joint session of Congress on September 11, 1990, President Bush described this era and its corresponding changes in terms of a "new world order" in which the United States would play the leadership role in the management of global crises.[1] Indeed, the new world order was almost claimed, defined, and consciously framed in the interest of the United States at its very inception.

The old world order was a world of superpowers, the cold war, and military, political, and economic clientalism. It was a world of ideologies, struggles for national independence, and political sovereignty. The old world order emerged as a result of World War II and as a result was a world driven by military, political, and economic rivalries coated in ideological suits.

Although the declaration of the new world order was made during the crisis in the Persian Gulf, the realities of this emerging world were shaped by the dissolution of Soviet power at home and abroad. With the policies of *glasnost* and *perestroika,* the Soviet Union planted the seeds of its own demise. This was the beginning of the end for the cold war and the threshold for the emergence of a new world order. On April 11, 1990, Gorbachev stated that "we are at the beginning of the road to a new world order." Given the framework of U.S. foreign policy as the leading force against Communism in the last four decades, the dramatic collapse of the Communist states necessitated a new definition of the U.S. role in the post–cold war era. Political changes resulting from such a collapse affected the balance and distribution of power within the international order in favor of the United States.

Although the collapse of the Soviet Union as a superpower is the most significant cause of the redefinition of the world order, it is a mistake to underestimate the role of other factors. These factors include global recessionary trends, which contributed to a general decline in the standard of living, increasing economic competition among nations, the internationalization of capital and markets, the failure of centralized economies, a tendency toward market-oriented economies, the revolution in information technology, the global environmental challenges facing all nations, mounting population pressures, the inability of the Third World market to absorb the surplus of consumer goods from the industrialized world, the declining significance of NATO, the unification of the Germanys, the prospects of a unified European market, and an explosive level of poverty in Third World nations continue to shape the realities of the contemporary, international political economy.

In the new world order, the Soviet Union has disappeared. Eastern European countries, as well as new republics in the former Soviet Union, have lost their Soviet patronage and are searching for new identities and alliances compatible with their national, ethnic, cultural, political, and economic ambitions. The economic conditions of most industrialized countries are far from satisfactory: The U.S. economy is marred by a deep recession, a huge budget deficit, an anemic savings rate, the increasing cost of health care, particularly in the face of a deadly disease called AIDS, and a shabby financial system. Germany is burdened with the cost of unification. Japan is confronted with its own excesses of the 1980s. While the collapse of the Soviet Union has apparently subdued the ideological battle between Communism and capitalism, the realities of low economic and high population growth,[2] increasing national debt, deteriorating environmental conditions, and an increasing demand for political participation by citizens in most Third World countries have forced governments to seek adjustments to new realities and accommodations to external and internal forces.

CHARACTERISTICS OF THE NEW WORLD ORDER

How new is the new world order? It is not far from the truth if we argue, with a Wallersteinian conceptualization, that the new world order is the same old world order only without the Soviet Union as a contending superpower. From a world system perspective, the changes are merely political, and the world system economically remains the same, that is, a capitalist world economy that demands increasing integration and uniformity. While the principles underlying the world economy have remained the same, the relative position of forces within the system, vis-à-vis each other, has changed. The new international economic arrangement has become more multipolar than before, due to the weakening of the economy in the United States relative to Japan and Europe. Politically speaking, however, the United States has become the world's single superpower. To the extent that the old world order was influenced by U.S. political and military power, "the new world order is a reformulation of the basic historical principles that have underlain U.S. [foreign] policy throughout the twentieth century."[3] This means that aside from ensuring the freedom of movement for U.S. capital and maintaining its access to markets abroad, the United States sees it as its responsibility to define the rules of international engagement. Speaking of the obligations imposed on America by its unique role, Krauthammer writes:

> Our best hope for safety is in American strength and will—the strength and will to lead a unipolar world, unashamedly laying down the rules of world order and being prepared to enforce them. Compared to the task of defeating fascism and communism, averting chaos is a rather subtle call to greatness. It is not a task that we are any more eager to undertake than the great twilight struggle just concluded. But it is just as noble and just as necessary.[4]

Such a view corresponds to a long historical pattern of behavior demonstrated by the United States in the international arena: defining and abiding by international laws as it wished, using them when they served its national interest, and ignoring them when they stood in its way.

While in many ways the world has remained the same, in many other ways it has changed. Although at this early stage, the new world arrangement seems to be driven by economic factors, it is not inconceivable that some of the nascent forces of distress in various communities around the world, such as nationalism, territorial disputes, and ethnic rivalry, may turn into major forces of change in the near future.[5] We are already witnessing the destructive influence of ethnic tensions in the former Yugoslavia, new republics in Central Asia, and, in a more subtle but divisive way, in the political atmosphere prevailing in Western European societies and America. Many argue that although the old world order could not eliminate nationalistic and ethnic attitudes, it was able to restrain them within the global tendency to remaining part of a political empire.[6] For John Lukacs, the disappearance of the old order brings about nasty varieties of nationalism.

The most salient feature of the new world order is that its forces are driven by market issues and capitalist tendencies. The homogeneous forces of market have become the organizing principles around which social needs and desires are formed.[7] The global movement of capital in search of cheaper and more efficient productive resources has become the hallmark of the new era. American and Western European corporations have already established a revolving door between their respective countries and Eastern European countries. The United States has signed a North American Free Trade Agreement with both Canada and Mexico, hoping to offset the advantages of her competitors in Europe and Asia. Closely related to the above development is the dominance of global capitalist institutions, such as the International Monetary Fund and the World Bank, in the new world order. The conditions these institutions are imposing on the grant of loans to poorer countries, known as the "Structural Adjustment Program," are basically capitalist prescriptions for market-oriented economic growth: balanced budgets, devaluation, privatization or rolled-back governments and public sectors, elimination of government subsidies, reduction of tariffs, an open attitude to foreign investment, and competitive free markets as the real sponsor for capital formation, price determination and exchange rate, resource allocation, and wage determination.[8] The World Bank continues to follow its earlier plan for "accelerated development," according to which the developing countries are to find a niche in the global division of labor by specializing in the production of commodities in which they have a "comparative advantage."[9]

Surprisingly, the most forgotten aspect of the new world order is its structural inequality at national, regional, and international levels. The discourse of the new world order has little in it dealing with issues of social equity and fairness. Basically, the world economic order remains the same, for example, that of rich nations and poor nations. The balance of political and economic power still favors the industrial capitalist countries. Third World countries continue to be affected by the same forces of political and economic dependence that worked against them during the past four decades.[10] The gap between rich and poor is widening all over the world, within and between nations. The champions of the new world order have been silent about patterns of economic exploitation and misery in the non-Communist countries. Given the market weaknesses of many Third World countries—partially resulting from four decades of unsuccessful experience with "dependent development"—the new trend toward further privatization may widen the existing gap between poverty and wealth in these countries. As development studies show, Third World debt in the past decade continued to increase and these countries experienced a negative net flow of capital and resources.[11]

A defining feature of the new world order, as mentioned earlier, is global military and political assertiveness by the United States. The growing economic competition from Japan and now the European Community has become a real challenge for the United States.[12] When seen in the context of a huge deficit and economic decline at home, this competition undermines the U.S. hegemonic position in the global capitalist system. The military and political dominance demonstrated by the United States during the Persian Gulf War should be seen in the light of this competition. Many have argued that one reason for U.S. military intervention in the Persian Gulf was to offset its economic weakness at home and fend off its economic rivals abroad. As sociologist James Petras has put it, "It was meant to define a new military-centered global order in which markets, income and resource shares are defined not by technological market power, but by political military dominance."[13] This intervention was meant, among other things, to ensure U.S. military leadership vis-à-vis its old and new allies and to define the direction of things to come for both the developed and underdeveloped worlds. As Robert W. Tucker and David C. Hendrickson have argued, the choice of a military solution to the crisis in the Persian Gulf was another example of the "imperial temptation" for using military might without taking responsibility for its ruins.[14]

Another aspect of political assertiveness by the United States is its increasing effort to utilize the United Nations to advance the geopolitical objectives of the powerful Western capitalist countries. If prior to the collapse of the Soviet Union, unilateral action around the world against Communism could be justified, in the post–cold war period it would be difficult to justify such actions in the name of preventing Soviet expansionism. The United Nations, which was under financial and political pressure from the Reagan and Bush administrations, respectively, has become an excellent cover for imperial actions in the new world order. Recent efforts initiated and orchestrated by the United States in the United Nations are indicative of a new world order in which the powerful Western countries coalesce with one another and make decisions for helpless Third World countries without any consideration for the sovereignty and rights of those small countries. The example of orchestrated efforts by the U.S., France, and United Kingdom against Libyan terrorists, regardless of the merits of the case, was the best example of how in the new world order all the cards are stacked against the powerless Third World countries.[15] The relentless efforts by which the United States has used the UN to destroy Iraq's military and industrial capabilities, in the face of the hardships of two wars, is another example of the United States seeking the UN's blessing for American foreign policy objectives.[16] It is this desire to use the UN as a conduit for control that has prompted some U.S. policy analysts to propose strengthening of "international agencies of all sorts . . . most particularly the United Nations Security Council," where the United States and her other European allies have permanent seats and veto power.[17]

To the industrial countries of Asia and Europe, the war in the Persian Gulf signaled the leadership and the resolve of the United States to remain the only military superpower. The symbolic aspects of creating an alliance for this war, despite many reservations that some European powers had, were very important. In the face of a new German and French desire to exercise their political will, the United States needed to demonstrate its intention of both maintaining presence in Europe and of making it clear that political dissent from powerful European countries would not prevent the United States from achieving its foreign policy objectives. The invasion of Kuwait by Iraq provided a golden opportunity to prove superiority by maintaining a tight control over the flow of oil in the Persian Gulf. The United States was determined to maintain its hegemonic position in global affairs by making sure that the flow of oil from the Middle East—which consists of about 80 percent of the exported oil in the world and more than one-third of the oil consumed in the industrialized world daily—is under its control.[18] Closer ties among the United States, Kuwait, Saudi Arabia, Egypt, and smaller Arab countries have been in this direction. Oil is the source of 85 percent of the world's energy. The control over the oil reserves in the Persian Gulf is probably one of the most effective ways in which the United States can exert pressure on the Europeans and Japanese, who are the main beneficiaries of Middle Eastern oil. Japan receives 70 percent of its needed oil from this region, the United States only 25 percent.

To the underdeveloped countries, the Gulf War showed that (1) the United States will protect its interests at any cost, even if it means sending thousands of its soldiers to an uncertain and hostile environment; (2) the United States will not allow a Third World country to become powerful enough to be a potential threat to its political and economic interests; and (3) it is important for the United States to remove any potential threat in the Middle East to the state of Israel, regardless of where it comes from.

What are the implications of the military and political supremacy of the United States for the so-called Third World countries, including the Muslim countries of the Middle East? Third World countries are militarily too weak and politically too vulnerable to be able to resist hostile pressures from within and without. This political vulnerability, coupled with an economic need for foreign capital and technology, will keep these countries in a subordinate position relative to the foreign policy objectives of the advanced industrialized nations, particularly to the United States. During the cold war, these countries played one superpower against the other to secure aid, developmental assistance, and security support. With the absence of the Soviet Union, such a game has ended. If during the cold war political factors were the major criteria for granting foreign aid to these countries, in the new global arrangement the quantity and quality of this aid will be determined more by economic factors. We have already begun to see much more stringent, market-oriented strings attached to loans given by the International Monetary Fund and the World Bank, where the United States plays a dominant role. In this non-competitive environment, the United States is in a stronger position to use aid as a means for achieving its own political and economic objectives.[19] The severity of this situation can be better understood when we take into account that the growing need for capital and technology in the

Third World is accompanied by a decreasing flow of these resources to Third World countries. Lower economic productivity in the United States, the pressing needs of the Eastern European countries and newly formed states in the former Soviet Union, and the recessionary economic trends in the United States, Europe, and Asia are creating a less generous environment for foreign aid to Third World countries.

THE NEW WORLD ORDER AND THE MIDDLE EAST

In the post–cold war era, the Middle East still remains an unstable region. The area is receiving more than two-thirds of the world's arms imports, still struggling with a recession that began with the world oil glut of the 1980s, and is burdened with religious militancy and political instabilities.[20] Although the Soviet influence has disappeared, the area is imbued with ethnic and political strife. The Palestinian and Kurdish peoples are still struggling for basic national rights. The civil war in Lebanon is far from over. Although Kuwait has been liberated from Iraqi conquest and the Iran-Iraq War has ended in a no-peace, no-war situation without a formal peace treaty, new hostilities are being fomented between Iran and its Arab neighbors. Inside the Middle Eastern countries, the killing, torture, assassination, or disappearance of political dissidents, detention without trial, and summary executions have not been abandoned by government forces. Dictatorship, repression, and religious fanaticism, whether traditional or modern, continue to be the rule rather than the exception. The new world order has done little to change these structural characteristics. If anything, it has actually made them worse.

Since World War II, American foreign policy in the Middle East has been guided by four objectives: (1) containing Soviet expansion and Communist influence in the region, (2) securing an uninterrupted flow of oil to the West, (3) ensuring stability of the region's markets for American goods and capital, and (4) protecting the state of Israel. To achieve these objectives, the United States has relied heavily on the friendly relationships with the repressive monarchies and ruling elites in the region. The choice of such an approach has added three other related objectives to U.S. goals in the area: (1) commitment to the security of friendly regimes, (2) maintaining open access to international waters, and (3) securing stability by reducing regional tensions.[21] While in the absence of the Soviet Union the first major objective has become irrelevant, and a new objective of containing the Islamic radicalism originating from Iran has been added to this list, the U.S. desire to maintain control over the flow of oil has remained strong and prominent. This U.S. objective has had, and will continue to have, serious implications for political and economic developments in the Middle East. The United States will resist any change in the political economy of the Middle East that jeopardizes its political and economic interests in controlling the oil flow to the West and in maintaining the stability and security of the state of Israel. Since the 1973 oil embargo, the United States has consistently prevented any one country in this region from gaining control over the flow of oil.

This foreign policy objective has had a devastating effect on internal political conditions in Middle Eastern countries. On several occasions after World War II (Iran in 1953, Jordan in 1957, Iran in 1978–79, and Iraq in 1991), opportunities for democratic political developments have evolved in the region. On each of these occasions, with the exception of Iran, the United States successfully opposed those opportunities and suppressed their potential realization. The United States also has done little in opposing the authoritarian nature of the political structures in these countries because the emergence of democratic governments in this area would open the door to many uncertainties that the United States does not welcome. The war in the Persian Gulf, which was waged under the name of "democracy" and "liberation," practically increased the Arab dependence on U.S. protection. Such patronage, as has been historically the case, often robs these countries of their ability to be masters of their own fate and translates into undemocratic practices in these countries. The new economic realities facing the capitalist industrialized countries in the West reduce the structural opportunities for people in the Middle East to throw out their undemocratic leaders. All Middle Eastern regimes except Saudi Arabia, the Emirates, and Kuwait are in need of foreign capital to boost their economies. This need for foreign capital, technology, and know-how will probably make them more vulnerable to U.S. pressures through various international monetary agencies. In the wake of the weakened economic position of the industrialized countries, resources available to these states will be limited, except where significant geopolitical factors coincide with the interests of the industrialized countries.

One of the most publicized aspects of the new world order is political democratization. Proponents of the new world order often make a masterful jump by associating the move toward privatization of productive forces with the democratization of a society. In other words, privatization of market and labor conditions is defined as a democratizing process. The extent to which these economic changes relate to political democracy is neither demonstrated nor adequately examined. The past history of economic liberalization in many Third World countries, and its effect on political freedoms, has not shown a strong correlation between political and economic liberalism. The greatest examples of economic growth in Asia—Asia's four "Little Dragons," that is, South Korea, Taiwan, Singapore, and Hong Kong—in the last decade were countries with authoritarian rule.

Unfortunately, the new discourse on democracy represents another twist in realpolitik whose real outcome remains to be seen. Unfortunately, the Muslim countries of the Middle East have not had the fortune of sharing the fruits of a sweeping movement toward democracy. From the moment of its inception, the new world order has reinstituted and beefed up the undemocratic structures in Iraq, Kuwait, Egypt, and Saudi Arabia. While Arab countries have played a crucial role in an implementation of the United States' political and economic agenda in opening up their markets and borders to foreign capital, the United States has done little in encouraging these countries toward opening their political system to all segments of the society. The United States has consistently been silent about the tyrannical political practices and violations of human rights in these friendly countries, including violations of Palestinian human and territorial rights in Israel.[22] This lack of serious commitment to the aspirations of Middle Eastern people has created serious doubts about the new world order even among friendly Arab nations.[23] Supported by and friendly with the United States, these regimes are not popular and their overthrow will jeopardize U.S. interests in the area.[24]

The fact remains that the existing dictatorships in the Middle East have failed to satisfactorily meet the basic social and economic needs of their people. The likelihood that these regimes will move toward genuine democratic processes is very small. All Arab countries, except Egypt, are ruled by patriarchal rulers not subject to public elections. In Turkey, Iran, and Egypt, where there are elections, political systems are filled with corruption and are not adequately accountable to the public. Opposition in all these countries is either suppressed or eliminated.

As for the Arab-Israeli conflict, given the requirements of its global political management, the United States has been anxious to put an end to this hostility. Prior to the Gulf War the United States tried to de-link the Iraqi takeover of Kuwait from the Palestinian question by declaring its intentions to solve this dispute once the war would be over. The Palestinian question has always been a thorny issue in the relationship between the United States and the Arab world. In a post–cold war era, the full integration of the Arab world into the new world order requires the removal of this problem. Also, the declining significance of Russia as a player in Middle Eastern politics, the weakening of the Iraqi threat to Israel, and other changes in the balance of power in the area have undermined the strategic significance of Israel as an ally for the United States.[25] The development of close alliances among the United States and Egypt, Saudi Arabia, Kuwait, and small Arab countries in the Persian Gulf have eliminated any serious threat to the security of Israel. At the same time, recessionary trends in Middle Eastern economies, coupled with an increasing division between secular and Islamic movements, have reduced Arab support for the Palestinian cause. These developments have assured both the United States and the Palestinians that the issue was no longer an Arab problem, but an internal Israeli problem to be solved by the mutual interaction of Palestinians and Israelis. Such a realization on the part of Palestinians produced the intifada. Changes in the political climate of the region prompted the United States to organize an international conference dealing with Arab-Israeli disputes. This effort was described by former President Bush as one of the U.S. objectives in the new world order in the Middle East.[26] Securing peace between the Arab countries and Israel and dealing with Palestinian grievances provide a more stable situation for further cooperative relations between Israel and the United States. The two countries have had a long relationship and the new arrangement in the Middle East will provide ample opportunities for further mutual operations, especially in case of military emergencies.

Any change in the U.S. attitude toward the Palestinian issue is bound to be related to a change in the configuration of U.S. interest in the region. There is no doubt that both Israel and America are interested in a peaceful resolution of this question. However, neither America nor Israel are willing to give what it takes to resolve it. Post–cold war events in the region have not worked in favor of the Palestinians due to the demise of Soviet support for the Palestinian cause, the improvement in relationships between Israel and the East European countries, the influx of Jewish immigrants to Israel, the emergence of Hamas as a powerful force in the Palestinian resistance, the relative loss of support by Arab states for the Palestinian movement, and Saddam Hussein's defeat in the Gulf War.

Given the new realities of the Middle East, the United States is no more interested in establishing a Palestinian "state" than Israel is interested in changing the status quo regarding the Palestinian situation. Until now, the United States and Israel have either rejected Palestinian demands or have asked for their redefinitions. In doing so, Israel saw time on its side. It often acted on the assumption that the more time passes the weaker the Palestinian position and the more they would have to concede. Therefore, Israel continued to maintain the status quo until it could solve this problem on its own terms. In the peace process, Israel has been negotiating the Palestinian question in the larger context of a series of bilateral or multilateral exchanges that would hopefully guarantee Israel's security and her access to water sources and Arab markets. "Negotiation" requires change and compromise. While Palestinians are interested in changing the status of occupation, Israel is more interested in changing the Palestinian position by reducing their "national rights" to "municipal rights." Having failed to crush the intifada, Israel used the weakness of the Palestinian position by proposing a peace agreement. In September 1993, an agreement in principle was signed between Israel and the PLO, according to which Israel would give the Palestinians control of Jericho and the Gaza Strip. With this agreement in hand, Israel has killed two birds with one stone: it has offered the Palestinians "land for peace" and has transferred its security problem in the Gaza Strip to the PLO. Given the density of the populations in the Gaza Strip (750,000) and strong Hamas support in this area, it remains to be seen how the PLO is going to achieve the national rights of the Palestinians and to establish a democratic government in acquired lands.

ISLAM AND THE NEW WORLD ORDER

*The Cold War is not being replaced with a new competition
between Islam and the West. It is evident that the
Crusades have been over for a long time.*

—EDWARD DJEREJIAN,
ASSISTANT SECRETARY OF STATE
FOR NEAR EAST AND SOUTH ASIAN AFFAIRS, JUNE 2, 1992

Although Western government officials deny any sense of threat from so-called Islamic fundamentalism, the foreign policy track of the United States and its Western allies reveals a different reality. Islamic movements, as they manifested themselves in Iran, Lebanon, Tunisia, Algeria, Egypt, and Gulf countries, have been no less than a source of discomfort and irritation to Western interests in Asia and Africa. There are many scholars and political observers who view Islam and/or the religious militancy of Islamic activists around the world as a substitute for the cold war and, therefore, as a real threat to the West.[27] Based on the assumption that "in the Islamic world, and especially in the Middle East, . . . Islam is emerging as . . . [a] new defining paradigm and the favored successor to Communism," Hunter argues that "there is a real risk that some kind of Western-Islamic confrontation may replace the Cold War."[28] Speaking of Islamic fundamentalism, Islamic historian Bernard Lewis argues that "it should be clear by now that we are facing a mood and a movement far transcending the level of issues and policies and the governments that pursue them. This is no less than a clash of civilizations."[29] Edward Luttwak goes a step further by arguing that the antagonistic and anti-Western character of the heavily militarized Middle East is a real threat to the stability and peace in Europe. He argues that wherever Islam meets non-Islam, the outcome is violence.[30]

In the same vein, Livingston views Islam as a real source of confrontation with the West, Taylor is concerned with the expansion of Islam and its strong appeal because of its anti-Western tendencies.[31] For instance, the increasing movement away from Russia and Communism has brought the Central Asian republics of the former Soviet Union closer to the Muslim world. The transfer of nuclear technologies and know-how from these republics to other Muslim countries, especially Iran, Syria, and Libya, has become the real nightmare for the United States and its Western allies. In late 1991, the Bush administration began a series of efforts to selectively establish ties with various new republics in the former Soviet Union in order to curtail Iranian influence on countries that have had cultural and linguistic affinities with Iran.[32] The strong resolve shown by the United States and its Western allies for the total destruction of Iraqi nuclear capabilities and the United States attempt to curtail arms shipments to Iran or Syria in the past two years are indicative of the willingness of Western countries to do anything to prevent the Islamic world from developing either a nuclear capability or any other strengths that might threaten Western interests.

Is Islam really a threat to the West? The answer to this question is certainly "no."[33] No matter how much Islamic militants wish the answer to be yes, and no matter how much political ideologues of the military-industrial complex in the Western countries attempt to give the appearance that the answer is yes, neither the Islamic militancy nor Islam as a religion represent a *real threat* to the West. There is nothing in Islam calling for the destruction of the West or Christianity. Islam has coexisted with Christianity and other religions for a long time. The new confrontation between Islamic activists and West emanates from the Western policies and the treatment of Muslim countries in the last century. Muslim activists are asking for the overthrow of undemocratic governments often supported by the United States and other powerful Western countries. They are rebelling against political and economic miseries inflicted by these governments upon their societies. They are using Islam as an alternative to Western liberalism, which has failed to respond to their needs and to overcome the problems of poverty and underdevelopment. In this sense, then, the rise of Islamic fundamentalism in the Islamic world certainly poses a *challenge* to the Western world. But such a challenge is far from a threat. The challenge for the West is to be able to find a balance between its interests in the Islamic lands and the rights of their people to political freedom, economic well-being, and cultural dignity. Several reasons can be offered for such an assessment.

As far as Islam as a religion is concerned, the West really need not be worried. First of all, the Islamic world is culturally heterogeneous, politically divided, and economically diverse. These features, coupled with the close political and economic ties that many of these Muslim countries have with the West, make it improbable that Muslim countries would act in unison. While cultural issues like the Rushdie book can cause universal reaction, responses to most political events in the Muslim world have been somewhat varied. Second, there are enough accommodations in Islam to assure a mutually respectable coexistence with the Western societies. There are many Muslims who, when dealing with the West, are interested in emphasizing the commonalities between Islam and the West rather than their differences.[34] As Robin Wright has argued, the implementation of Islamic laws (*sharia*) does not conflict with Western interests, as is the case in Saudi Arabia and Pakistan.[35] As a matter of fact, it might be in the interest of the West to find these commonalities rather than to focus on the few, perhaps insignificant, differences. Third, we need to distinguish between Islam as a religion and Islam as an ideological tool in the hand of Islamicists. Islam as a religion will remain strong in the Middle East and does not pose a threat to the West. The West should fear Islam and the Islamic world less and understand them more. Islam cannot be effectively shaken by foreign manipulations. As a world religion, it commands its position in world affairs and should not be underestimated. Historically, Islam has proven its capability to adjust to the changing realities of competing ideologies and politics.

However, Islam as a political tool used by Islamic activists is a different issue and has a different agenda. Islam as used by Islamic militants is a rallying cry for a disadvantaged Muslim population to express their disenchantment with Western liberal economic policies, which not only have failed to relieve their economic misery but have also increased their sense of frustration and alienation. The continued support given by Western powers to monarchs and dictators in the Muslim world has convinced these Muslims that they have no chance of representation in the national political process. Islam gives them such a chance.

Given this predicament, if Muslim people continue to be left out of the political process, if their views and concerns continue to be suppressed, and if their alienation from national politics continues, as the events of 1991 and 1992 in Algeria have demonstrated, they will probably continue their political agitations and, if circumstances allow, remain a source of revolutionary aspiration for the disenchanted masses. For instance, the suppression of Islamic sentiments and the lack of any opportunity for the various political forces to participate in national politics laid the ground for the overthrow of the Shah and the eventual establishment of an Islamic state. The West cannot continue to use a double standard of accusing Muslim forces of undemocratic views while treating them undemocratically. Indifference to the plight of Muslims in Bosnia, Palestinians in refugee camps in Gaza and the West Bank, and the Iraqi population suffering under Saddam Hussein's dictatorship, as well as from hardships caused by the UN-imposed embargo, are often cited as examples of lack of any seriousness or sincerity by the West in its treatment of Muslims.[36] Such indifference to the "social injustice" endured by the Muslim people is even acknowledged by U.S. Assistant Secretary of State Edward P. Djerejian.[37]

While the West does not need to embrace Islam, it should not deny the political and cultural rights of those who believe in it either. Ignoring Muslim forces in these societies will actually increase their popularity and appeal.[38] If given an equal chance in a democratic setting, along with the other social and intellectual forces, the real attraction of Islamic fundamentalism as the only force of change will diminish. Islamic fundamentalists will, like other groups, be tested and have their appropriate share of power in a democratic process. Such a public participation exposes these groups to the same trial and errors, and successes and failures, experienced by other political parties. Despite their ideological claims, the Islamic activists are very practical. They live in a mundane world and are interested in the political and material gains of this secular world.[39] In the course of events in the past decade, they have shown an ability to adjust themselves (and an interest in doing so) to practical political changes necessary for their survival. Islam as a religion provides enough ideological ammunition for these activists to shift their position from revolutionary to accommodationist and vice versa.

It has been 16 years since the Islamic revolution in Iran encouraged the spread of fundamentalism in the Muslim world. Except for the West's losing a loyal friend in Iran, what else has really happened to the Islamic countries? Are they in any better position in the world political economy today than 16 years ago? Both economic and political conditions in many of these countries are in much greater disarray than they were in the 1970s and 1980s. Iraq is a divided country and in ruins. The economies of the Arab countries in the Persian Gulf, heavily dependent on oil revenues, are faced with serious deficit problems resulting from extravagant spending and the heavy costs of financing the Iran-Iraq War and liberating Kuwait. These regimes are also very closely tied to U.S. geopolitical interests and those ties make them politically vulnerable at home. Egyptian and Jordanian economies are performing at their worst. Lebanon has not fully recovered from the torment of the civil war. Sudan and Somalia are facing horrendous starvation and internal wars. Libya is confronted with political and economic pressures, partly due to the decline in oil prices and partly due to the various sanctions imposed by the UN. Pakistan has been experiencing internal political instability. The newly formed Islamic Republic of Afghanistan is still experiencing factional political strife. The newly independent Muslim countries of Central Asia are ridden with ethnic and political struggle. The Algerian economic system is weak and its political structure is fragile and unstable. Bosnian Muslims are butchered by Serbs, while the world remains indifferent. So which of these countries really presents a serious threat to the West? What common sociological, political, and economic thread can unite these countries against the West? Surely, Islam provides these countries with a common symbolic expression of their pride and identity. But the political demands and strategic position of Islamic activists in these countries are so diverse that one cannot respond to them uniformly. The real challenge for the West, as Stephen Rosenfeld has noted, is to deal with the political use of Islam by the militant Islamic activists case by case.[40] This means that if the West is determined to respond to the challenges posed by the Islamic fundamentalists, it should correct those conditions that are the source of fundamentalist grievances.

CONCLUSION

After the invasion of Kuwait by Iraq, the United States moved its troops to the Persian Gulf and created a multinational force for liberating Kuwait. The invasion of Kuwait was used by the United States as an opportunity to redefine its role in the post–cold war era. America defined the new world order in terms of its own power and image and pronounced the dawn of the American century. Such a declaration was not unconnected to numerous pressing issues confronting the United States at home and abroad. In the face of these problems, to assume the world leadership of the United States seems premature. To continue to enjoy its prominence over the global capitalist system, the United States has to solve effectively various structural concerns that have contributed to the lowering of its global status. These issues include, among others, a prolonged recession at home, deterioration of its industrial infra-structure, increasing environmental challenges and concerns that restrain U.S. capital's need to move uninhibitedly around the globe, a staggering debt that limits future economic growth, and an increasingly competitive international market in which a unified Europe and Japan act as major economic competitors. In the global capitalist competition, the United States has lost its economic and scientific edge. Today, Japan produces the equivalent of 70 percent of America's GNP, has increased its share of the global equities from 10 percent to 55 percent (the United States decreased from 40 percent to 20 percent), controls 50 percent of the microprocessors market (the United States' share is 38 percent), has a higher annual per capita income (4.3 percent compared to 1.8 percent for the United States during 1981–89), saves 18 percent of disposable income (the United States saved 2 to 2.5 percent during 1986–87), and had 7.8 percent manufacturing productivity for 1984–89 (the United States had 0.3 percent).[41] The area in which the United States still enjoys global superiority is in military technology and political clout. But the postindustrial, postmodern world is the world of ideas, science, and technology. It is a world in which military might has a much more lim-ited effect than in earlier periods. In today's interdependent world, hav-ing the strongest economy and the most advanced technology are far more important than having the strongest army. Thanks to the revolu-tion in communications, the world has become much smaller than it used to be. In a multipolar world, only those countries that have strong technological, scientific, and economic power will be able to demonstrate political influence.

According to former president Bush, the new world order was to bring prosperity, democracy, arms control, and scientific and economic cooperation and development to the Third World. Unfortunately, the prospect for such progress is poor. The Third World began this decade with tremendous economic disadvantages: declining per capita income, increasing debt ($1,200 billion in 1990), increasing fluctuation and decline in commodity prices, declining foreign aid, increasing population, catastrophic environmental damages, increasing ethnic and religious rivalry, and rising health care costs. The combined effects of these problems have been poverty, malnutrition, disease, and political repression in many of these countries. To deal with these concerns, many countries have wholeheartedly accepted the solutions prescribed by the International Monetary Fund and World Bank: deregulation, devaluation, desubsidization, privatization, and trade liberalization. In the absence of a structural policy to protect the unprotected, to help the helpless, and to eliminate mass poverty, experience shows that these measures result in more riots, economic disruptions, military coups, emigration, economic displacement, and sociopolitical alienation.[42] Economic growth is definitely an important ingredient of development. However, a major precondition to sustained economic progress is a broadening of access to resources and purchasing power in these countries. The privatization programs often have resulted in strengthening only the influential and wealthy classes in these societies.[43]

In the Middle East, the United States failed to achieve four of its five objectives in initiating the Persian Gulf War. The United States has been successful in restoring Kuwait but has failed (1) to promote democracy in the region, (2) to create a meaningful framework for resolving the Palestinian question, (3) to overthrow Saddam Hussein, and (4) to stop the arms race in the area. Middle Eastern politics today are not any more democratic than they were prior to the war in the Persian Gulf. The United States has done little to change the status quo. In some ways, the U.S. presence in the region has contributed to the strengthening of governmental measures for silencing opposition to the U.S. presence. The United States, along with other European powers, has also been responsible for increasing the arms race in the region. In 1991, half of the $30 billion in arms transferred to the Third World by the United States went to the Middle East. The United States has used weapons as a means of

(1) creating a balance between various countries in the region, (2) making friends with various countries, and (3) profiting financially. The new world order, so far, is a militarized order absorbing tremendous amounts of financial resources of Middle Eastern countries. The danger of this militarization is that it is taking place in the context of growing hostility between and within the nations in the area. Increasing tensions between Iran and its Arab neighbors, along with the attacks by restless Islamic activists on established governments in the region, have created an explosive situation.

As for Islam, there is no substantive evidence that Islam in the post–cold war era should be viewed as a threat to the Western world. If America defines the new world order in terms of her own interests and views Islam as a force contradicting those interests, then we will see a great deal of tension arising between the Western world and Islamic world. Such pressures can obviously be faulted on the unilateral redefinition of world affairs in terms of the United States national interest and on the inappropriate understanding of Islam and the Islamic world. The continuing conflict between the West and Islamic activists around the world in the past decade is caused more by the political and economic consequences of the United States' relationship with the Islamic world than by Islam as a religion. The real causes of Islamic activism in the Muslim world are political repression, economic deprivation, cultural alienation, and the social isolation experienced by the Muslim people in their countries. To deal with these concerns, the West should abandon the policy of isolating and suppressing these activists. Instead, it should look for policies and options that encourage participation by these Muslims in their national politics, improve their economic situations, and provide them with a sense of control over their lives.

NOTES TO CHAPTER 3

1. See *New York Times*, October 2, 1990.

2. See International Monetary Fund forecast in *New York Times*, April 23, 1992.

3. Roger E. Kanet and James T. Alexander, "The End of the Cold War and the 'New World Order': Implications for the Developing World," *The Iranian Journal of International Affairs*, vol. 4, no. 2 (Summer 1992): 250.

4. Quoted in Keith Melville and Matthew Yeo, *America's Role in the World: New Risks, New Realities* (New York: McGraw Hill, 1992), 11.

5. George Melloan, "Global View: Stirring the West's Postwar Alphabet Soup," *Wall Street Journal,* 1 June 1992, 1; Tom Wicker, "Today's Threat to Peace Is the Guy Down the Street," *New York Times,* 2 June 1991.

6. John Lukacs, *The End of the Twentieth Century and the End of the Modern Age* (New York: Ticknor & Fields, 1992); Benedict Anderson, "The New World Disorder," *New Left Review,* no. 193 (May/June 1992).

7. Jacques Attali, "Line on the Horizon: A New Order in the Making," *New Perspectives Quarterly* (Spring 1990).

8. See reports on G7 and IMF in *Financial Times* (London), 27 April 1992.

9. World Bank, *Accelerated Development in Sub-Saharan Africa: An Agenda for Action* (Oxford: Oxford University Press, 1981); World Bank, *World Development Report, 1986* (Oxford: Oxford University Press, 1986); see also James Morgan, "Rip Van Winkle's New World Order," *Financial Times* (London), 25-26 April 1992.

10. Tom Wicker, "A Not-So-New Order," *New York Times,* 5 June 1992.

11. E. Wayne Nafziger, *The Debt Crisis in Africa* (Baltimore, Md.: Johns Hopkins University Press, 1993); Jeffry A. Frieden, *Debt, Development, & Democracy: Modern Political Economy & Latin America, 1965–1985* (Princeton, N.J.: Princeton University Press, 1992); Cheryl Payer, *The Debt Trap: The IMF & the Third World* (New York: Monthly Review Press, 1975).

12. Jeffrey E. Garten, *A Cold Peace: The Struggle for Supremacy in the Post–Cold War World* (New York: Random House, 1992).

13. James Petras, "The Meaning of the New World Order: A Critique," *America,* no. 11 (May 1991): 513.

14. Robert W. Tucker and David C. Hendrickson, *The Imperial Temptation: The New World Order and America's Purpose* (New York: Council on Foreign Relations Press, 1992).

15. This orchestrated effort resulted in the passage of UN Security Council Resolution no. 848.

16. Alton Frye, "How We Can Contain the Mideast Arms Explosion," *Washington Post,* 16 June 1991, Section B1.

17. McGeorge Bundy, "Our Country's New Role in the World," *Life*, vol. 15, no. 8 (August 1992): 51.

18. Christic Institute, *Covert Operations, the Persian Gulf War and the "New World Order"* (Washington, D.C.: Christic Institute, 1991).

19. Roger E. Kanet and James T. Alexander, op. cit., 275.

20. Jane Friedman, "US 'Lukewarm' on Arab Democracy," *Christian Science Monitor*, 6 August 1991.

21. Washington Institute, *In Search of Peace; American Strategy for Arab-Israeli Peace Negotiations* (Washington, D.C.: Washington Institute, 1992)

22. Thomas L. Friedman, "What the United States Has Taken on in the Gulf, besides a War," *New York Times*, 29 January 1991.

23. Carol Berger, "Mideast Critics Say 'New World Order' Ignores Arab Aspirations," *Christian Science Monitor*, 14 February 1991.

24. Mohammed Akacem, "A New World Order for Oil," *Middle East Policy*, vol. 1, no. 3 (1992).

25. Clyde Haberman, "Israeli Worry That US Will Need Them Less in New Global Realignment," *New York Times*, 3 August 1992; George D. Moffett III, "Era of Automatic U.S. Assistance to Israel May Be Drawing to Close," *Christian Science Monitor*, 10 February 1992.

26. See *New York Times*, 7 March 1991.

27. David D. Newsom, "The New 'Crusades' of Islam," *Christian Science Monitor*, 27 January 1988; Mark Juergensmeyer, *The New Cold War? Religious Nationalism Confronts the Secular State* (Berkeley, CA: University of California Press, 1993).

28. Shireen T. Hunter, "The Transformation of the Soviet Union: Impact on the Northern Tier Countries," *The Iranian Journal of International Affairs*, vol. 4, no. 2 (Summer 1992): 383; see also Robin Wright, "Islam, Democracy, and the West," *Foreign Affairs*, vol. 71, no. 3 (Summer 1992).

29. Quoted in Rushworth M Kidder, "The Islamic War Against Modernity," *Christian Science Monitor*, 7 May 1990, 13. See also Bernard Lewis, *Islam and the West* (Oxford: Oxford University Press, 1993).

30. Edward Luttwak, "The Shape of Things to Come," *Commentary*, no. 89 (June 1990): 17–25.

31. Neil Livingston, "Islam: Confrontation with the West," in *Soldier of Fortune*, Persian translation in *Iran Times*, vol. 22, no. 25 (4 September 1992); Trevor Taylor, "What Sort of Security for Western Europe?" *The World Today* (August–September 1991): 138–42.

32. See Editorial, *Christian Science Monitor*, 20 February 1992.

33. See John L. Esposito, *The Islamic Threat: Myth or Reality?* (New York: Oxford University Press, 1992).

34. Mowahid H. Shah, "A New Cold War with Islam?" *Christian Science Monitor*, 30 July 1990.

35. Robin Wright, op. cit.

36. Ibid.

37. See *Washington Post*, 30 May 1993.

38. Shireen T. Hunter, op. cit., 393.

39. David D. Newsom, op. cit.; Howard Lafranchi, "Reconciling Islam and the West," *Christian Science Monitor*, 1 April 1992.

40. Stephen S. Rosenfeld, "Rhetorics and Realities in the Islamic World," *Washington Post*, 22 November 1992.

41. Abu K. Selimuddin, "Will America Become Number Two?" *USA Today Magazine* (September 1989).

42. Julius O. Ihonvbere, "Africa and the New World Order: Prospects for the 1990s," *The Iranian Journal of International Affairs*, vol. 4, nos. 3 and 4 (Fall and Winter 1992).

43. Frances Moore Lappe, Rachel Schurman, and Devin Danaher, *Betraying the National Interest* (New York: Grove Press, 1987).

IRAN AND THE PERSIAN GULF: STRATEGIC ISSUES AND OUTLOOK

Hooshang Amirahmadi

The international political economy is going through a period of rapid change, which, along with domestic changes, is resulting in a redefinition of foreign policy strategic concerns and outlooks of a number of nation-states as they search for new regional and geo-political alliances. The Islamic Republic of Iran is very much a part of this phenomenon. In the post–cold war period, a number of strategic issues have emerged whose intricate dynamics are likely to affect Iran's status as a dominant actor in the Persian Gulf area. These concerns are: the intervening role of great power relations, Iran-Arab relations, the arms race, Islamic movements, oil politics, regional collective security, and relevant domestic factors including demographic and economic trends.

This chapter, in seven parts, focuses on an examination of current trends in these strategic issues and indicates how mutations in them are likely to affect Iran and its foreign policy in the foreseeable future. It also presents an analysis of how Iran's regional neighbors to the south and a few great powers—especially the United States—would respond to changes in these issues. It is through their responses that these actors are likely to shape the stability of the Persian Gulf in the post–cold war period. The chapter argues that, unless such reactions are measured and collectively acceptable, a conflictual and near-bleak future would await the Persian Gulf. My arguments and speculations are primarily based on several interviews and discussions I have had with a number of foreign policy leaders of Iran in 1992 and 1993. Needless to say, I have also used, and have been influenced by, various spoken and published sources in Iran and in the West.

1. RIVALRY AND INTERVENTIONS OF THE GREAT POWERS

Although nominally a nonaligned nation, for most of the cold–war period, Iran remained an ally of the West and used the U.S.-Soviet rivalry to its strategic advantage in political and economic spheres. The policy of "negative equilibrium" was officially introduced by the nationalist prime minister Mohammad Mosaddeq in 1951. It grew out of Iran's experience with rivaling Russo-British interests in the nineteenth and early twentieth centuries. The policy dictated that Iran should not grant concessions to superpowers, but instead use their assistance for furthering its objectives. The tradition continued, with some moderation, under the Shah Mohammad Reza Pahlavi (1941 to 1979). In particular, the Shah introduced what became known as "positive equilibrium," which allowed the government to enter into concessionary economic relations with superpowers in an attempt to improve relations and economic ties. Accordingly, Iran, as a "strategic buffer zone," enjoyed significant, although mostly titular, autonomy to maneuver between the East and the West. This position allowed Iran to make demands on both sides and obtain political relief from pressures that would have otherwise handicapped its domestic and foreign policies.

This policy orientation underwent some changes in the postrevolutionary period, initially toward the old "negative equilibrium" policy and then back in the direction of a "positive equilibrium." In particular, early in the postrevolutionary period, Iran-Soviet relations remained tenuous even though the Soviet Union was an adversary of the United States and relations between Iran and the United States had dangerously deteriorated. The Soviet entanglement in Afghanistan prevented it from developing a closer relationship with Iran. Indeed, the initial "Neither East, Nor West" foreign policy of the new regime in Tehran could be viewed as a noncooperative and conflictual version of the "negative equilibrium" policy except that it placed the concept in an Islamic propagandist garb instead of a nationalistic one. This change in policy approach did not necessarily reflect the impact of the regime's revolutionary Islamic ideology. Rather, it could be viewed as an approach based on Iran's self-image as a powerful nation that was never colonized and, more often than not, played rival superpowers against each other to its advantage.

In the post-Khomeini and post–cold war era, as Iran focused on reconstruction of its economic base, its return to the pre-revolution policy of "both East and West" became more evident.[1] In other words, the Islamic Republic's recent foreign policy has become increasingly similar to the Shah's "positive equilibrium" policy. Again, there is a difference: While the Shah's policy had no fixed ideological framework and was quite consistent, the Islamic Republic has wavered and placed the policy in an Islamic propagandist garb. For instance, large contracts have been signed with a variety of countries representing all areas of the ideological spectrum at the same time that the regime in Tehran has remained steadfast about its ideology. Notable among such countries are China and the former Soviet Union at one extreme and Japan, Germany, and Turkey at the other. Even trade with the United States has expanded significantly since 1990.[2]

Needless to say, indigenous regional developments and future developments in other parts of the globe are decisive in shaping the great power rivalry in the Persian Gulf. For instance, China's decisions regarding the magnitude and the modalities of its involvement in the Gulf have a great deal to do with its global ambitions. Similarly, Russia's perceptions of its future role as a major military power and an oil producer, or Japan's willingness to extend its role as an economic superpower in the Pacific to other regions of the world, or the potential intensification of U.S.–Western Europe economic differences, are bound to affect the future dynamics of their involvement in the Persian Gulf as well as in other global areas.[3]

Still another critical issue is the evolution of the U.S.–Commonwealth of Independent States (CIS) relations. Although the rigid bipolar system that characterized the international political economy since World War II has changed significantly, it is debatable whether the present cooperative atmosphere in U.S.-CIS relations will continue in the future. The collapse of Communism alone, even if it was to be considered a fait accompli, cannot guarantee a sustained cooperation. There are also old ethnonationalistic interests that may lead to conflicts between the major players in international politics. Indicative of this phenomenon is the increasing opposition in Russia to Yeltsin's pro-Western posturing.

In addition, Moscow has expressed its desire to maintain a prominent role in Middle Eastern affairs.[4] Russia's sponsorship of an Arab-Israeli peace conference in Moscow in 1992 was a clear indication of such aspirations. Russia also seems intent on enhancing its strategic leverage in the Persian Gulf. The possibilities for Russia to increase its influence in the region are enhanced with the collapse of Communism, since it was seen as abhorrent to Islam and threatening to traditional monarchies of the area. Moscow has, for instance, developed cordial relations with the Gulf Cooperation Council (GCC) states including Saudi Arabia, which never established full diplomatic relations with the former Soviet Union. The Persian Gulf crisis was a turning point. The GCC states awarded the former Soviet Union large loans and other types of financial assistance for its support of the anti-Iraqi coalition. Furthermore, the CIS states have not thus far renounced the USSR-Iraq defense pact and are attempting to forge new coalitions and trade ties with other Persian Gulf states, such as Iran and Kuwait. With Iran, they signed a multibillion dollar economic and military pact in 1989. It must also be remembered that the Russians have traditionally given top priority to sales of weapons to the Middle East on which they depend for a sizable portion of their foreign exchange earnings.

American-European relations with respect to the Persian Gulf have been oscillating between full cooperation, as witnessed during the recent war with Iraq, and lively competition, as in arms sales to the Gulf states. One recent episode involved the Kuwaiti purchase of American military equipment after they were pressured by the Bush administration to abandon a plan to place a similar order with the British arms industry.[5] The possible emergence of the European Community as an integrated entity would create a new pole that could pose a threat to U.S. hegemonic aspirations in the Persian Gulf region. The EC will, in all likelihood, want to pursue its own economic and political policies in the Persian Gulf, independent of the United States. This tendency is already evident in the Community's lack of enthusiasm for an American proposal to further restrict sales of high-technology items to Iran.[6]

Notwithstanding these possible future challenges, the United States remains the most prominent and influential foreign power in the Persian Gulf. The U.S.-led coalition's victory against Iraq, the ensuing series of bilateral defense arrangements with Saudi Arabia, Kuwait, and Bahrain, the near monopoly of arms sales to the GCC states, and the dominance in Kuwaiti reconstruction contracts have guaranteed an active American presence in the region for the foreseeable future. In addition, ensuring the flow of oil, attempting to keep the recurrent ethnonationalist sentiments at a manageable level (as has been done in the northern and southern parts of Iraq after the Gulf War), and preserving the fragile Gulf monarchies are of utmost importance to the United States. These developments and concerns attest to the very real possibility of a growing U.S. involvement in the Persian Gulf.[7]

Iran remains skeptical of the American involvement in the region in the 1990s. Since the revolution in 1978, relations between the two nations have been tainted with misperceptions of each other's intentions, mutual distrust, and, at times, even hostility. Episodes such as the hostage crisis, the Iran-Iraq War, the Iran-contra scandal, and the downing of an Iranian passenger jet have played major roles in worsening relations. The coalition war against Iraq had the potential to ameliorate tensions between Iran and the United States. Iran's assistance in securing the release of Western hostages in Lebanon could have helped improve the country's fractured image and might have resulted in the initiation of at least businesslike relations. However, among other factors, subsequent developments relating to arms purchases, the Abu Musa islands, Iran's alleged renewed support for certain Islamic movements in the Middle East, and Tehran's opposition to the Arab-Israeli peace conferences created a reverse trend. Presently, the United States continues to view Iran as a potential source of regional instability and terrorism.

From the preceding, it appears that the United States will remain the undisputed foreign power in the Persian Gulf in the near future. In the longer term, however, American dominance of the region faces challenges from the rising powers in Europe and the Pacific Rim. Great power alliances and rivalries will in the future be less influenced by ideological considerations and more by economic strength, as measured by competitiveness in trade and technological development. This is largely because of the partial demise of Communism and the emergence of nonmilitary superpowers such as Japan and Germany. China and Russia seem determined to remain major arms exporters and are likely to strengthen their domestic military sectors. This might use a major part of their resources and will constrain their ability to become major economic powers. While arms production and export will continue to be a dominant factor in economic growth and political power, it may not, in the last analysis, be sustained without a strong domestic economic base. From this perspective, Japan and the EC appear to have a better prospect for becoming major players in the Persian Gulf. If America is to meet such challenges successfully, it needs to redefine its domestic priorities toward emphasizing economic growth. It is equally important for the United States to focus on improving its relations with Iran.[8] As the largest and strongest state, as well as the largest market in the region, Iran can uniquely provide any major power with facilities that could significantly enhance its regional role.

2. IRAN AND THE ARAB WORLD

Interstate realignment based on the frequently changing nature of rivalries and interests has been a major feature of the Middle East since
World War II. It will undoubtedly remain unchanged in the post–cold
war period. This is particularly true of the Persian Gulf area where, in
slightly more than a decade, two major interstate wars have been fought
and international borders still continue to remain disputed among all
states.[9] The Persian Gulf region also holds two-thirds of the world's
proven oil reserves and in the past this precious commodity has, more
often than not, been a divisive factor in Iran-Arab relations. Other
major factors contributing to regional tension include ethnonationalist
and ideological inclinations. It is, however, misleading just to focus on
differences among states in the region, as they also have significant commonalities. For example, a common religion—Islam—has historically
been a major bond between Iranians and Arabs. Other potentially con-
cordant factors include geographic contiguity; centuries of social inter-
actions; economic relations, as with OPEC; and population movement
across the Persian Gulf. Arabs and Iranians have also had common
enemies, such as the colonial powers, and a shared purpose, as with a
homeland for the Palestinians. In addition, the two peoples are grappling
with similar developmental needs and aspirations.

Yet, as history well indicates, these same solidarity-generating factors
have at times been acutely divisive. It is for this reason that a better
understanding of regional relations requires a more thorough examination of the tension-generating factors. In what follows, a brief survey of
past and present sources of harmony and discord between the Iranians
and the Persian Gulf Arabs is given, with a special emphasis on tension-
generating forces.[10]

Islam—as the common religion of Iranians and Arabs—could and
should be a major source of harmony between the two peoples. Yet it is
more often than not a source of tension. To begin with, the Sunni-Shia
division reduces the solidarity-generating potential of Islam. Iran is predominantly Shia, and Shiism has been intertwined with Iranian nationalism. Arabs are predominantly Sunni, and Sunnism is ultimately linked
with Arab nationalism. The dispute over the Hajj ritual in Mecca, Saudi
Arabia, reflects this ideological rift. Instead of bringing Muslims together
in a show of solidarity and common purpose as was the original intent,
the ritual became an arena of politico-religious contest between the
kingdom and the Islamic Republic. In a demonstration during the 1987
Hajj, some four hundred Iranian pilgrims were killed by the Saudi

troops; the event led to a severance of diplomatic relations between Saudi Arabia and Iran for the next four years.

On the economic side, OPEC could be a bond between Arabs and Iranians. In reality, it is a major source of conflict. In 1986, during the Iran-Iraq War, a Saudi-"engineered" oil glut, helped by Kuwait and the United Arab Emirates (UAE) and encouraged by the United States, reduced oil prices from around $28 per barrel to below $10 per barrel in less than two months. The Iranian economy is yet to fully recover from the devastating impact of that Saudi "treason."[11] Iran's expected oil revenue of $15 billion dropped to an actual $5.8 billion. Also, after the cease-fire in 1988, Arab members of OPEC backed Iraq's demand for parity in production quota with Iran. After some initial resistance, Iran accepted the new condition; this was inequitable as Iraq's share had always been lower, and Iran's economy and population are about three times larger than those of Iraq.

Iran-Arab tensions are also rooted in ethnic and cultural differences. Despite the commonality of religion, Iranian and Arab cultures are marked by significant differences. They speak distinct languages, they have separate calendar years, and they celebrate several unique national holidays. Nor are their tastes in food, music, or apparel similar. Differing national identities have led to contrasting national purposes and rivalries. Exacerbating these differences is a long history of conflict and coexistence since the forced introduction of Islam in Iran in A.D. 637. Unfortunately, tensions crystallized in the near racist ideologies of pan-Arabism and pan-Iranism (as distinct from Arab and Iranian nationalism).[12]

Territorial disputes, largely a legacy of colonialism in the region, also divide Iranians and Arabs (as well as Arabs themselves). These include the Iranian province of Khuzistan, the three Persian Gulf islands of Abu Musa, the Great Tunb and the Small Tunb, and the Shatt al Arab waterway. Arabs also reject the name of the Persian Gulf, referring to it as the "Arabian Gulf." Khuzistan, a southern province of Iran, is also called "Arabistan." Yet, the Persian Gulf has been called so since ancient times, and Khuzistan has always been an Iranian territory, part of which was called Anzan or Anshan under the historic Achaemenid Empire.[13] Territorial disputes among the Arab states also influence Iranian-Arab relations as was demonstrated during the Iraqi invasion of Kuwait and more recently in reaction to Saudi-Qatari border skirmishes.

The Iranian and Arab governments, as well as outside powers, are also part of the problem. Using religion and ethnicity, or political and ideological differences, they have played a divisive role in Iran-Arab relations. They can utilize these factors effectively because Arabs, Iranians, Shiites, and Sunnis live on both sides of the Persian Gulf and they come from differing socioeconomic backgrounds. Sunnis account for more than 7 percent of the Iranian population, and ethnic Arabs number about 500,000. At the time of the Iraqi invasion of Kuwait, about 30 percent of Kuwait's l.7 million population were Shiites. In Iraq, Yemen (north), Bahrain, and Saudi Arabia, Shiites account for 52, 50, 65, and 10 percent of the population, respectively. The Iranian popula- tion of these nations varies from 4 percent in Kuwait to 10 and 8 percent in Qatar and Bahrain. Iraqis of Iranian decent are also significant. In the last two decades, the Iraqi government has deported these people by the thousands, seemingly for national security reasons. Shiites have also been discriminated against in the Arab world where they generally rep- resent the lower classes. The same is true of Sunnis and Arabs in Iran.

Governments have used ethnic and political divisions to intervene in the internal affairs of other countries. Iraqis gave active support to Iranian Sunni Arabs and Kurdish nationalists and the People's Mujahedeen Organization, among other opposition forces, against Tehran. The Iranian governments under the Shah and since the Islamic revolution, in turn, supported the anti-Baghdad Kurds and Shia oppo- sition in Iraq. The Islamic Republic also used Shia radicals in Lebanon against the United States and Israel and, during the Hajj, against the Saudi government. More recently, the United States and its largely Western allies in the Persian Gulf War of 1991 have used Saddam Hussein's abuse of human rights against the Iraqi Kurds and Shia pop- ulation as a pretext to delineate two "no-fly" zones in the country. States have typically justified their interventions in internal affairs of others by citing ideological and national security/interest considerations.

The Islamic Republic is suspected to have attempted to export its rev- olution to neighboring states in the 1980s. This antagonized almost all Arab states, most notably Iraq, Saudi Arabia, Kuwait, Egypt, Algeria, and Jordan. The reaction of these governments led to a deterioration or suspension of diplomatic relations with Iran, and in some instances, triggered retaliatory actions. Iraq imposed a war on Iran. Saudis along with Kuwait and other Gulf Arab states financed Iraq for $50 billion, and Egyptians along with Jordanians sent military support. The oil-produc- ing Persian Gulf Arab states weakened Iran within OPEC and harmed its economy by manipulating OPEC oil production and prices. They also involved the United States in the so-called tankers war in the Persian Gulf against Iran in 1987. After the Iraqi defeat by the U.S.-led forces, even Syrians who had supported Iran during the Iran-Iraq War approved a proposal for a peacekeeping force in the Persian Gulf that excluded Iran; a strong Saddam Hussein was no longer a threat to Hafiz al-Assad. Significantly, the Iran-Iraq War did not cause a major rift in the Arab world as the Iraqi invasion of Kuwait did. Most Iranians viewed this as evidence of Arab hostility toward Iran.

Finally, the Arab-Israeli conflict, another legacy of the Western powers in the region, is also a source of both tension and solidarity. Iranians sympathize with Palestinians because they are mostly Muslims, mistreated, and homeless. The Islamic Republic has focused particularly on Israel's occupation of "holy Jerusalem" and on its "Zionist expansionist designs." This attitude toward the conflict increased Arab-Iranian solidarity. Yet the conflict also created tensions. As Arabs, most Palestinians took the Arab side in Iran-Arab conflicts, including the Iran-Iraq War. This reduced Iran's solidarity with their cause. Although the Arab-Israeli conflict contributes to regional tensions, its resolution is secondary to Iran's main concerns in the region, namely security of the Persian Gulf and Iran's traditional leadership position in the area. Iran did not favor linking the Palestinian question with the Persian Gulf crisis and opposed the recent peace conferences between the Arabs and the Israelis.

3. THE ARMS RACE AND MILITARY BALANCE

Concern over regional arms buildup in the Persian Gulf has rightly reached meteoric heights.[14] Major American newspapers frequently publish front-page articles regarding this matter. In fact, the arms race has been a significant contributing factor to the present state of tensions among Persian Gulf states. Two devastating interstate wars and a plethora of civil wars and border skirmishes attest to this fact. In the post–Gulf War period, attentions have increasingly focused on Iran's actual arms purchases and the potential for future military development, including concerns for technology transfer and training of scientists and technicians. Unfortunately influenced by the "Iraqi syndrome," the recent news coverage has been for the most part biased, and as a result a more balanced and accurate assessment of this multifaceted and potentially explosive issue has not emerged.

From Iran's perspective, present trends in the arms race are certainly counterproductive if not catastrophically dangerous. This is based on its experience with the war with Iraq and the Gulf War of 1991. Its own experience has taught Iran that a deterrent force is the only alternative to an ironclad collective security arrangement. In addition to war-related experiences, regional developments such as the extravagantly sophisticated arms purchases on the part of the Saudis, bilateral defense pacts between the United States and most Persian Gulf Arab states, and the continuing political chaos in Iraq and Afghanistan have shaped Iran's approach to defense matters. Other factors include the emergence of largely unstable northern neighbors and the intensification of ethno-nationalistic struggles.

There are two major aspects of Iranian arms buildup—domestic production and imports. Development of Iran's arms industries predates the Islamic Republic. Under the Shah and with the assistance of the West, particularly a number of American multinationals (Northrop, Lockheed, General Electric, Grunmenn, and Bell Helicopter), a rapidly growing arms industry was in place by the mid-1970s, focusing on air power. These included helicopter industries, missile repair and modification facilities, jet engine maintenance industries, and armament factories manufacturing a wide variety of small arms. The Shah also sought, unsuccessfully, to expand Iran's nuclear power–generating capacity. Meanwhile, the country became the largest importer of military hardware in the Middle East, with the possible exception of Israel. At the time of the revolution in 1978, Iran was committed to multiple contracts with American arms producers worth $17 billion. One of the first foreign policy initiatives of the Islamic Republic was to cancel these contracts. Iran also let its military industries go into inaction, reduced the period of conscription from two years to one year, and cut in half its standing army and its budget. These factors, along with other policy shifts, moved Iran away from military buildup.[15]

The Iran-Iraq War was an unfortunate awakening and maturing process for the Islamic Republic. Both the leadership and the public were caught off guard when Iraq suddenly launched an all-out offensive into Iranian territory in September 1980. More surprising, perhaps, was the ensuing lack of response by the international community. The United Nations failed to condemn Iraq, and the two superpowers appeared relieved. The Arab states actively and belligerently supported Iraq. Saudi Arabia along with Kuwait and other Gulf Arab states gave some $50 billion to Iraq in loans and unilateral aid. Egypt and Jordan sent military support. Meanwhile American-led sanctions (for example, Operation Staunch) made it very difficult for Iran to procure arms at the time it needed to defend itself against an aggressor that was superiorly armed and continuously supplied. Both superpowers, perhaps for the first time in the cold war era, sided with and militarily supported the same party in the conflict, namely Iraq. Toward the end of the conflict, the United States became directly involved, bombarding Iranian oil platforms in the Persian Gulf and downing an Iranian passenger plane. The United Nations eventually declared Iraq an aggressor but only well after it had invaded Kuwait and was forcefully repelled.[16]

As a consequence, Iran began, although belatedly, to revitalize its existing military industries, targeting maintenance and service of its existing stockpile. Soon, however, Iraq initiated its "war on cities" strategy using long-range missiles. To reciprocate, and in the absence of an easy-to-access arms market, Iran rejuvenated its missile production. It also expanded its capabilities in production of light arms, ammunition, mortars, howitzer and artillery barrels, and aircraft parts.[17] Meanwhile Iran was also importing a certain amount of armament from a variety of sources, including black markets. Yet its military stockpiles were in steady decline, reaching a critically insufficient level by the end of the war. To give an indication of the decline in military imports, in the last two years of the war (1987–88), the total figure for Iran stood at less than $1.5 billion. Comparable figures for Iraq and Saudi Arabia were $8.2 billion and $5 billion respectively. In the next three years, the gap between Iran and the other two widened even further. Thus, Iran's total military imports bill for the 1987–91 period was $2.8 billion while those for Iraq and Saudi Arabia had jumped to $10.3 billion and $10.6 billion.[18] Measured in per capita terms, the gap becomes considerably wider as Iran's population is 60 million as compared to 17 million for Iraq and 14 million for Saudi Arabia. This gap notwithstanding, in the immediate postwar period Iran still did not emphasize military buildup. On the contrary, it directed attention and resources to economic reconstruction and deployed its military to that end. It was only after the Persian Gulf War of 1991 that Iran began to reconsider its defense strategy and replenish its military hardware.

The present strategy is focusing on both domestic production and imports. On the domestic side, the noticeable change is an emphasis on the use of modern technology in a variety of production areas. Using examples of navigational, avionic, electronic, and information technologies—radar-testing devices, oscilloscopes, logic analyzers, fiber-optic cables, digital switches, high-speed computers, remote sensors, and jet engines—the Western media and governments have stressed the "dual use" or "military use" of these technologies and Iran's potential as well as intention to apply them toward military buildup.[19] Iran has utilized these technologies in projects that could have both civilian and military use, such as airports, port facilities, industrial units, power generation, and communication networks. Yet the dual-use nature of these projects cannot be taken to indicate Iran's militaristic intent, particularly in the absence of sufficient evidence. Moreover, the limited scope of such dual-use projects should serve as evidence of the constraints on the Iranian ability to become a regional threat in the foreseeable future. Besides, that country has demonstrated its commitment to international rules of conduct on technologies of mass destruction. For example, the International Atomic Energy Agency (IAEA) investigated Iran's nuclear projects and materials and, along with U.S. government officials, cleared Iran of any ill intention.[20] That agency is also to monitor the Sino-Iranian nuclear energy project, which has become another rallying point for anti-Iran lobbyists in the West and in the region.[21]

On the imports side, Iran was (in the 1980s) reportedly in the process of acquiring military aircrafts from both Russia (Mig 29s, Su24) and China (F-7), tanks (T-72) from Russia and Eastern European countries, ballistic missiles and rocket-guidance systems from North Korea and China (gyroscopes), satellites, gear, and three small, used, and diesel-powered submarines from Russia.[22] It should be noted, however, that according to some American intelligence experts, the total import bill is still far below the outlay the Shah devoted to peacetime military buildup. The total of $2 billion a year in military imports is also less than 10 percent of Iran's total import bill of $28 billion for the 1991–92 fiscal year.[23] In comparative terms, Iran's current annual military expenditures are only about 40 percent of what Iraq was spending per year on weapons after the Iran-Iraq War, and only a fraction of a single Saudi-U.S. aircraft deal of $9 billion.[24]

As for the rationality behind Iran's current defense policy, a number of regional and global developments merit attention. The general impression, particularly among Western observers, is that the outcome of the Gulf War was beneficial to Iran in at least two ways: it substantially weakened Iraq's military power, and it strengthened Iran's air-defense system as a number of Iraqi aircrafts defected to Iran. Implied in this assertion is that Iran did not need its military build-up. From Iran's perspective, however, the Gulf War introduced new elements of risk and uncertainty in its relevant regional environment. To begin with, the war led to increased U.S. involvement in the region through a series of bilateral defense arrangements with Saudi Arabia, Kuwait, Bahrain, and UAE.

The war also escalated an arms buildup by Saudi Arabia, Israel, and Kuwait, among other states in the region. For example, from 1987 to

1991, Saudi Arabia imported $10.6 billion worth of major conventional weapons;[25] its purchases for 1992, were, however, much higher. In one shot it purchased 75 units of F-15 jets from the United States at $9 billion.[26] To use another indicator, Saudis consistently have maintained high military expenditures throughout the last decade, ranging between $14.5 and $26.2 billion each year.[27] In a single deal in 1992, Kuwait purchased some 236 American M1-A2 advanced battle tanks, which with the spare parts and training involved will eventually cost Kuwaitis some $4 billion.[28]

The Gulf War introduced political chaos in Iraq to the point of possible disintegration. In particular, it emboldened the Kurdish separatists, who with the help of the West, have established a semi-independent state in northern Iraq and are demanding recognition from the UN and its member states. The de facto Kurdish state boasts a guerrilla force of some 200,000, a major force by all standards.[29] The Kurdish issue is particularly relevant since Iran's large Kurdish minority has in the past expressed similar aspirations. Despite this, Iran continues to remain concerned with Iraqi threat to its security as long as the Baath Party and its strongman, Saddam Hussein, are still in power. The Iraqi military maintains its technological potential and the state remains militaristic in its orientation. Moreover, the People's Mujahedeen Organization of Iran, the main guerrilla opposition force to the regime in Tehran, is securely based in Iraq and enjoys the full support of the Iraqi regime as well as a number of major political figures in Western Europe and the United States.

Iran also saw itself excluded from several proposed collective security arrangements by the United States, while Arab states, even nonregional actors, were included. One such example was proposed in Damascus and was subsequently known as "GCC plus two formula" (or the Damascus Declaration). This agreement called for an "Arab peacekeeping force" with the participation of Syria, Egypt, and the GCC states. Iran was excluded, the pretext being the preservation of Arab identity of the force. The United States also excluded Iran from its proposed regional security arrangements throughout the Gulf crisis. Iran's efforts to join the GCC as a member were also rebuffed by the organization. From all this, Iran has reached the obvious conclusion that the Gulf states and other major actors are systematically attempting to marginalize it into irrelevance. This perception must have had some impact on Iran's determination to enhance its defensive capabilities.

Another major influence on Iran's defensive strategy includes the emergence of a new political configuration on its northern frontier—the

Commonwealth of Independent States. Some of these states have nuclear capabilities without appropriate controlling institutions. Others maintain significant conventional military technology and force in the context of declining economies and sociopolitical instability. A few are experiencing disorder stemming from political factionalism and ethnic infighting. The ethnic issue is particularly disconcerting to Iran as some of these ethnic groups also reside in Iran (Azaris, Turkomans, and others). If the Soviet, Afghani, and Iraqi experiences serve as examples, the possibility of ethnic divisions challenging the territorial integrity of a country is a very real threat for the Iranian leadership. With the future of political developments across all Iranian borders remaining uncertain, possessing the capability to defend international borders remains a top priority.

There are also some domestic prerequisites that guide Iran's defense policy. The prohibition of desperately needed arms during the war with Iraq drove Iran toward a policy of increased reliance on domestic production of conventional weaponry. It soon became evident that expansion of this industry has many advantages. Even though precise figures are not available, it is well known that Iranian defense industries have created many well-paying jobs. For an economy suffering from the adverse effects of economic sanctions, war destruction, and consistent decline in real oil prices, this development could not be ignored or precluded. In addition, the resulting technological innovations that emanate from defense-related R & D serve Iran's economic aspirations as much as that of any other country. The targeted industrial sector, in particular, continues to benefit substantially from such research, as do the electronic and consumer goods industries. The scientists who conduct these activities can in turn contribute significantly by training future engineers and technicians, thus rendering the country capable of lessening its dependence on others.

One other issue that deserves attention is the current coverage of Iran's defense policy by the Western media. Iran's recent arms purchases have received singular attention, but what has been consistently missing is an analysis regarding the need to replenish weaponry destroyed during the lengthy war against Iraq. For a country as large and as populated as Iran, having gone through a devastating eight-year war and being situated in such a volatile region, replenishing its defense capabilities to a minimal level of efficacy and balance is an absolute necessity. Another example of reckless journalism pertains to Iran's purchase of three used submarines from Russia. One should not forget that other countries in the region also possess submarines and that Iran's location also exposes it to naval developments of Indian Ocean states, many of which possess highly advanced naval capabilities. Iran's declared policy to dock these submarines in its ports on the Sea of Oman should in no way threaten the relative security of the Persian Gulf, especially since the average depth of the Persian Gulf waters is not conducive to submarine navigation. Finally, the Western media remained conspicuously silent when Iran became a signatory of a major treaty banning chemical warfare in Paris on January 13, 1993. Unfortunately, Arab states did not participate, citing Israel's stockpile of chemical weapons as a pretext.

4. OIL POLICY POLITICS

Iran's oil and regional security policies have been closely linked ever since revenue from this single-export commodity became a major economic resource for the country in the 1950s. The Formation of OPEC, globalization of oil, and intensification of regional tensions in subsequent years have braced the link by further integrating Iran into the world political economy. Under this condition, domestic and foreign policies have largely merged, and balancing economic and security interests have become a complicated task as they are often contradictory.

The fact that oil has become Iran's economic and security lifeline is not difficult to demonstrate. More than 95 percent of the country's foreign exchange is earned through oil, which pays for Iran's sizable imports of industrial inputs, defense procurements, and food. Specifically, industry requires some $8 billion a year to operate at a zero-growth level, food imports at the minimum will need some $4 billion a year, defense procurements will cost between $3 billion to $4 billion in peacetime, and some $1 billion to $2 billion is required for miscellaneous expenses relating to foreign operations of the government. The total figure for a nongrowth scenario comes to some $17 billion to $18 billion a year. Another $7 billion to $8 billion will be needed for a 5 to 6 percent economic growth. In 1991, Iran's total imports bill reached $28 billion, resulting in an economic growth rate of about 8 percent. These figures must be viewed in relation to a population of 60 million that is growing at 3.2 percent a year, and an economy that experienced a 50 percent decline in per capita income (in real terms) between 1979 and 1989.[30]

Recognizing the significance of oil for Iran's economy and national security, the Shah adopted what I wish to call a linkage policy, whereby his government linked oil, regional politics, and economic growth within a single policy framework. Oil was used to finance both economic growth and military buildup, which were in turn used to sustain sizable oil exports and near-dominant leadership within OPEC and in regional security affairs. Iran's friendship with the United States, and accommodation of oil companies, and the Shah's carrot-and-stick policy toward the Arab states contributed to the success of this linkage policy approach.

The Islamic Republic changed this policy by de-linking Iran's oil, economic growth, and security interests and replaced it with a combative approach based on the primacy of ideology and revolutionary zeal. Thus oil revenue and economic growth were de-emphasized as security tools, and military strength was considered insignificant in the presence of a potent Islamic ideology. As Ayatollah Khomeini used to say, the Islamic revolutionaries would fight imperialist powers with their "fist." Instead, attention was focused on exporting the revolution to neighboring states, challenging the superpowers within a "Neither East, Nor West" foreign policy, contesting OPEC's production and pricing policies, exercising more control on downstream operations, and expanding spot oil markets. By terminating production and marketing agreements with a number of Western oil companies, the new regime caused a further disintegration of the international oil regime in the beginning of the 1980s.

The de-linking approach, along with the war with Iraq and the American hostage episode, among other factors, soon brought the Islamic Republic in direct conflict with all of the major players in the oil and regional security markets. With a further decline in the economy, destruction caused by the war, and the realignment of forces at the regional and international levels, including the formation of GCC and the emergence of Gorbachev, the Islamic Republic lost its ability to sustain this approach. As a response to these changes, it decided to gradually move away from its initial ideologically based oil and security policy toward a more pragmatic and depoliticized one. This trend was accentuated in the period following the cease-fire with Iraq in August of 1988 and Ayatollah Khomeini's death in June of 1989 when postwar reconstruction became a priority. However, a total shift in policy occurred only after the 1991 Persian Gulf War was concluded. That event radically changed the Islamic Republic's perception of its security, making it keener on developing a deterrent military force. Thus, as was the case under the Shah, oil revenues are being used to spur economic growth and military strength, which will in turn be used to ensure a leading role for the Islamic Republic within OPEC and in regional security matters.

Accepting the linkage among oil, economic growth, and regional security interests, the government manifested a more accommodative attitude toward the major players in oil and regional security markets and adopted a reconstruction plan that was heavily dependent on oil revenue. The first five-year plan (1989–93), which hoped to achieve an annual 8 percent growth, was based on a foreign exchange budget of some $147 billion for the entire plan period, or around $28.1 billion per year. Some $27 billion was to be borrowed from long-term capital markets, another $17 billion was to be earned from non-oil exports, and the remaining $103 billion from oil (to be complemented by short-term credits). Economic reconstruction and military buildup required technology and foreign exchange that could be earned largely by oil exports. Thus oil revenue predictability and price stability became important for the Islamic Republic, and these factors could only be brought about under a condition of sustained producer-consumer cooperation. Regional political stability and good neighborly relations thus became a prerequisite.[31]

Already in 1988 an international conference on the Persian Gulf had been organized to underline Iran's quest for friendship with its Arab neighbors on the other side of the Gulf. Two subsequent conferences on the Persian Gulf also focused on themes of stability, unity, and solidarity in the region.[32] It was, however, the May 1991 conference on "Oil and Gas in the 1990s: Prospect for Cooperation" in Isfahan that was used as a platform to promulgate the new oil policy. The conference followed the end of the Persian Gulf crisis during which Iran had cooperated with the anti-Iraqi coalition in an attempt to rebuild its fractured image in the West as a terrorist and unlawful state. Among the participants of that conference were 7 oil ministers including the Saudi oil minister, 60 executives of major Western oil companies, representatives of Western media giants, and a few academics. Iranian participants included the ministers of foreign affairs, oil, and economy and finance, directors of the Central Bank and Plan and Budget Organization, and a special message from the president.[33]

The subsequent disintegration of the Soviet Union and intensification of Islamic movements in Algeria, the Sudan, the Central Asian republics, Egypt, and Turkey has led the Islamic Republic to rethink its foreign policy of moving away from ideology. These developments, along with uncompromising Saudi persistence to maintain a high level of production, made it difficult for Tehran to continue its accommodative policy or to conform to the rules that are being set by OPEC or the international oil market. However, the effect of such re-ideologization on Iran's oil policy has thus far been minimal. It continues to cooperate with the Saudis within OPEC and is agreeable to prices and quotas set by the organization. Iran is also honoring its commitments to its oil partners, be they purchasers of its crude oil or firms involved in upstream and downstream contractual projects.

The Islamic Republic's new oil policy is based on a number of considerations. Price stability and revenue predictability are said to constitute the government's major areas of concern. For these to be achieved, it is argued that OPEC must cooperate with market forces in determining a "fair price" for oil, the so-called invisible handshake concept. Iran needs to cooperate with Saudi Arabia and oil companies ("consumers") if this is to be achieved. Another important policy concept is "reciprocal supply security." It means security of supply for consumers and security of demand for producers. The supply or "energy security," which was ingrained in OPEC's constitution from day one, was hardly accepted by the Islamic Republic prior to 1990. Specifically, it requires that OPEC guarantees adequate flow of oil at fair prices to its consumers, particularly at times of crisis. Storing oil close to consumer markets, in the West in particular, is one major way of achieving this objective. Investment in upstream projects is another measure of providing for supply security. This, however, requires foreign investment in OPEC member countries by big oil companies.

Demand security, on the other hand, addresses the concerns of oil producers. Specifically, it should lead to easy access by oil producers to stable markets at fair prices. Consumer governments should make no attempt to limit this demand unless such a limit has been well planned in accordance with the revenue needs and production levels of oil producers. A major concern of OPEC members at present is the West's attempt to impose an additional gasoline tax. In 1990, for example, average excise taxes levied on a barrel of oil in Western Europe was $49 and in Japan, $39. Net receipts from taxation of oil products in the West is higher than the export earnings of the oil-exporting countries. There are such demand-limiting measures as export duties, energy conservation policy, investment in alternative fuels, environmental concerns with oil production and use, and consumer countries' refusal to provide information on the size and direction of their demand. This data transparency problem also exists on the suppliers' side but with lesser consequences for consumers. Another area of concern with demand security is the elimination of "spontaneous chaos" that is usually created by competition between short-term and long-term interests of OPEC producers.

Finally, recognition of the growing interdependency between the upstream (producers) and downstream (buyers) segments of the oil market is critical for maintaining demand security. This latter concern is being increasingly addressed in the debate for re-integration of international oil markets. Another major component of the new oil policy is a new production policy. The government intends to increase production to 4.5 million barrels a day by 1993, from the present (late 1992) level of about 4.2 million barrels a day. To achieve this target, Iran has given contracts in numerous reconstruction, exploration, and expansion projects to Western oil companies, including American firms. To complete the job, some $5 billion in investment is needed, a level of expenditure that Iran will not find easy to afford particularly since another $3.5 billion is also needed for development of Iran's huge gas resources. Attempts to sell oil in forward markets have been only partially successful. Contracts with Phibro Energy A.G., a Salomon Brothers, Inc., oil-trading unit, Mark Rich, and Total CFP are neither significant nor inexpensive. Attempts to borrow or to induce foreign investment—despite a new law that intends to facilitate foreign investment in mines—have not succeeded significantly.

The new oil policy is also based on a new marketing strategy. In particular, the government is now eager to enter into markets that are stable rather than selling oil in spot markets or markets with less predictability of demand. It also prefers to sell oil for hard currency whenever possible, as opposed to barter, and where oil money can be used to purchase modern technology and know-how. As a consequence, Western markets are given priority and, as a policy, large quantities of oil are made available in storage close to these markets in Rotterdam and a port in France. Indeed, according to Gholamreza Aghazadeh, Iran's oil minister, the Islamic Republic now has two channels for exporting its oil: Kharg and Rotterdam. To facilitate better implementation of this policy, the government sells oil at lower prices to companies that provide storage or other similar facilities. Another aspect of the policy includes selling more crude to European refineries (some 1.5 million barrels per day in 1992). The new marketing also involves extensive use of oil traders as sales agents, as opposed to the previous policy of direct sale.

Iran has also attempted to open up to the American market. By 1992, Exxon Corporation had "become the largest U.S. buyer of Iranian crude, purchasing about 250,000 barrels a day, which would be worth $1.8 billion on an annual basis."[34] The Houston-based Coastal Corporation was the second largest with half Exxon's level of purchases.

Mobil Corporation, Texaco Inc., Chevron Corporation, and an overseas joint venture of Texaco and Chevron, Caltex Ltd., were buying an average of 50,000 barrels a day. Phibro Energy A.G. was also purchasing an unknown quantity. Most these firms buy Iranian crude on a "terms contract" ranging from six months to a year, take delivery directly from Iran's Kharg Islands and use their crude in retail and refining operations in Europe and Asia. Most such contracts were issued in 1991 after the Persian Gulf War but a few were also signed prior to that event. Coastal and Chevron purchased quantities of Iranian crude much earlier but only under the U.S. government's condition that the proceeds be deposited in an escrow account in the Hague. While most Western countries have increased their purchase of Iranian oil, Japan has reduced its purchases, as have Pakistan, Indonesia, and South Korea.

Gulf oil will remain strategic in the future and the industrialized countries are expected to take whatever measures are necessary to control its flow and price. Therefore, the politics of oil policy will continue to be central in the future of the Persian Gulf. As major producers, Iran and Saudi Arabia are bound to remain vulnerable to global oil politics, and the interstate aspect of this politics will play itself out within OPEC. As things stand now, prospects for an Iranian-Saudi conflict are very real in the near future. First, even Iran's new oil policy, which is based on accommodating Saudis and Americans in some major ways, has become a source of concern to them insofar as this policy links oil revenue with Iran's alleged military buildup. This concern could potentially become conflictual given that the Israelis also share the same anxiety with the Saudis and Americans. Second, Saudis have consistently shown reluctance to lower their production to pre–Gulf War levels. As long as Iraq and Kuwait are not exporting any significant amount of oil and the price remains stable at around $18 per barrel, Iran can afford to tolerate the Saudi resistance. Tensions will rise when these countries enter the oil market again and oil prices decline significantly.

5. ISLAMIC MOVEMENTS

Radical political Islam may be viewed as a crystallization of Muslim disenchantment with the increasing corruption of both capitalism and socialism. An absolute majority of Muslims around the world, including those in the oil-rich Middle East, live under conditions of economic misery and political oppression. The movement is, however, more than just a reaction to these Western political, economic, and ideological systems. Islam also presents an alternative, in certain ways an authentic one, as it is endogenously rooted in national cultures and seeks to reintegrate marginalized groups into the mainstream of a homegrown development process.[35] Revolutions in communication technologies and increasing public awareness of their plights were some of the factors that enabled radical Islamic movements to gain popularity in a number of Middle Eastern countries. Moreover, the success of the Islamic revolution in Iran became a source of inspiration, and at times support, for these movements.[36]

Whether or not Iran has any significant role in current Islamic movements, and regardless of the nature of its influence on them (moderating or radicalizing), it is greatly impacted by them because of the sheer fact that it also espouses a similar ideology and supports their anti–status quo posture in a number of Middle Eastern polities. But with the worsening of domestic law and order that stems from the activities of these movements—as in Algeria and Egypt—Iran's influence over them reduces significantly. In some instances, as in the preceding examples, the popularity of the Islamist forces might be the direct result of the acutely inept economic policies of the existing governments. At times, however, such impacts are the direct result of Iran's own behavior and policy, as in the case of the Hajj in Saudi Arabia, the Lebanese Hezbollah, and the Rushdie affair. In the case of Hezbollah in Lebanon, Iran might have only become an institutional source of support for a sector of the population that has been historically excluded from the political process. Here, however, Iran's ultimate influence has been to moderate the force. In yet another example, the Rushdie affair, Iran might have only expressed forcefully the anger of the Muslim world for a blatant case of disrespectful writing. The notable fact that such an expression of anger came in the form of a religious decree, not a political statement, is again ignored. As far as an impact on foreign policy is concerned, the Islamic movements provide Iran with significant opportunity to boost its domestic image and international bargaining power. But at the same time they also became a source of tremendous constraints on Iranian relations with the West and neighboring states. A better understanding of this contradictory influence of Islamic movements on Iran is at the heart of developing a more realistic perspective on the future course of events in the Persian Gulf.

On the enabling influence of the Islamic movements on Iranian foreign policy one may distinguish three interrelated factors: (1) Islamic movements as power boosters and bargaining tools; (2) Islamic movements as identifying and legitimizing tools; and (3) Islamic movements as sources of strategic purpose and direction. The power-boosting function of the Islamic movements stems from the fact that they are popular and, as such, stand against mostly unpopular regimes in the Islamic world. They could, therefore, be easily utilized as a source of pressure on domestic politics. The Islamic nature of the state in Iran affords it a better position to manipulate the movements for its regional diplomatic aims. As such these movements have the potential to increase Iran's bargaining power vis-à-vis the unpopular states or their foreign protectors.

The magnitude of the gain for Iran, however, will depend on how intelligently this enabling function of the Islamic movements is utilized. Generally speaking, whenever Iran's support of these movements paralleled the West's interests, it contributed more productively to Iranian foreign policy, as in the cases of Afghanistan and Iraq. The gain also depends on the nature and extent of the movements themselves. In particular, the more popular and extensive the movements are, the higher their power-boosting utility for Iran. In sharp contrast, movements identified with terrorist actions have proven the most damaging to Iran's image and prestige. The power-boosting function of the Islamic movements for Iran takes an even more significant role in the Persian Gulf area, where most states are small and generally weak. Moreover, the geographic spread of these movements affords Iran significant maneuverability in directing its foreign policy.

The identifying and legitimizing functions of the Islamic movements for Iran emanate from their ideological specificity. In particular, the collapse of the cold war bipolar ideological system has given the Islamic movements an opportunity to define themselves as a new non-Western pole. The new pole is further strengthened by the endogenousness and authenticity of the movements. As long as Iran and the Islamic movements espouse the same ideals and radical ideology, this congruity of purpose will enhance the visibility of Iran and its strength in international politics. This ideological similarity and its attendant solidarity also enable Iran to claim worldwide leadership of these movements in much the same way that the former Soviet Union claimed international leadership of Communist movements. In addition, the popular nature and geographic spread of these movements have legitimized Iran's own struggle to create an Islamic model state, which, in turn, is hoped to become a source of aspiration and emulation by all Muslims. This is certainly the case in the Middle East, and the Persian Gulf in particular, where Muslims dominate and are politically active. The result for Iran is increased political strength and diplomatic maneuverability in the region.

The Islamic movements are also a source of strategic purpose and direction for the Islamic Republic. For one, these movements are indicative of a revitalized and dynamic ideology. They also function as a reminder whenever there is a tendency in the leadership to drift from its ideological commitments. The recent re-ideologization of Iran's foreign policy after a period of pragmatism and moderation is a case in point. This change, as was previously noted, was the result of political developments in Central Asia, Algeria, Egypt, and Afghanistan, indicating a growing strength in Islamic movements.

Moreover, the ideological uniqueness of the Islamic camp creates a given space for Iran in international relations and breeds coherence. This in turn gives Iran a certain identity and creates a distinct framework for its behavior and policies. Iran's attempts to expand its relations with the Islamic nations is a reflection of this sense of Islamic direction. In reality, however, such attempts have not been always successful because this sense of Islamic purpose and direction often comes into contradiction with the interests of the states in the Muslim world where most regimes are antithetical to radical Islamic movements. Moreover, the perceived Islamic pole and Iran's self-appointed leadership of it has led to a new Western paradigm of an Islamic and Iranian threat very much in the same way that Communism and the Soviet Union were seen as dangerous to Western interests.

The disabling impact of Islamic movements for Iran emanate from three sources: (1) tensions in relations with the West, (2) tensions in relations with neighboring states, and (3) tensions with domestic or expatriate secular intellectuals and scientists. The perceived "Islamic threat" that causes tension between Iran and the West is rooted in a set of objective and subjective factors that include both real and imaginary sources. The fictitious side of this perceived threat is largely a product of certain media leaders and Orientalists who explain the present-day tension between the Western and Muslim worlds as partly reflecting an alleged classical Islamic view that regards the two as inherently inimical. One such example comes to us from the historian Bernard Lewis: "In the classical Islamic view, to which many Muslims are beginning to return, the world and all mankind are divided into two: the House of Islam, where the Muslim law and faith prevail, and the rest, known as the House of Unbelief or the House of War, which it is the duty of Muslims ultimately to bring to Islam."[37] That this recklessly abstract characterization of Islam is held nowhere in the Muslim world today by any serious individual, group, or institution is irrelevant to these ideological pundits. Even the late Ayatollah Khomeini, a much-maligned leader of modern Islamic movements, is not known to have espoused such an extreme and obsolete view.

However, and aside from this subjective side, there exists an objective basis for the West's concern with the Islamic threat. This relates to the West's access to oil and its concern for the survival of the conservative regimes in the region. As for the oil factor, some 75 to 77 percent of the world oil is located in the Muslim world, where the majority has become poorer and more helpless over the last several decades and lives in a state of spiritual turmoil. Some 66 percent of this oil comes from the Persian Gulf region, where corrupt and antidemocratic regimes rule by decree and face problems ranging from economic malaise to political instability. The region also holds more than two-thirds of the world's oil reserves and contains a good part of the world's natural gas. The Gulf reserves will also last the longest among the known world reserves and cost the least to produce. Iran is the second-largest oil producer in the region and its natural gas reserves are second only to Russia. The West depends on this oil for a significant portion of its increasing energy needs, making its economy potentially vulnerable to disruptions in the supply from the region. Therefore, an anti-Western Islamic control over oil could become dangerous for the West.

Yet the West's dependency on the flow of oil from Muslim countries must be viewed in relation to an equally critical dependency of the Muslim oil producers on oil revenues and on Western markets. Almost all Muslim states face tremendous economic hardship and depend on oil revenue for 90 to 99 percent of their foreign exchange earnings. Oil revenue is needed to pay for a ballooning imports bill for goods, industrial inputs and military purchases and to recompense debt services and other foreign obligations. From rich Saudi Arabia and other Gulf Arab states to poorer Egypt and Algeria, from war-devastated Iran and Iraq to the more radical Libya, this dependency on oil revenue is such that it makes it impossible for any of these states, even when they fall in the hands of Islamic radicals as in Iran, to use oil as a weapon against the West. This is particularly so because for most, if not all of them, Western oil markets are the only major alternative or nearly so. Iran is no exception.

As long as the Islamic movements and the Islamic Republic are connected through their ideological stand—whose two chief traits are anti-Westernism and anti–status quo orientation, especially in the Persian Gulf but also in the Middle East—the West will have difficulty in its relations with Iran. This creates a problem for Iran's foreign policy because the subjective side of the West's fear of Islam and Iran is hardly resolvable in the immediate future. The objective side must be, however, carefully assessed and addressed by the Iranian leadership. It is only through changing the nature of this objective concern that Iran would be able to mitigate its difficulties with the West in the short run. This implies a more realistic policy within OPEC and in relations with oil-producing nations of the Persian Gulf.

This latter point is particularly important because another objective source of the West's concern in relation to Iran is the political stability of its neighboring states. What makes this concern of the West very prominent is the fact that these small states are also quite vulnerable to Islamic movements. Moreover, the Gulf Arab states have in the past had difficulty with the Islamic Republic when it threatened to export its revolution. The sources of Iranian-Arab tensions also played a major role in raising their fear of Iran. Under these conditions, Iran could not formulate a long-term, sustainable foreign policy for the region. Natural outcomes of this inconsistency in policy emerged in the form of volatility, unpredictability, and political instability in the region. The perceived Iranian threat—which was related to the peninsular states' vision of Khomeini's Iran—also invited foreign intervention in the region during the last phase of the Iran-Iraq War. A resurgence of such a threat might also result in a development in the future, something which is hardly in the national interests of Iran.

Finally, another major way that the Islamic movements influence Iranian politics is through their impact on secular intellectuals and scientists. One way this impact occurs is through a permanent re-ideologization of the state by the radical Islamic movements. The secular forces do not necessarily share the same ideals as the Islamic forces. Besides, they have often been restricted by the Islamic Republic on the basis of Islamic teaching, laws, and values. Such obstructions have been particularly felt at sociocultural levels. As a consequence, some of these forces have withdrawn from cooperating with the regime and others have worked only halfheartedly. Although the impact is more felt at the domestic level, its foreign policy implications cannot be underestimated. Of particular interest here is the opportunity cost to the nation of underutilized scientists and intellectuals at a time that the nation is struggling to rebuild its economy and to make advances in technological innovation. The total impact of the resulting social tensions and economic costs has been increased difficulties in advancing Iran's national power, with far-reaching implications for its regional standing.

6. COLLECTIVE SECURITY

In the past, several models of so-called collective security systems, such as the Baghdad Pact and CENTO, have been tried; they have all failed in managing regional conflict because they were organized by one group of nations against another group. A more stable and effective regional security arrangement should include all parties involved and must be sensitive to their national interests; only then can one hope for a better future in the Persian Gulf.[38] Is it possible to create such a system in the foreseeable future? The answer is a categoric no given the current state of regional affairs and the kind of obstacles that militate against regional cooperation, particularly between Iran and its Arab neighbors. The dilemma facing both Iran and the Arabs is that "there will be no [workable] regional security system in the Gulf without Iran and Iran cannot join it without playing the game."[39] In the remainder of this section a brief discussion will be provided of the recent failed attempts and their underlying causes, focusing on Iran's relations with the Gulf Cooperation Council (GCC) and the future of Iraq.

The GCC was established in 1981 as a "third pillar" to contain the Iranian power, the Iraqi power, and radical political Islam. For most of the 1980s, the Islamic Republic applied a stick policy, with some carrot, to the GCC states. Relations with the Saudis became particularly antagonistic. Five factors underlaid the tension: (1) differences over Islam, (2) struggle for OPEC leadership, (3) quest for supremacy and leadership in the Persian Gulf, (4) the U.S.-Saudi alliance, and (5) the Iran-Iraq War. The inevitable symbiosis that gradually developed between the GCC and Iraq ran into difficulty when Iran took the upper hand in the Iran-Iraq War during 1985–87. The GCC then developed a symbiosis with the United States, causing the latter's direct intervention in the war on the side of Iraq. Consequently, Iran's relations with the GCC deteriorated to an all time low and the confrontation with the Saudis reached a dangerous point in 1987 when some four hundred Iranian pilgrims were shot to death on Mecca's street during a political demonstration. In August 1988, after the cease-fire with Iraq, Iran launched a "charm offensive" to improve relations with the Gulf Arab states.

By the time of the Kuwaiti crisis, the confidence-building measures had resulted in a steady upturn in the relations between the two. Some GCC leaders even expressed hopes that Iran and Iraq would soon earn observer status within the GCC. In its turn, the Islamic Republic reaffirmed its respect for the sovereignty of Iran's neighbors in a National

Security Council resolution that was issued only a few days before Iraq invaded Kuwait. Such a selective disengagement from Khomeini's hard-line position sprang from the recognition that a more stable regional environment was needed if Iran wanted to resolve its problems with Iraq and to accomplish its domestic economic goals. Iran's steadfast opposition to the Iraqi annexation of Kuwait further helped improve Iran-GCC relations. Significantly, diplomatic ties between Tehran and Riyadh were re-established in March 1991.

In the aftermath of the Kuwaiti crisis, negotiating a new regional order with the GCC states became Iran's postwar priority.[40] First, however, Iran needed to gain the organization's cooperation. To this end, Iran emphasized GCC's own concepts of "self-reliance" and "Gulfanization." This discursive strategy, Iran hoped, would reduce the GCC's foreign dependency and its reliance on the United States in particular and would solidify Iran's image as the guardian of autonomy and conscience of the GCC. Another tactic entailed the creation of an interlocking relationship between the GCC and the Economic Cooperation Organization (ECO). At the time, Iran's main concern remained with establishing a regional "balance of power" among various parties in the Persian Gulf.

However, Iran's balancing strategy soon clashed with the plans of other players. The Syrian-Egyptian-sponsored "GCC plus two formula" (Damascus Declaration) in March 1991 was aimed at creating an "Arab peacekeeping force" with the participation of the GCC, Syria, and Egypt.[41] The GCC itself emphasized the "Arab" identity of any security arrangement but insisted on the participation of Iran and Turkey in a broader nonmilitary union. Against this background, Iran abandoned its balancing idea in favor of a collective security order. Accordingly, in response to the "GCC plus two formula," Iran called for the inclusion of both Iraq and Iran in the GCC. Iran did, however, realize that as long as Saddam Hussein remained in power, Iraq's inclusion would remain a moot issue. In pursuit of shared security arrangements with the GCC, Iran even made an explicit pitch for formal inclusion within the organization.

The sudden prospects of cooperation between Iran and the GCC states dismayed the United States, whose long stay in the region could only be legitimized by its military protection of the Gulf Arab states. In the absence of a nonthreatening Iraq, Iran was to be portrayed as the regional threat to the sheikhdoms. However, before the Iran-GCC dialogue could develop into any specific plan, the United States offered the GCC its own terms for regional security. Specifically, former president

George Bush indicated that the United States wished: "to create shared security arrangements in the region." This would entail, he said, "American participation in joint exercises involving both air and ground forces." This design was realized in the form of bilateral security arrangements with a number of Persian Gulf sheikhdoms.

Deprived of its plan, Iran focused on confidence-building measures via enhanced communication and increased bilateral economic ties with various GCC states. Meanwhile, Iran intensified its policy of creating free economic zones in its Persian Gulf islands of Qeshm and Kish, hoping that the policy would further increase Iran-GCC economic relations. Nevertheless, GCC's military dependency on the United States— its de-autonomization—ran contrary to Iran's growing desire for cooperation with a self-reliant GCC. Some factions of the Iranian leadership also remained suspicious of ultimate American objectives in the Persian Gulf.[42] To de-align the United States and the Gulf states, Iran emphasized the principle of self-reliance as enshrined in GCC's charter. Most observers saw the Islamic Republic's de-alignment strategy following naturally from the "anti-Western" hegemonic predilection of its Islamic ideology. Yet the strategy largely reflected Iran's nationalistic and historical view of its leadership position in the Gulf.[43]

Determined as they were in their opposition to the Western powers' presence in the Gulf, foreign policymakers also realized the futility of a de-alignment strategy in the light of American influence in the region. This realization together with the de facto partnership of the United States and Iran against Iraq, and the advantage Iran saw in the stability-generating presence of American forces in the area—thanks to the Gulf emirs' "rent a superpower" approach—gave the accommodationists within Iran the upper hand in a debate that was ignited between them and the hard-liners. The accommodationists had argued that Iran should cooperate with the United States on Gulf security matters and join the GCC as this policy would reduce the risk of a new round of hostilities between them, institutionalize the competition between Iran and Saudi Arabia, and limit American influence in Persian Gulf affairs.

A complex web of historical, geopolitical, ideological, and cultural factors worked against the development of security cooperation between Iran and the GCC states. Despite a constructive engagement that brought Iran and the GCC closer during the Kuwaiti crisis, it did not go far enough to eliminate the GCC's suspicion of Iran.[44] The territorial dispute that recently surfaced concerning the islands of Abu Musa and the Tunbs is an example of factors that feed into such a suspicious attitude.[45]

Moreover, the Arab states—particularly members of the U.S.-led anti-Iraq coalition—have yet to be fully convinced of the durability of Iran's emerging pragmatic foreign policy. They also feared that Iran's membership in a Persian Gulf security system would inevitably lead to its dominance of the collective in the long run. As an Arab diplomat contended, the security arrangement "comes down to whether we want a Middle East order, or a new Arab order [without Iran] with the West as a shield."[46] The GCC-plus-two formula reflected this latter Arab option.

America's new powerful position in the Gulf, along with the diminished threat related to Iraq, reduced the GCC's incentive to lean on Iran for protection. For the maximalist notion of collective security (*amniyat-e dast-e jam'e*) to become meaningful, Iraq had to be a participant. But this was not possible as long as Saddam Hussein was in power. Significant divisions of opinion also existed between Iran and the GCC states about the role of the "out of area" states in the security affairs of the region. The military weakness of the GCC states made them too dependent on Western security guarantees to afford a regional solution to security issues. The pre-existing mutual suspicion based on ethnic, religious, political, and historical factors between Iran and the GCC states presented additional difficulties. The American proclivity against collective security and its preference for creating a patchwork of overlapping bilateral alliances proved a major stumbling block. Finally, lack of enthusiasm on the part of Iran for membership in a collective in which its primacy could be jeopardized by a potential American interference also worked against development of security cooperation between Iran and the GCC.

This last point deserves further elaboration as it reflects Iran's bifurcated, and often contradictory, approach to Persian Gulf security. While collective security demands that Iran participate in the multilateral system as an equal to others, Iran has continued to underscore its power and primacy among the Gulf states, a notion that lurks behind the balancing model. Thus, according to President Ali Hashemi Rafsanjani, if there is one country that can provide peace and stability, and can serve as a guardian (*negahban*) in the Persian Gulf, it is Iran. "Iran has had the role of guardian (*negahban*) in the Persian Gulf . . . there is only one power that can provide the peace and stability of the Persian Gulf and that is Iran's power."[47] Since such statements often coincided with a renewed emphasis on collective security, Iran's commitment to the latter approach was often questioned; Iran was also at times accused of expressing its willingness to participate in collective security only in an attempt to hide its predilection to form a Pax Iranica, or to prevent smaller states from employing the protective service of outside powers against Iran's hegemonic tendency. The United States has also utilized the seeming contradiction to forge alliance with Arab states as a countervailing force in the Persian Gulf. Rather than helping Iran, emphasis on primacy became ammunition for the U.S.-Arab alliance as a countervailing force in the Persian Gulf.

It should be noted, however, that Iran's emphasis on its primacy is in part a reaction to similar claims by its main regional rivals, namely Saudi Arabia and Iraq. Although Iran may be in a better position to back up such claims due to its sizable population, large economy, and relatively strong army, the other two countries also possess considerable potential: Saudis on the economic side and Iraqis in military technology. In the 1970s, a three-power entente was established to preserve regional stability. In the 1990s, a similar arrangement may again become necessary, for a number of developments point toward the need for this arrangement: the nationalist and Islamic reaction to the destruction of Iraq by the West is gaining momentum in the region, Gulf monarchies remain vulnerable to demand for democracy and reform, and most people, including antimilitaristic forces, view the present military spending by the Saudis and the Kuwaitis as unacceptable and a sellout. Under these circumstances, the current significance of Saudi Arabia could be short-lived, while Iraq's diminished military power may grow again.

The current de facto two-power détente between Iran and Saudi Arabia could, therefore, become obsolete in the near future. Iran, thus, needs to plan for a reinvigorated Iraq, whose strategic interests are dangerously at odds with those of Iran. In part, it is this view of Iraq's future and the need to contain the militaristic state that drives Iran's current military buildup. If Saddam Hussein were to survive the present domestic and international pressures, Iran-Iraq relations will become even more hostile in the future. However, Saddam's departure will not reduce such potential tensions unless the Baath Party also loosens its grip over Iraq. Moreover, if Saddam is successfully replaced by a pro-Western leader, there is a good possibility that Iraq will rise to prominence even faster than predicted. Ironically, Iran cannot afford a weakened central government in Iraq for it would result in its disintegration as a country. A dangerous example may then be set for a multiethnic Iran, and the country's own Kurdish population may pose threats to its internal stability.

Although Iranian interests dictate that Iraq remain intact, the leadership in Tehran is well aware that a stable and nonthreatening Iraq must empower its large Shia population and its Kurdish minority. President Rafsanjani's March 8, 1991, speech urging Saddam to "step down and give in to the will of the people of Iraq"[48] reflected this Iranian perspective. Iran, which has publicly opposed the presence of American troops in the region, has signaled its desire to have American troops help the grassroots opposition to Saddam's rule. In a candid admission of Iran's views, Mohammad Jafar Mahallati, a former Iranian ambassador to the United Nations, urged the United States to discard its "phobia" about Shia Islam and help them earn their due weight in Iraqi political discourse.[49] This position was stated more forcefully by the Iranian foreign minister, Ali Akbar Velayati, when he urged the United States to use its forces to prevent the Iraqi air force from launching attacks against Kurdish and Shia cities inside the country.[50]

7. CONCLUSIONS AND POLICY IMPLICATIONS

This chapter has discussed a number of strategic factors that are bound to influence Iran's future Persian Gulf policy. The United States will remain the undisputed foreign power in the Persian Gulf in the near future. In the longer term, however, American dominance of the region faces challenges from the rising powers in Europe and the Pacific Rim. Great power alliances and/or rivalries will in the future be less determined by ideological considerations and more by economic strength as measured by competitiveness in trade and technological developments. As the strongest state and the largest market in the region, Iran can uniquely provide any major power with facilities that could significantly enhance its regional role. The trends concerning superpower rivalry and intervention indicate that Iran needs to pursue a two-tier policy with long-term as well as short-term foci. In the immediate future, Iran seems to have little realistic alternative but to work out its difficulties with the United States by focusing on the issues that divide them. In the longer term, however, Iran must have its eyes on the emerging economic and technological forerunners in the world.

The state of Iran-Arab relations remains tenuous and dangerously volatile. This implies that no immediate remedies may be sought and that a candid acknowledgment of such tensions is an essential first step toward an eventual resolution. This could lead to mutual understanding and an enhancing of the solidarity-generating forces in the interim. Over time, an institutionalized process of conflict resolution could be established to address more structural problems. The arms race is another major tension-generating factor. Unless a comprehensive, all-inclusive defense arrangement can be worked out in the Persian Gulf, Iran is expected to pursue a policy of defense buildup capable of withstanding any potential foreign threat. Perhaps the time has come for the Persian Gulf states to rely on existing international norms and regimes to guide and assist their mutual relationships. They should also move away from antagonistic posturing and reliance on nonregional actors. In the absence of these developments, the arms race will only intensify, and with oil money to finance it, arms suppliers will be more than willing to fuel it, especially since there aren't too many willing and financially capable arms buyers left in the post–cold war world.

Gulf oil will retain its strategic significance in the future and the industrialized countries are expected to take whatever measures that are necessary to control its flow. Therefore, the political economy of oil will continue to be central in the future of the Persian Gulf. As major producers, Iran and Saudi Arabia are bound to remain vulnerable in global oil politics. Their own clashing strategic perspectives will also have to play themselves out within OPEC. As things stand now, prospects for an Iranian-Saudi conflict are very real in the near future. As long as Iraq and Kuwait are not exporting any significant amounts of oil and the price remains stable at around $20 per barrel, Iran can afford to tolerate the Saudi refusal to lower their production rates. The tension will rise when these countries enter the oil market again. A triangle of contention over oil policy could develop among Iran, Iraq, and Saudi Arabia. Under this circumstance, the UN is likely to play an important role, especially if the issues of war-related Iraqi compensation to Kuwait and other actors were to remain unresolved, as it controls Iraq's oil exports.

With respect to Islamic movements, Iran's foreign policy faces two challenges: to control the damaging impact of disabling factors while improving the influences of enabling forces. A major difficulty relates to dealing with the subjective side of the West's perception of the Islamic threat. The most effective way to minimize this perception is to properly manage the objective sources of such threat. Iran must be prepared to show flexibility and the willingness to negotiate in good faith while focusing on its national interests. Another aspect of such management is for Iran to let its rivals understand that the ideological similarity between Iran and the Islamic movements does not necessarily imply any political-military or financial connections. Finally, Iran must understand and be sensitive to the interests of its rivals in the region and deal with them accordingly. Otherwise, the complex political environment in the Persian Gulf could convert opportunities into constraints for Iran.

Negotiating a collective security system for the Persian Gulf has become an almost impossible thing to do. If the current trends of distrust and animosity among states continue, bilateral defense relations and a balance-of-power model will prevail, leading to an intensified arms race. In the absence of a comprehensive collective security arrangement, the current de facto two-power détente between Iran and Saudi Arabia could also become obsolete in the near future. Iran needs to plan for a reinvigorated Iraq, whose strategic interests are dangerously at odds with those of Iran. If Saddam Hussein survives current domestic and international pressures, Iran-Iraq relations will become even more hostile in the future. However, Hussein's departure would not reduce this potential conflict unless the Baath Party also loosens its grip over Iraq. Moreover, if Hussein is successfully replaced by a pro-Western leader, there is a good possibility that Iraq will rise to prominence even faster than predicted and perhaps stronger than Iran can easily contain. Although Iran's interests dictate that Iraq remain intact, the Iranian leadership is well aware that a stable and non-threatening Iraq must empower its large Shia population and its Kurdish minority. However, one may argue that a similar development is also required in multiethnic Iran for otherwise it can be expected to face political instability, with far-reaching implications for its Persian Gulf policy.

There are also several other domestic concerns that may act as guidelines for and limitations on Iran's future Persian Gulf policy. One of the most distressing developments facing Iran is its excessive rate of population growth. At a rate estimated at 3.2 percent, Iran's population will double in less than 20 years, to 120 million by the year 2010. Already demographic constraints are creating severe problems for the government and the country as a whole. The domestic and imported food supply is barely meeting the minimum dietary needs of the Iranians and their three to four million refugee "guests." The population factor affects foreign policy by way of increasing the nation's urgency to expand its infrastructures, including ports in the Persian Gulf, and its need for rapid economic growth as well as for better defense mechanisms. Added security will mean an increased emphasis on defense industrialization. Part of the economic growth would require expansion of oil production and sales, which may create conflicts with OPEC or its main producers, Saudi Arabia and Iraq.

Population pressures can also add to an increased emphasis on the economic role of the Persian Gulf, not just as a trade route but also as a production hub as indicated by Iran's push to make the Persian Gulf Islands into new centers of regional trade and industry. To meet its food requirements, Iran is also becoming increasingly dependent on Gulf fishing and the agricultural products from the land bordering the Gulf. The environmental consequences of the Gulf War, especially the hazardous smokes emanating from the burning of Kuwaiti oil fields, significantly affected the Iranian food chain. Population pressures will continue to further degrade the Gulf's environment, a problem that could become a point of contention among nations that depend on the waterway. All these indicate an ever-increasing, inevitable reliance on an immutable environment in the Gulf. This realization, which is slowly but surely dawning on the Iranian leadership, highlights one of the very critical areas of interaction between Iran and other regional and foreign actors in the Persian Gulf. The irreversibility of such demographic developments in the short term and in the near future may incline Iran's Persian Gulf policy toward cooperation and accommodation. If this moderation is acknowledged and reciprocated, a potential window of opportunity will exist for the creation of a stable, peaceful environment.

Finally, the analyses in this chapter point to a conflictual and near-bleak future for the Persian Gulf. If this prediction is even partly true then serious thought needs to be given to forces, trends, and events that are shaping politics in the region. More research, better understanding, and realistic policies are needed in the areas of superpower interest in the region, interstate relations, arms race, oil politics, Islamic movements, collective security, and domestic dynamics, particularly population pressure, environmental degradation, increasing poverty, and the widening gaps among states in the region and social classes within these states. Careful planning needs to be done for better management of conflicts in all parties' interests.

NOTES TO CHAPTER 4
◆

In writing this chapter I have benefited from the assistance of Mehdi Khajehnouri and Freydoun Nikpour, both Ph.D. candidates at Rutgers University. I am also grateful to E. M. Ahrari for his comments on an early draft. However, I remain solely responsible for any errors or omissions.

1. On Iran's foreign policy before and after the revolution, see the following publications: Asadollah Alam, *The Shah and I: The Confidential Diary of Iran's Royal
   Court*, introduced and edited by Alinaghi Alikhani (New York: St. Martin's Press,
   1992); *Neither East nor West: Iran, the Soviet Union and the United States*, Nikki R.
   Keddie and Mark J. Gasiorowski, eds. (New Haven, Conn.: Yale University Press,
   1990); Amin Saikal, *The Rise and the Fall of the Shah* (Princeton, N.J.: Princeton
   University Press, 1980); *Iran and the Arab World*, Hooshang Amirahmadi and
   Nader Entessar, eds. (London: Macmillan Press, 1993); *Reconstruction and Regional
   Diplomacy in the Persia Gulf*, Hooshang Amirahmadi and Nader Entessar, eds.
   (London: Routledge, 1992); R. K. Ramazani, *Revolutionary Iran: Challenge and
   Response in the Middle East* (Baltimore. Md.: Johns Hopkins University Press,
   1988); Shireen Hunter, *Iran and the World: Continuity in a Revolutionary Decade*
   (Bloomington: Indiana University Press, 1990); and James A. Bill, *The Eagle and
   the Lion: The Tragedy of American-Iranian Relations* (New Haven, Conn.: Yale
   University Press, 1988).

2. Steve Coll, "U.S. Firms Buying Oil from Iran," *Washington Post*, 8 November 1992.
   See also *Iran's Business Monitor* (a monthly publication of the Center for Iranian
   Trade and Development, New York City), vol. 1, no. 1 (February 1992).

3. Hooshang Amirahmadi, "Global Restructuring, the Persian Gulf War and the U.S.
   Quest for World Leadership," in *The United States and the Middle East: A Search
   for New Perspectives*, Hooshang Amirahmadi, ed. (Albany, N.Y.: State University
   of New York Press, 1993), 363–429; Noam Chomsky, *The New World Order*
   (Westfield, N.J.: Open Magazine Pamphlet Series, 1991); Yoichi Funabashi, "Japan
   and the New World Order," *Foreign Affairs* (Summer 1992): 58–74; and Gerd
   Nonneman, ed., *The Middle East and Europe: An Integrated Communities Approach*
   (London: Federal Trust for Education and Research, 1992.)

4. Vladislav Zubok, "Tyranny of the Weak: Russia's New Foreign Policy," *World Policy
   Journal* (Summer 1992): 191–217; and Shahram Chubin, "A New Soviet Role in
   the Gulf," in *The Gulf, Energy, & Global Security*, Charles F. Doran and Stephen W.
   Buck, eds. (Boulder, Colo.: Lynne Rienner, 1991), 131–51.

5. "Kuwait Will Buy Tanks Made in U.S.," *New York Times*, 13 October 1992.

6. "U.S. Hopes to Broaden Ban on Arms Sales to Iran," *New York Times*, 18
   November 1992.

7. Amin Saikal, "The United States and Persian Gulf Security," *World Policy Journal*
   (Summer 1992): 515–31.

8. Lee H. Hamilton, "A Democratic Look at Foreign Policy," *Foreign Affairs* (Summer
   1992): 30–51.

9. Amirahmadi and Entessar, op. cit., 1992; Amirahmadi and Entessar, op. cit., 1993.

10. For details see Hooshang Amirahmadi, "Iran and the Persian Gulf Crisis," in Amirahmadi and Entessar, op. cit., 1993; Ramazani, op. cit., 1988; and Hunter, op. cit., 1990. See also Eric Hooglund, "Iranian Populism and Political Change in the Gulf," *Middle East Report,* no. 174 (January–February 1992): 19–21.

11. See Amirahmadi, "Iran and the Persian Gulf Crisis," op. cit.

12. Ibid.

13. Ibid.

14. Michael Collins Dunn, "Arms and the Gulf: The Gulf Regional Arms Race to the Turn of the Century," in Doran and Buck, eds., op. cit.

15. Hooshang Amirahmadi, *Revolution and Economic Transition: The Iranian Experience* (Albany, N.Y.: The State University of New York Press, 1990).

16. United Nations Security Council, *Further Report of the Secretary-General on the Implementation of Security Council Resolution 598 (1987),* S/23273 (9 December 1991).

17. Amirahmadi, *Revolution and Economic Transition,* op. cit., 148.

18. *SIPRI Yearbook 1992, World Armaments and Disarmament* (Stockholm: International Peace Research Institute, 1992), 273.

19. *Washington Post,* 8 November 1992.

20. *Washington Post,* 28 March 1992.

21. *New York Times,* 11 September 1992.

22. *Wall Street Journal,* March 1992.

23. *Washington Post,* 8 November 1992.

24. *New York Times,* 30 November 1992.

25. *SIPRI Yearbook 1992,* op. cit., 273.

26. "Jet Sale to Saudis Approved by Bush, Saving Jobs in U.S.," *New York Times,* 12 September 1992.

27. *SIPRI Yearbook 1992*, op. cit., 260.

28. *New York Times*, 13 October 1992.

29. *New York Times*, 16 September 1992.

30. On Iranian economic problems and policies see Hooshang Amirahmadi, "Toward a Multi-Gap Approach to Medium-Term Economic Growth in Iran," *Orient*, vol. 33, no. 1 (January 1992): 97–117; and Hooshang Amirahmadi, "Economic Destruction and Imbalances in Post-Revolutionary Iran," in Amirahmadi and Entessar, eds., op. cit., 1992. See also Jahangir Amuzegar, "The Iranian Economy Before and After the Revolution," *Middle East Journal*, vol. 46, no. 3 (Summer 1992): 413–25.

31. On Iran's five-year plan, see Hooshang Amirahmadi, "Iranian Economic Reconstruction Plan and Prospect for Its Success," in Amirahmadi and Entessar, op. cit., 1992. See also M. R. Ghasimi, "The Iranian Economy After the Revolution: An Economic Appraisal of the Five-Year Plan," *International Journal of Middle East Studies*, vol. 24, no. 4 (November 1992): 599–614.

32. For the proceedings of the conference see *The Iranian Journal of International Affairs*, vol. 2, no. 1 (Spring 1990).

33. For the proceedings of the conference see *The Iranian Journal of International Affairs*, vol. 3, no. 2 (Summer 1991).

34. *Washington Post*, 8 November 1992.

35. Robin Wright, "Islam, Democracy and the West," *Foreign Affairs* (Summer 1992): 131–45.

36. On Islamic movements see John L. Esposito, *The Iranian Revolution: Its Global Impact* (Miami, Fla.: Florida International University Press, 1990); and Dilip Hiro, *Islamic Fundamentalism* (London: Paladin Grafton Books, 1988).

37. Bernard Lewis, "The Roots of Muslim Rage," *Atlantic Monthly* (September 1990).

38. M. E. Ahrari, ed., *The Gulf and International Security: The 1980s and Beyond* (New York: St. Martin's Press, 1989); and Doran, F. Charles, "Gulf Security in Perspective," in Doran and Buck, eds., op. cit., 189–208.

39. Richard C. Hottelet, "Iran's Part in Gulf Puzzle," *Christian Science Monitor*, 21 March 1991, 18.

40. James A. Bill, "The Resurrection of Iran in the Persian Gulf," in *Middle East Insight* (1992): 28–35.

41. *Iran Times*, 15 March 1991.

42. *Iran Times*, 8 March 1991.

43. See Amirahmadi, "Iran and the Persian Gulf Crisis," op. cit.

44. R. K. Ramazani "Iran's Foreign Policy: Both North and South," *Middle East Journal*, vol. 46, no. 3 (Summer 1992): 393–412.

45. Anoushirvan Ehteshami, "Iran Rides Out the Storm in the Gulf," *Middle East International*, no. 395 (March 8, 1991): 23.

46. *Christian Science Monitor*, 1 March 1991.

47. See *Tehran Times*, 19 December 1990.

48. *Kayhan* (Tehran), 9 March 1991.

49. Mohammad Jafar Mahallati, "The U.S. Should Work Closely with the Iraqi Opposition," *Christian Science Monitor*, 27 March 1991, 19.

50. "The Today Show," NBC TV, 5 April 1991.

IRAN IN GLOBAL PERSPECTIVE

Siamack Shojai

INTRODUCTION

The 1990s began with dramatic—some unexpected—changes. The Persian Gulf War and the liberation of Kuwait, the dissolution of the former Soviet Union, the emergence of democracies in Eastern Europe, the creation of the Commonwealth of Independent States (CIS), the reunification of Germany, and emerging regional trade agreements, such as the North American Free Trade Agreement (NAFTA), all indicate that the world is in transition and is currently undergoing rapid changes that will bring about a new world order.

In Iran, Ayatollah Khamenei was selected as the supreme leader of the Islamic Republic following the death of Ayatollah Khomeini. Also, Hojjatoleslam Hashemi Rafsanjani was elected president and the position of prime minister was eliminated, which provided the president more power than before. President Rafsanjani began his administration based on a new premise. His cabinet included Western-educated technocrats who assumed responsibility with a mandate to rebuild the economy and demonstrate the constructive side of the Islamic regime. The end of the cold war, the defeat of Saddam Hussein, and the dynamic changes in Europe and in other parts of the world have all added new dimensions to the governance of Iran.

This chapter provides a brief analysis of Iran's policy choices and its place in the new world order. The next section explores the meaning and implications of the new world order for the international community; it envisions two possible scenarios that could describe the future of the world. The third section is a brief overview of economic, social, and political conditions in contemporary Iran. The fourth section deals with Iran's potential strategic choices.

THE NEW WORLD ORDER

A rapid proliferation of literature on the future of the world and its political and economic order has emerged since the end of the cold war. In his State of the Union address on January 29, 1991, former President Bush stated: "And tonight we lead the world in facing down a threat to decency and humanity. What is at stake is more than one small country; it is a big idea—a new world order where diverse nations are drawn together in common cause to achieve the universal aspirations of mankind: peace and security, freedom, and the rule of law."[1]

The former president's description of the new world order contains interesting ideas, which lend themselves to diverse interpretations. A liberal interpretation, founded on the diversity of the nations, suggests that the common aspirations of mankind—democracy, human rights, and freedom—must be achieved through global law and multinational institutions rather than through nation-states. This notion of the new world order can impose significant restraints on the sovereignty of nation-states. However, the U.S. leadership position can be secured only if the citizens of the world see a clear connection between the demise of Communist regimes and the proclaimed moral supremacy of capitalism.

A realist view on the emerging world order defines order in terms of the balance of power among major nations. It argues that the military supremacy of the United States was underscored by the Desert Shield/Desert Storm operations and the military defeat of Saddam Hussein, a victory that came about with the complete cooperation of the former Soviet Union and China under the auspices of the United Nations. The U.S. military triumph legitimizes its claim to leadership of the global village, however, its military supremacy is being overshadowed by economic challenges and rivalries from Japan and Germany—countries with no significant military power at this time.

The Islamic Republic of Iran has not officially reacted to the notion of a new world order. However, various government and religious leaders have commented on the issue. The hard-liners have rejected the new world order as described by former president Bush. According to them, the new order is nothing but a complete domination of the world by the United States. They have not shied away from encouraging Muslims to challenge the notion of the new order and the United States' interests all over the world. Even the more pragmatic leaders in Iran have offered similar interpretations. In a recent news conference in Iran, the newly elected Speaker of the Islamic Parliament, Hojjatoleslam Ali Akbar Nouri, stated that the new world order means nothing more than American expansionism and domination of the world.[2]

Unlike the aftermath of World War II and the resulting distribution of power based on the military triumph of the allied forces, a balanced distribution of power cannot be created in the 1990's and beyond based on military supremacy alone. The existing distribution of economic power, the immense industrial capacity of all countries, the proliferation of global communications, finance, and production limit the ability of one nation to claim a leadership position based solely on military might. In other words, the conditions that allowed the United States to become the sole leader of the West do not exist today. The United States of America emerged triumphant from World War II with its military and economic power intact. Europe and Japan lost their military and economic positions and had to accept the leadership of the United States for many reasons. The main reason was the rivalry between capitalism and Communist ideology, which led to the costly and long cold war.

The 1990s started with the collapse of Communism as a crusading and salvaging ideology. Many idealogues of Communism questioned the relevance of Marxism-Leninism and paved the way for its rejection even in the former Soviet Union. In Iran, prominent Communists, such as Ehsan Tabari, spent the last days of their lives writing rejections of the Communist ideology that had dominated their intellectual and political lives for so many years. But whether the demise of the Soviet Union is a victory for liberal capitalism remains to be seen.

The cold war has ended with the world being different in three major ways. First, the era of dogmatic pursuit of an ideology seems to be over. Second, the global economy is faced with excess capacity and fierce economic competition. Finally, multinationalism seems to be on the rise, as witnessed by the actions in Somalia and the Persian Gulf and inaction in Bosnia. More recently, lack of multinational support hampered the U.S. plans for Bosnia, demonstrating the limits of the only military superpower in the new global arena.

The nations of the world are faced with momentous decisions that will eventually bring about a new world order and a new balance of power. The ultimate choices are globalism or regionalism. The nations of the world can either join hands and create a new world order based on global law, respect for human rights, a fair global absorption of economic resources, protection of the environment, freedom, and global democracy, or pursue a narrow-minded, nationalistic, isolationistic, and protectionistic policy that could lead the world to regionalism and trade wars.

A global approach that leads to the transfer of technology across nations, higher productivity, economies of scale, more international trade, global environmental policies, joint efforts in solving common human problems, and new frontiers in science and technology will be gratifying to many peace-loving citizens all over the world. The success of such a global system in addressing human rights problems, freedom, economic development, elimination of poverty, and human suffering is dependent on how far the major players are willing to go to eradicate the notions of supremacy and pure self-interest. The pursuit of self-interest as a driving force to promote competition and economic vibrancy is acceptable. However, a stable global village needs to create institutions that are universally acceptable and have the means and power to enforce collective global decisions. The existing multinational institutions can provide the foundation for new and more vibrant global institutions. The leader of the global economy in the minds and hearts of billions of people in the less-developed parts of the world will be the nation that can offer them a dignified way out of their poverty and economic backwardness. The era of ideological competition should be replaced with an era of economic, social, political, and military cooperation among the industrious people of the world.

A regional approach to contemporary economic challenges can induce creation of a tripolar system with three trading blocs—the North American, the European, and the Asian-Pacific poles. Under such a scenario, each trading bloc may attempt to gain more economic power by pursuing a policy of beggar-thy-neighbor. The resulting trade diversion can easily reduce the volume of international trade and engender a welfare loss in all countries concerned. Production and consumption inefficiencies will hurt the global as well as the national economies for many generations to come.[3] Regionalism could provoke trade wars with fierce competition over access to strategic commodities such as oil. The world can be brought to major military confrontations over ultimate economic supremacy and leadership.

The developing nations are also faced with difficult choices. For many decades they suffered from the cold war; their economies and social fabrics were undermined by the rivalry between the superpowers. They were caught between two ideologies, capitalism and Marxist-Leninism, each offering them a model of economic development and social salvation. In spite of the collapse of the USSR, there does not seem to be an end to their miseries yet.

CONTEMPORARY IRAN

Alienated by the Communist ideology, the Iranian revolution took a different course. It ostensibly relied on the Islamic philosophy for salvation, economic self-sufficiency, and political independence. Islam provided millions of Iranian youth and others an alternative to Western and Eastern ideologies. The late Ayatollah Khomeini led them to a great victory against the well-armed forces of the Shah and promised them a new society fully salvaged by adherence to the Islamic theocracy. The strengths and weaknesses of the Promised Land were overshadowed by the charismatic and projected superhuman personality of the Ayatollah. However, as is the fate of all revolutions, soon after the victory voices of dissent were heard across the new Islamic Republic, forcing the government to employ earthly means to bring order and conformity to the new republic.

A long and expensive war with Iraq and the death of the Ayatollah provided an opportunity for a renewed debate among the followers of the Ayatollah over the strategic choices of the Islamic regime. President Rafsanjani, allied with Ayatollah Khamenei, envisioned a more pragmatic approach in the pursuit of the revolution's objectives. His approach was perceived by many segments of Iranian society to be more in tune with the goals of the revolution. Still, as of today, there is no consensus in the Iranian society on the goals and the purpose of the revolution. The nonreligious factions see their revolution hijacked by the clergy. The revolution was supposed to bring about freedom, democracy, and a modern society capable of competing globally in all arenas. Their shattered dream of a free and modern Iran puts them at odds with the ruling clergy.

Economic conditions in Iran deteriorated rather rapidly after the revolution. Despite some recent token gains in oil and agricultural output, the economy has been stagnant for most of the postrevolutionary period due to a prolonged war and mismanagement of the economy. Manufacturing has suffered from inadequate imported raw materials due to insufficient foreign exchange earnings. The construction industry is still a major contributor to the gross domestic product, however, shortages of raw materials and high housing costs have hampered the government's efforts to make significant improvements in chronic housing shortages. This problem has been exacerbated by an alarming population growth since the revolution.

Crude oil exports, as always, are the major source of foreign exchange earnings despite the recent non-oil export promotion policies of the government. Traditionally, non-oil exports are primarily composed of dry fruits and Persian carpets. However, more recently the government has encouraged the export of fresh fruits and vegetables at the expense of domestic absorption. This has become another source of discontent and criticism among the Iranian people.[4]

The oil industry suffers from inadequate investments and is in need of a massive infusion of capital and state-of-the-art technology. This important task cannot be done adequately without cooperation by foreign financial markets and a transfer of foreign technology. Despite the nationalistic rhetoric about indigenous technical know-how, the country has no prospect of self-sufficiency in science and technology. Inadequate refining and transportation facilities have contributed to chronic shortages of home-heating fuels and other oil products. To millions of Iranians, energy shortages in a nation that sits on an ocean of oil are incomprehensible.

The Islamic government has been more forceful in levying and collecting new taxes. However, huge budget deficits financed through borrowing from the Central Bank exist in the country. This has contributed to massive liquidity expansion and high inflation rates. The credit policy of the government has been hostage to budget deficits. The government earns foreign exchange proceeds from oil exports and allocates them based on government priorities. Recently, a three-tier foreign exchange rate system was replaced with a single foreign exchange rate system following a huge official depreciation of the Iranian rial. The new system is expected to curtail profiteering activities of speculators and government agencies, which take advantage of the market by purchasing government-allocated foreign currencies at lower rates and selling them at substantially higher prices. The elimination of foreign exchange budgets may help bring more efficiency to the economy, however, it will also contribute to large price increases for many basic consumer products and food causing discontent among Iran's lower class.

The Iranian economy will suffer from chronic shortages of foreign exchange, government budget deficits, high inflation, and shortages of food and other necessities for the unforeseeable future unless dramatic steps are taken to reassess the political, social, and economic fabric of

Iranian society. Economic policy changes alone cannot resolve these huge problems. Past government economic policies of price controls, subsidies, and rationing will only postpone facing the real problems and not solve them. A sharply rising population, rapid urbanization, and lack of consensus on the future course of the country taxes heavily the entire socioeconomic and political fabric of the nation.

The Current Political Atmosphere

Until recently, President Rafsanjani managed to promote his pragmatic policies of opening the country to the rest of the world, in particular the Western industrialized nations. In contrast to the first decade of the Islamic Republic, he has embarked on an accommodationist path. The Islamic government was influential in securing the release of Western hostages held in Lebanon. It cooperated with the international community in its struggle against Iraq's invasion of Kuwait and it agreed with the recommendations of the International Monetary Fund (IMF) and the World Bank in such matters as the elimination of foreign exchange budgets, reduction of subsidies, and the establishment of a single exchange-rate system.

Rafsanjani, in collaboration with Ayatollah Khamenei, managed to consolidate the Revolutionary Guard and other armed forces under a central command. He initiated renewed talks about an open-door policy for Iranians abroad in order to encourage the millions who left the country after the revolution to return. He also managed to promote more pragmatic and educated candidates in the parliamentary elections. Social life for nonorthodox Muslims started to become more bearable as a consequence of the open policies initiated by Rafsanjani. However, soon after the defeat of radical candidates in the parliamentary elections, major riots broke out in a few highly populated cities. The Islamic government took immediate steps to arrest and execute the alleged leaders of the rioters and started to roll back its openness policies. In short, Rafsanjani attempted to win the support of war-weary Iranians by promoting a policy of openness based on a market economy, privatization, Islamic culture with limited tolerance, and an authoritarian sedo-parliamentary political system capable of perpetuating the Islamic reign, some of this at odds with the totalitarian fundamentalists who adhere to heavy government involvement in economic affairs.

CONCLUSION AND POLICY IMPLICATIONS

Iran, an Islamic country with a rich culture, has survived many invasions by outside forces and cultures. It has always managed to protect and retain positive Iranian values and culture. The Islamic government has tried to promote a version of Islamic culture that is highly influenced by Arabic cultures and traditions, a culture that is as alienating to some sectors of Iranian society as Western culture has been to others. The heroic defense of Iran during eight long years of war with Iraq is seen by Islamic factions as a defense of Islam. However, millions of Iranians defended their country on purely nationalistic grounds. At times, when the war efforts were not as successful as expected, the Islamic government appealed to Iranian patriotism as opposed to their religious convictions. Iranian peoples with different degrees of religious orthodoxy can be motivated and mobilized through a combination of Islamic appeals and nationalistic aspirations. History will testify that the time has come for Iran to address all these issues in terms of its strategic goals and needs. The strategic choices are not as divisive as they may seem on the surface. Whether one adheres to Islamic ideology or a nationalist agenda, or both, the policy choices of Iran are surprisingly similar.

Iran needs to define its security, economic, and foreign policies in terms of a truly global perspective as opposed to a regional approach. It must resist the delusion that it can become a major global or even regional power by promoting its religious ideology. Its political and military ambition must be to defend and protect Iran's territorial integrity. Security issues in the 1990s are far more complex than they were during the cold war era. The Soviet threat has been removed, but potential adversaries and challenges exist that may threaten the territorial integrity of the country. Iraq, Russia, and even some newly independent states in Central Asia may challenge Iran in the future, based on nationalistic aspirations. A defense strategy must be put in place based on mobilization of indigenous forces as well as reliance on transnational institutions. Regional military pacts, which Iran is seeking in the Persian Gulf, can be easily overshadowed by global necessities during times of major multinational crisis. The success of this strategy can be guaranteed only if Iran is not seen as an aggressive country with political and territorial ambitions beyond its boundaries. A careful planning and implementation of this strategy could save the country billions of dollars in defense spending.

Domestically, Iran needs to develop its economy based on full participation of all indigenous forces, including the clergy as well as laypeople.

Economic and political participation cannot and must not be under the domain of any group. A modern progressive Iran can be built based on freedom of economic activity with minimum government interference. Democracy must be cherished and promoted through democratic institutions capable of adapting to the Iranian and Islamic culture. Perhaps for the first time in the modern history of Iran, the Islamic government has managed to achieve a peaceful transfer of power. However, this is mainly due to the extraordinary character and charismatic leadership of the late Ayatollah Khomeini. His careful scrutiny of his potential successor before his death and the people's admiration of his personality prevented an open dispute over the succession issue. Strategically, Iran needs a democratic, plural multiparty political system capable of continuity, adaptability, and a peaceful transfer of power. The political system needs to be capable of identifying and recognizing competent, self-assertive younger leaders who can address the intergenerational political issues of the day.

Social and political life has always been influenced by Islamic values even during times when secularism was on the rise. Those who advocated a secular society found, to their surprise, that secularism is only a theoretical matter to large segments of the society. Those who have tried to impose fundamentalist Islamic rule on the nation have been equally surprised by the resistance they have received from diverse segments of Iranian society. Even among the ruling clergy the issue of religious leadership and political leadership has not been settled yet. Since the death of Ayatollah Khomeini, it has been extremely difficult to nominate someone who is qualified to succeed him as the Supreme Leader as well as the religious leader. This demonstrates that even in a nonsecular Iran the issues of political leadership and religious leadership can be separate. There are a few Grand Ayatollahs who prefer to attend to religious matters and remain outside the political arena.

Contrary to the views of some political activists, the strategic issue is not whether a secular system is preferred to a nonsecular one. The political deadlock that is observed in Iran is mainly due to the unwillingness of some to do away with authoritarian tendencies disguised under Islamic rules or secular aspirations. The existing political institutions are too rigid and exclusive with too many inhibitive preconditions that deny large segments of the Iranian population the opportunity to serve their country. President Rafsanjani has a golden opportunity, during his second term in office, to address some of these issues and change the course of history by providing a mechanism for the creation of an all-inclusive, modern, and progressive political system capable of providing an honorable and meaningful place to those who would like to serve their country regardless of their political affiliation and orientation.

The past policy of limited tolerance, whereby a dominant group grants to members of nondominant groups some but not all rights and privileges enjoyed by its own members, is an impediment to full participation of all Iranian forces in the political, social, and economic affairs of the country.[5] By the same token, secularism will exclude many capable religious leaders from active participation in political life. Separation of church and state may work in Western democracies but it becomes a source of fragmentation and political disenchantment in societies like Iran. The strategic goal of all Iranians, whether religious or nonreligious, must be equality among all groups in the Iranian society with complete freedom of participation in the economic, political, and social affairs of the nation. This is the only way to build a modern, progressive, and strong Iran based on Iranian culture and Islamic aspirations. The clergy and laypeople must become equal partners in leading Iran into the twenty-first century. A policy of coexistence must replace the existing limited tolerance strategy of the Islamic regime.

NOTES TO CHAPTER 5
◆

1. Strobe Talbott, "Post-Victory Blues," *Foreign Affairs*, vol. 71, no. 1 (1992): 53–69.

2. *Iran Times International* (Washington, D.C.), vol. 22, no. 14 (19 June 1992).

3. *Policy Implications of Trade and Policy Zones* (Kansas City, Kans.: The Federal Reserve Bank of Kansas City, 1991).

4. Central Bank of the Islamic Republic of Iran, *Economic Report and Balance Sheet,* various issues.

5. Lewis Bernard, "Muslims, Christians, and Jews: The Dream of Coexistence," *The New York Review of Books*, vol. 39, no. 6 (March 26, 1992), pp. 48–52.

REALPOLITIK AND TRANSFORMATION OF IRAN'S FOREIGN POLICY: COPING WITH THE "IRAN SYNDROME"

Nader Entessar

Good will begets good will.

—GEORGE BUSH,
PRESIDENTIAL INAUGURAL ADDRESS,
JANUARY 1989

When President George Bush stated, "Good will begets good will" during his first presidential inaugural address, it was clear that he was signaling the new American administration's desire to improve relations with Tehran if the Iranian government would use its influence in Lebanon to free the American hostages being held by groups sympathetic to the Islamic Republic. President Bush further stated that such assistance would long be remembered by his administration. In response to President Bush's statements, the influential Tehran daily, *Ettela'at,* published an editorial urging the Iranian government to help the United States obtain the release of American hostages in Lebanon. The editorial stated:

> During the imposed war [Iran-Iraq War], we learned a very
> important and costly lesson. [Iran's confrontationalist foreign
> policy] led to a situation whereby virtually all countries in the

> world either proclaimed neutrality or supported the aggressor
> Iraq. In spite of this, our side prevailed. . . . The peace period
> is different than the war period. Policies we pursued in the
> course of the war cannot be pursued successfully during peace-
> time. . . . We must be prepared to respond positively to oppor-
> tunities that may present themselves if we wish to remain
> victorious in peace as well.[1]

The English-language *Tehran Times,* which has traditionally echoed the
sentiments of the foreign ministry and other pragmatic elements in the
Iranian government, endorsed the aforementioned sentiments by calling for the adoption of a new approach to U.S.-Iranian relations.[2] The
paper did not specifically mention President Bush's inaugural speech;
however, the paper's editorial gave a relatively strong endorsement to
the adoption of a fresh approach to the United States because the new
U.S. president was "acting wisely" and distancing himself from the negative posturing of the Reagan administration.

Although Iranian intervention was largely responsible for the release
of U.S. hostages in Lebanon, the hoped-for improvements in U.S.-
Iranian relations have not materialized. Nor has the military defeat of
Saddam Hussein's Iraq by the allied forces yet engendered any warm-
ing of relations between Washington and Tehran. Both of these events,
however, aided and reflected changes, albeit gradual, that have been
occurring in the Islamic Republic's foreign policy orientation. This chapter will examine the impact of these developments, particularly the U.S.-
led war against Iraq, on the changing patterns of Iranian foreign policy.
A major thesis of this chapter is that the Persian Gulf War accelerated
the de-Khomeinization of Iranian foreign policy and its evolving realignment with the policies of the pro-Western Arab states in the region. At
the same time, it solidified U.S. intransigence and rigidity in its posture
toward the Islamic Republic.

Although Iran remained neutral during Operation Desert Shield/
Storm, and even sought, albeit unsuccessfully, to prevent the occurrence
of a major war in the region, it was evident that certain pragmatists
within the country's ruling hierarchy favored military neutralization of
Iraq's Baathi regime. Iraq's devastating war against Iran in the 1980s and
Saddam Hussein's attacks on the Shia holy cities of Najaf and Karbala
in southern Iraq further caused the Islamic Republic to adopt a policy
posture that was akin to that of the West and its Arab allies.

Furthermore, the security of the Persian Gulf, which Iran has traditionally considered as vital to its own security, compelled the Islamic

Republic to shed much of its Khomeini-era radical rhetoric and to reestablish diplomatic relations with all Gulf Arabs as well as with European countries. Notwithstanding these major transformations in Iran's foreign policy thinking and practice, major problems continue to hamper improvements in Iran's relations with certain key countries, including the United States. As will be discussed later, the United States' and Iran's bellicose attitude and policies toward each other, Washington's near total disregard for what Iran considers to be its legitimate defense needs, and the United States' overall policy of military, political, economic, and cultural containment of Iran may in the long run serve as catalysts for major future crises with far-reaching implications for Iran's foreign policy and the country's relationship with regional and international actors.

THE NEW WORLD ORDER AND THE PERSIAN GULF

The Persian Gulf region is arguably the most volatile and militarized region in the Third World. The combination of political volatility and militarization has made the region susceptible to outside intervention and regional power plays. The eight-year war between Iran and Iraq, Iraq's invasion and occupation of Kuwait in August 1990, and the subsequent deployment of more than 500,000 American troops in Saudi Arabia in defense of American foreign policy objectives and the Saudi monarchy are concrete examples of this reality.

The crisis in the Persian Gulf generated by Iraqi president Saddam Hussein's gamble on Kuwait has, in the words of one analyst, provided the United States a window of opportunity to establish "strategic bridgeheads, secure the Gulf, and ensure that it retains a virtual monopoly on global violence."[3] The U.S. troop deployment in the region and Washington's dominant role in leading an allied military attack on Iraq was the first major test of the so-called Bush Doctrine. This doctrine envisioned a post–cold war global arrangement dominated by the United States, with Western Europe, Japan, and perhaps Russia, acting as junior partners. In other words, without the deterrent effect of the former Soviet Union's military power, the Persian Gulf has also become a testing ground for Washington's search for a new "global order" and its apparent determination to augur a new era of Pax Americana.[4]

The emergence of the post–cold war unipolar world has been hailed by some American commentators as an auspicious phenomenon for world order. Thus, political commentator Charles Krauthammer contends that the best hope for global safety and security lies in "American strength and will—the strength and will to lead a unipolar world, unashamedly laying down the rules of world order and being prepared to enforce them."[5] Similarly, Michael Vlahos, former director of the U.S. State Department's Center for the Study of Foreign Affairs, stated: "If we [the United States] marched right into Baghdad, brought Saddam Hussein back in a cage and paraded him down Pennsylvania Avenue, the world would take notice. We would have great freedom of action in the world for the next 10 to 20 years, . . . people would truly respect us, and if we said we didn't like what they did, they'd sit up and take notice.[6]

In a less strident fashion, an editorial in the *Wall Street Journal* reasoned that in the post–cold war world, the only alternative to Pax Americana is a balance-of-power system, which is not a realistic option in today's world in light of the preponderant military position of the United States vis-à-vis other major actors in international affairs. Given this reality, the editorial justified Pax Americana in the following terms: "Insecure regional powers will respond to the U.S. retreat by arming to the teeth, causing their neighbors to do the same; the U.S. will end up playing one against another. . . . This is precisely the policy the U.S. pursued in the 1980s in the Persian Gulf, building up Iraq to balance Iranian power. Saddam proved to be even more dangerous."[7]

These commentaries and statements, which represent the main thrust of thinking among Washington's foreign policy establishment, have contributed greatly to the revival of the misguided notion that the United States has the responsibility to act as the world's policeman. When former President Bush triumphantly declared after the end of the Gulf War that the United States had finally "kicked the Vietnam syndrome," he was implying that his administration had swept aside any lingering reluctance to use maximum force to achieve his version of a "new world order."[8] Although the U.S. military achievement in the Persian Gulf War appears to have allowed the country's political leadership to overcome the "Vietnam syndrome" for the short term, Washington's greatest problem in formulating its Gulf policy remains its "Iran syndrome," which has prevented it from improving its relations with Tehran. It is Washington's "Iran syndrome," reflected in a mixture of demonization and containment policies, that have to a large extent affected Iran's foreign policy decisions and options. As the United States seeks to construct a new world order in the region, "the hand of [the late] Ayatollah Khomeini, architect of rather a different order, still hangs over the White House."[9]

THE PERSIAN GULF WAR AND IRAN

The Islamic Republic has since its inception opposed the stationing of foreign forces in the region, particularly those forces that it has viewed as inimical to its security interests. American support of Iraq during the devastating course of the Iran-Iraq War, its troop skirmishes with Iranian naval forces in the latter part of this war, and the shooting down of Iran Air Flight 655 by the cruiser USS *Vincennes* in July 1988 (killing 290 passengers) were among the factors that compelled Iran to oppose a major American troop deployment in Saudi Arabia so close to Iran's southern regions.

The Islamic Republic's initial antipathy toward the stationing of Western troops in the Persian Gulf was reflected in a myriad of statements and speeches given by Iranian officials on this topic. For example, in a talk given to the families of those killed during the Iran-Iraq War, Iran's supreme religious leader, or *faqih,* Ayatollah Ali Khamenei, expressed Tehran's perspective on the American military deployment in the region:

> This region's security is the business of this region's nations. You [Americans] are buyers of the oil belonging to these nations, so you had best line up outside and refrain from interfering in their affairs. . . . If you see the region as insecure today, then you are responsible. It was you who armed Iraq and you who encouraged him [Saddam Hussein] to feel strong and attack Kuwait. . . . If you had not helped [Saddam Hussein] as much as you did . . . then the region would not now be facing this insecurity. . . . Utter shame on those governments which allow aggressive America to come here in pursuit of its own interest.[10]

Ayatollah Khamenei's expression of serious concern about the stationing of a large number of American troops in the Persian Gulf region was echoed by a number of *Majlis* (parliament) deputies associated with the so-called radical faction of the ruling hierarchy. Their condemnation became more vociferous after Saddam Hussein's desperate bid for Iranian support of his policies and after offering unilateral concessions to Iran on the boundary disputes between the two countries, including his acceptance of the *thalweg* line (midchannel) in the Shatt al-Arab waterway. *Majlis* speaker Hojjatuleslam Mehdi Karrubi predicted that the Muslim nations would "eject American troops from Saudi Arabia ignominiously."[11] Other "radical" parliamentary deputies denounced both the al-Sabah ruling family in Kuwait and the al-Saud monarchy in

Saudi Arabia for inviting non-Muslim and anti-Muslim forces to the land of the Prophet Mohammad. It is important to note that the "radicals" remained equally contemptuous of Saddam Hussein's invasion of Kuwait and his expansionist policies.

The pragmatists among the ruling hierarchy in Iran remained suspicious of the Iraqi overtures toward Iran and were ambiguous about foreign troop buildup in Saudi Arabia. They remained in touch with the ousted al-Sabah family and, according to one report, kept the Kuwaitis abreast of Iraq's "peace overtures" toward the Islamic Republic.[12] The two leading pragmatists, President Ali Akbar Hashemi Rafsanjani and Foreign Minister Ali Akbar Velayati, continued to pursue several avenues for the peaceful settlement of the crisis. Through close contacts with Syria and Turkey—two key Muslim states that were participants in the coalition against Iraq—the pragmatists remained abreast of developments of the crisis. When Syrian President Hafiz al-Assad visited Iran in late September 1990, President Rafsanjani took advantage of this opportunity to establish a joint Iranian-Syrian commission for maintaining a direct channel of communication with his Syrian counterpart throughout the crisis.

Although the pragmatists continued to subscribe publicly to the official government policy of neutrality, and continued to portray the crisis as a conflict between two equally guilty aggressors, it was evident that they also sought to take advantage of the window of opportunity and reestablish Iran's credentials as a responsible key player in regional affairs. In a meeting with a group of Tehran University students shortly before the onset of the allied war against Iraq, Foreign Minister Velayati stated that since Saddam Hussein was not going to leave Kuwait peacefully, the presence of foreign troops in Saudi Arabia was justified so long as those troops were stationed there for limited security purposes.[13] This was a clear departure from previous public statements of Iranian officials on the Gulf Crisis, and it signaled the ascendancy of the pragmatists in the foreign policy domain.

Furthermore, the pragmatists took advantage of the uncertainties generated by the Persian Gulf Crisis to curtail the power of some of their more prominent "radical" opponents. For example, Rafsanjani and his allies in the Council of Guardians—the twelve-man body responsible for supervision of elections and having veto power over legislation passed by the *Majlis*—orchestrated a move that led to the virtual disqualification of several key radicals from running as candidates for the Assembly of Experts. This was engineered through requiring all candidates to pass a rigorous examination in Shia jurisprudence. Several noteworthy radical *Majlis* deputies, including Ali Akbar Mohtashemi and Sadeq Khalkhali, failed the above examination and were thus excluded from becoming members of the Assembly of Experts, the body responsible for, among other things, selection of the *faqih*. Rafsanjani and his associates managed to weaken the influence of the "radicals" again when the Council of Guardians disqualified a number of prominent "radicals" from running as candidates for the April 1992 parliamentary elections.

During the course of the allied war against Iraq, Iraqi air force pilots flew more than 130 of their planes to Iran. They were either defecting or flying their planes there for safekeeping. These included some of the best combat aircraft in the Iraqi air force, such as Su-24 Fencer bombers and an assortment of trainers and transport planes. Initially, some Western analysts feared that Saddam Hussein had struck a deal with Tehran in order to preserve some of his best aircraft for later use against the allied forces. The Iranians, however, consistently claimed that no such deal had been made and that the Iraqi pilots were defectors. Tehran further asserted that neither the pilots nor the aircraft would be released until after the Persian Gulf War was over. Subsequent events seem to have borne out Iranian claims of neutrality during the war. As military analyst Norman Friedman has noted:

> The fact that many [Iraqi] aircraft crashed on landing suggested that their pilots were inexperienced, that they had stolen aircraft in order to defect. Early in the mass flights, some aircraft peeled off as they approached the border. That was initially interpreted as the departure of escorts that had accompanied officially sanctioned flights, but later it was theorized that these airplanes had turned back when they were painted by Iranian air-defense radars, that is, when they became subject to interception. That certainly pointed the way toward something other than Iranian connivance in an Iraqi plan.[14]

In the immediate aftermath of Iraq's military defeat, the Shia majority in the south and the Kurdish minority in the north rebelled against the central government in Baghdad. They were encouraged to do so partly due to CIA-run broadcasts of the so-called Free Voice of Iraq radio station operating from Saudi Arabia. The Shia region of Iraq had already borne the brunt of the allied saturation bombing runs during the Persian Gulf War. However, given the history of their persecution by the

Baathi regime, the Shias were anxious to lead a revolt against the Baghdad government. Ayatollah Sayyid Mohammad Baqir al-Hakim, the chairman of the Tehran-based Supreme Assembly of the Islamic Revolution in Iraq (SAIRI), took the lead in encouraging a Shia uprising against Saddam Hussein, with "the evident support of President Rafsanjani, who effectively put Iranian broadcasting facilities at the disposal of the rebellious Iraqi Shiites."[15] However, the anticipated outside logistical support for the Iraqi Shias never materialized, and Saddam Hussein was able to launch a major devastating offensive against Shia strongholds, including the holy cities of Najaf and Karbala. It is evident that an exaggerated fear of the coming to power of an Islamic government in Iraq and the concomitant "Iran syndrome" compelled the United States to take an inactive position at that time regarding the massacre of Iraqi Shias.

During Saddam Hussein's attacks in the south, heavy damage was inflicted on some of Shia Islam's holiest shrines, causing Iran to intensify its encouragement of the Shia uprisings in the south and the Kurdish revolt in the north. However, the Iranian government took pains to project an image of active neutrality in the Iraqi civil war. Although Iran's interests dictate that Iraq's territorial integrity remain intact and that a stable and nonhostile government be established in Baghdad, the Iranian leadership is well aware that a stable and nonthreatening Iraq must empower its large Shia population and its Kurdish minority. In this vein, President Rafsanjani's March 8, 1991, speech urging Saddam Hussein to "step down and give in to the will of the people of Iraq"[16] was a reflection of Iran's desire to maintain Iraq's territorial cohesion while undermining the Baath Party's authority.

In turn, Saddam Hussein accused Iran of supporting the "saboteurs of the south [the Shias] and the stooges and agents of foreign enemies in the north [the Kurds]."[17] The extent of Iran's material help to Iraq's opposition groups is difficult to determine. On the one hand, Tehran has long nurtured various Shia anti-Saddam groups, such as the SAIRI. On the other hand, given the tortuous contours of Iraqi domestic politics, Iran has remained somewhat aloof from direct involvement in political restructuring in Iraq. Furthermore, Iraqi opposition leaders have endeavored to minimize the Iranian dimension of the Shia uprisings. As M. al-Rubaie, a spokesman for the underground al-Daawa Party asserted: "We asked Iran to refrain from interfering inside Iraq. We want an Arab dimension and flavor, not Persian. It's of paramount importance that we approach our [Arab] brothers in Saudi Arabia especially."[18]

It is clear that Saudi Arabia does not favor a Shia-influenced government in Iraq. For this reason, the Saudis initially backed two alternatives—the National Salvation and the Free Iraq Council. These groups represent diverse elements within Iraq's Sunni community, some of whose members have held high-level positions in the Iraqi government in the past. In the Saudi-supported groups, one could find such individuals as Talib Shabib, a former Baath Party leader, General Hassan al-Naqib, a close ally of President Assad of Syria, and even Abdul Rahman Arif, a former Iraqi president who was overthrown by the Baathis in a 1968 military coup. Neither these individuals nor the Saudi-supported groups have the necessary mass-based support to spearhead a popular uprising against the Iraqi government. If they do manage to come to power, it will be through a military coup and the machinations of foreign powers, most likely the United States and Saudi Arabia.

Iran, signaling a drastic change from its oft-stated opposition to foreign military involvement in the Persian Gulf, has at times encouraged the United States to help grassroots opposition to Saddam Hussein's rule. In a candid admission of Iran's views, Mohammad Jafar Mahallati, a former Iranian ambassador to the United Nations, urged the Bush administration to discard its "phobia" about Shia Islam. He pointed out that many prominent Shias in Iraq have an established record of "moderation on Middle Eastern issues and on questions of international relations over the past decade. These influential figures believe that the only way for countries in the Middle East to get out of the prevailing miserable situation is to rid the region of all sectarian political frictions and frustrations."[19] Mahallati, like many members of opposition groups inside Iraq, argued that the United States can help preserve the territorial integrity of Iraq by giving the Shia majority their due weight in Iraqi political discourse.[20] This position was stated more forcefully by the Iranian foreign minister, Ali Akbar Velayati, when he urged the United States to use its military forces in the area to prevent Iraqi helicopters from launching attacks against the Kurdish and Shia cities.[21]

Iran's exhortations to the West to use its military might to contain Saddam Hussein further strained Tehran's relations with Baghdad. Iran's policy also seems to contradict the Saudi objective of denying Shias any significant power that they would have in any future democratically elected government in Iraq. The military defeat of Saddam Hussein has "indeed provided opportunities and pitfalls for changing the course of Iranian-Arab relations."[22]

NEITHER MILITARIZATION NOR OUTSIDE HEGEMONY

A byproduct of the swift and decisive victory of the U.S.-led forces against Iraq has been the lessening in importance of the region's "oil weapon" in dealing with the industrialized West. Those arguing for the total destruction of Iraq's military potential and the unconditional surrender of Iraq's forces in the aftermath of the Persian Gulf War posited, among other things, that such an outcome would result in the expansion of the U.S. role in the region and the weakening of OPEC.[23] Elie Kedourie, an Israeli-British scholar, contended that the weakening of OPEC was not only desirable for the West but also necessary to prevent another war in the Persian Gulf.[24] The argument that OPEC power must automatically be translated into weapons power is spurious at best and ignores the overwhelming responsibility of the West, especially the United States, in perpetuating the arms buildup in the region.

The irrationality of the arms buildup in the Persian Gulf stems from regional perceptions of strategic threats. As I have argued elsewhere, the acquisition of sophisticated weapons by the littoral states of the Persian Gulf has not resulted in a stable balance-of-terror situation that would lead to regional equilibrium and maintenance of regional security.[25] What has existed in the Gulf in the past two decades has been an asymmetrical military balance against either one major regional player or a group of countries in the area. In the 1970s, Iran maintained an edge over Iraq and Saudi Arabia in terms of its weapons imports and the size of its armed forces. Beginning in the late 1970s, Iraqi arms purchases from abroad surpassed those of Iran.[26] Throughout the 1980s, the former Soviet Union alone transferred arms valued at $20 billion to the Baathi government of Saddam Hussein.

The eight-year Iran-Iraq War and the American arms embargo against the Islamic Republic further deteriorated Iran's military posture vis-à-vis Iraq, thus creating the military asymmetry that partly made Iraq's search for regional hegemony and its invasion of Kuwait possible. The destruction of Iraqi military capabilities by the United States has created another vacuum that may in the long run prove to be destabilizing. Realizing the potential for instability, the United States has embarked upon a two-pronged policy that may, ironically, contribute to regional instability and bring Tehran and Washington onto a collision course.

On the one hand, the United States and its allies have embarked upon the demilitarization of Iraq while promoting further arms sales to Saudi Arabia, Egypt, and other Arab participants in Operation Desert

Storm. Notwithstanding the post–Gulf War reestablishment of diplomatic ties between Iran and Saudi Arabia, Tehran still views a highly militarized and resurgent Riyadh, backed by the military power of Washington, as a potential source of threat to its national security interests. After all, it was Saudi Arabia that supported, both financially and militarily, Saddam Hussein's invasion of Iran in September 1980 and his devastating war against the Islamic Republic. The human cost of the war to Iran (more than 350,000 casualties), and the economic war damages (some $400 billion) are staggering figures that will have long-lasting effects on the Iranians' psyche and their perception of threat to their national well-being. The psychological impact of the Iran-Iraq War will undoubtedly play a significant role in shaping Iranian foreign policy toward the Arab world, in particular, and the West, in general. The potential Saudi military threat against Iran was enhanced when the Bush administration announced shortly after the end of the Gulf War its intention to sell to Riyadh an additional $21 billion worth of such advanced weapons as M-2 Bradley fighter vehicles, TOW and Hellfire missiles, UH-60 Blackhawk and Apache helicopters, M-1A2 and M-60A3 tanks, and F-15C and F-15D fighters. Between March 1991 and March 1992 alone, the United States concluded arms agreements totaling $11 billion with Middle Eastern countries, many of which were government-to-government agreements with pro-Western Arab sheikhdoms of the Gulf. If commercial sales and military construction projects are added to this total, U.S. military sales to the Middle East for fiscal year 1991 reached $23 billion.[27]

The second element of the current U.S. policy in the Gulf is reflected in the evolving plan to maintain a relatively significant direct military presence in the region. This military presence, especially if it is accompanied by bellicose posturing toward and policy announcements against the Islamic Republic, will affect Iranian foreign policy actions and may make a U.S.-Iran rapprochement more difficult. Moreover, as Iran specialist Shireen Hunter noted, "the onset of a major U.S. military presence, 20 years after Britain's departure, is simply too reminiscent of old colonial days. It could hardly be heralded as the dawning of a new world order."[28] Washington can contribute to the long-term stability of the region not by maintaining an overwhelming military presence in the region that heightens anxiety about its possible interventionist motives but by adopting a policy of "constructive disengagement" in the regional affairs.[29]

As a major player on the global scene, the United States cannot pursue an isolationist policy and still maintain its superpower status. On the other hand, Washington need not become a prisoner of its own rhetoric, which could lead to the adoption of an interventionary foreign policy in the Persian Gulf and permanent confrontation with one of the region's most significant players—the Islamic Republic of Iran. As political analyst Earl Ravenal has observed:

> Under the circumstances, American [Persian Gulf] policy should be to "quarantine" regional violence and compartmentalize regional instability. But this is not to be done by active intervention. . . . At most, American policy should be to encourage regional balances of power, whether bipolar or multipolar. And not necessarily neat and precisely calibrated balances; rough and messy ones will do. Yet, in the case of the Persian Gulf and Southwest Asia, incessant and feckless American intervention not only has, in the past, antagonized and neutralized potentially effective power balancers—such as Iran, which is still the obvious hegemon in the area—but also has, in the present instance, largely preempted the power-balancing role that intraregional countries should perform.[30]

In short, Washington's apparent disregard for a regional balance of power and Iran's defense needs may make the position of pragmatists within the ruling hierarchy more tenuous.

Notwithstanding the Western media's reporting on the "ominous Iranian threat," the fact is that Iran remains one of the least military-equipped countries in the Middle East relative to its size and potential power. In 1992 alone, Saudi Arabia had earmarked $18 billion and Kuwait $10 billion for the purchase of new sophisticated military equipment from the West. In contrast, Iran's military procurement budget in its five-year economic plan is only $10 billion.[31] Iran's inventory of weapons include 700 antiquated tanks and 213 combat aircraft, most of which are old and have been rendered unserviceable due to lack of maintenance and/or unavailability of spare parts. In contrast Saudi Arabia has some 700 advanced tanks and more than 250 combat aircraft. Turkey and Egypt, two countries that rival Iran in terms of population size and economic potential, have 4,000 advanced tanks and 425 combat aircraft, and 3,200 tanks and 288 sophisticated military airplanes, respectively.[32] Neither of these two countries have encountered the type of military force that has threatened or been used against Iran since the onset of the Islamic Republic in 1979.

COLLECTIVE SECURITY AND IRANIAN FOREIGN POLICY

Regional security can best be guaranteed when all countries in the Persian Gulf have a stake in stability. Of course, confidence-building measures are needed before any collective security arrangement can work. In the Persian Gulf, a complex set of regional and international factors have been at work to determine what role, if any, Iran should play in the post–Gulf War regional security schemes. In the heat of the Gulf War, Secretary of State James Baker alluded to Iran's role in maintaining Gulf security.[33] In fact, improvements in Iran-Arab relations after the Gulf War and the reestablishment of cordial relations with most Gulf Arabs have made Iranian-Arab cooperation in security matters more feasible. Notwithstanding lingering mutual Iranian and Gulf Arab apprehensions about each other's motives, it is clear that there will be no lasting "regional security system in the Gulf without Iran and that Iran cannot join it without playing the game."[34]

The concept of creating a collective security arrangement in the Persian Gulf region is not new. In February 1981, Saudi Arabia, Kuwait, Qatar, Oman, Bahrain, and the United Arab Emirates established the Gulf Cooperation Council (GCC), partly as a shield against the spillover effects of the Iran-Iraq War.[35] Because of the Saudi dominance over the GCC, and the Saudi-Iranian tensions during the course of the Iran-Iraq War, the GCC became predominantly an anti-Iranian security arrangement with backing from the United States. In the aftermath of the Gulf War, the GCC had an opportunity to change its policy direction and serve as a truly regional organization in light of Iranian attempts to curry favor with it.

Despite Iranian overtures toward the GCC states, the first post–Gulf War security talks to expand the GCC did not include Iran. When the six GCC members met in Damascus on March 5–6, 1991, they drew up a plan for an all-Arab security arrangement. This six plus two meeting (six GCC states plus Syria and Egypt) resulted in the drafting of the Damascus Declaration, which called for, among other things, the establishment of a "new Arab order" emphasizing the safety of Arab states to be guaranteed by an army of 100,000 men dominated by Syrian and Egyptian troops. Although perfunctory and oblique references to Iranian interests were included in the Damascus Declaration, Iran was effectively excluded from playing any role in a region whose stability cannot be separated from its own security. Realizing this fact of geography and Iran's geostrategic location, Syrian president Assad sought to allay Iranian fears of encirclement by stressing the provision in the Damascus Declaration that stated that the new arrangement would not be directed against any other party and would leave the door open for dialogue and cooperation with other Muslim countries, such as Iran.[36]

The six plus two security arrangement, however, never came to fruition as Iran lobbied the GCC states against it, and as the GCC countries began to develop separate security arrangements with Western allies. In the first post–Gulf War summit meeting of the GCC states, held on Christmas Day, 1991, the GCC brushed aside any hope of stationing Syrian and Egyptian troops in the region, a concept against which Iran had lobbied. The final communiqué recognized positive developments between the GCC states and Iran and expressed a strong desire to improve those ties. However, it did not envision direct Iranian participation in any collective security scheme for the region. In a separate interview, Abdullah Bishara, the former secretary general of the GCC, spoke of a role only in terms of the security of waters of the Persian Gulf but not including the land areas of the Arab states of the Persian Gulf. As Bishara put it, Iran's role would be "limited to the sea and other navigation routes because Iran is a major partner in the Gulf waters."[37] For its part, Iran announced that it had no desire to station troops in any GCC states, nor would it object to their signing of security agreements with the West.[38] This reflected a major reversal of the Iranian position on Western involvement in maintaining the security of the GCC states and signaled another victory for the pragmatists in the country's leadership. The Iranian position, announced by Deputy Foreign Minister Ali Mohammad Besharati, however, reiterated that the security of the Persian Gulf is not an exclusively Arab concern and that Iran and the GCC have a mutual interest in maintaining the security of the area. Continuing improvements in Iran-GCC relations in all spheres, especially in the expansion of economic ties, have been the most significant developments in Iranian foreign policy after the Gulf War.

CONTAINMENT REVISITED

The demise of the Soviet Union and the end of the cold war have coincided with a search for a new global enemy "around which the United States can orient its foreign policy."[39] Ironically at a time when Iranian foreign policy has exhibited genuine signs of moderation and pragmatism, the United States has become more ideological and myopic in its dealings with a key Middle Eastern and Muslim political actor. Invoking the specter of the so-called fundamentalist Islam, American strategists have embarked upon what appears to be a concerted effort to confront Iran. The term *containment* has been increasingly used in the same fashion as it had been during the heyday of the U.S.-Soviet cold war, with the "Communist menace" giving way to an equally perceived menace— fundamentalist Islam. Iran has been singled out as the torchbearer of this "menace" whose influence must be "contained." It is within this context that one needs to examine U.S. attempts to scrutinize Iranian foreign policy in all of its dimensions, from the Islamic Republic's relations with the Muslim states of Central Asia to its alleged nuclear arms projects and conventional weapons acquisitions. Similarly, it is within the context of U.S. containment policies that we need to examine the contours of Iran's post–Gulf War foreign policy goals.

Since the end of the Persian Gulf War, numerous American officials and commentators, ranging from the former CIA director Robert Gates to news commentators and editorial pundits have warned us about the alleged nuclear weapons programs underway in Iran.[40] In this vein, American pressure on Argentina and Germany caused these countries to cancel their nuclear agreements with the Islamic Republic.

Although U.S. officials have consistently maintained that they have clear indications that Iran's nuclear ambitions are directed toward developing atomic weapons, Washington "has failed to identify any clandestine facilities in Iran that might be part of a secret nuclear weapons program."[41] In October 1991, the Western press quoted Attaollah Mohajerani, Iran's vice-president for legal and Parliamentary affairs, as having confirmed Iran's intentions to acquire nuclear weapons to counter those possessed by Israel. This statement received wide publicity in the West.

Earlier in June 1991, Mojahedin-e Khalq, an Iranian opposition group operating from bases inside Iraq, claimed that the Islamic Republic was engaged in an ultrasecret nuclear weapons project under the direction of the Revolutionary Guards corps. The Mojahedin further claimed that their information had been obtained through intelligence access to Iran's decision-making circles. In particular, the Mojahedin's report singled out a purported nuclear research center in Mo'allem Kelayeh in the northwest mountainous region near the city of Qazvin as the centerpiece of Iran's nuclear weapons project.[42] However, the International Atomic Energy Agency (IAEA) has refuted claims made by outsiders regarding alleged Iranian nuclear programs. In a February 1992 visit to Iran, the IAEA's inspection team visited several centers of nuclear research

in Iran, including the so-called secret research centers. The IAEA's final
report read in part:

> We are pleased to confirm that there does not seem to be a
> shred of evidence on the allegations that were made in the
> [Western] media. . . . As a rule, we have confined our nuclear
> activities within the framework of Nuclear Non-Proliferation
> Treaty. . . . As far as nuclear matters are concerned Iran has
> been compelled to establish the fact that all allegations leveled
> against its nuclear activity are without foundation.[43]

This does not mean that Iran is not involved in nuclear research and
activity. After a hiatus of six years following the victory of the Iranian
Revolution, Iran began to revive nuclear research programs developed
under the Shah's government. After the Gulf War, Iran obtained a calutron
from China, heightening speculation that the Islamic Republic intended
to duplicate Iraq's efforts in using calutron to enrich uranium for nuclear
weapons projects. However, Iran's calutron, unlike that of Iraq's, was
described by U.S. officials as "desktop sized" and useful only for producing isotopes that would be "irritated in the reactor and converted into
radioactive materials useful in research and medicine."[44] Furthermore, in
contrast to Iraq's calutrons, which were designed to reach currents up to
600 milliamps, Iran's calutron current is only one milliamp. This will render it useless for enriching bomb-grade uranium. The nature of Iran's
nuclear programs, if any, will undoubtedly remain a matter of concern
and speculation. As of this writing, Iran remains under a nuclear embargo
by the West. This makes it extremely difficult for the Islamic Republic to
rely on nuclear energy for peaceful purposes, such as nuclear medicine
research and power generation. What is clear is that the United States
and Iran will remain at loggerheads over this issue, with negative consequences for improvements in their relations.

Iran's conventional arms policy is another important determinant of
the country's foreign policy decisions. The United States has also confronted Iran over this issue in the aftermath of the Persian Gulf War.
High-ranking Iranian leaders have consistently reiterated their intention
to reequip the country's armed forces with conventional weapons, many
of which were lost during the Iran-Iraq War. In fact, they have stressed
the fact that Iran, like every other country, has the right to defend itself
against a host of potential adversaries. In a March 1992 speech to a
group of graduating air corps cadets, President Rafsanjani stated: "There
is no doubt that defense of our borders cannot be achieved without

adequate modern weapons. You should rest assured that your country's leadership will do its utmost to equip you with the best weapons that can be within our means."[45] In the post–Gulf War period, Iran's major weapons purchases have been limited to importing Scud missiles from North Korea and, until its dissolution, tank, artillery, and airplanes from the Soviet Union. The Islamic Republic has reportedly purchased 48 MiG-29s (with no guarantees of spare parts) and three outmoded Kilo-class submarines from Russia as part of the now defunct agreement negotiated in 1989 between Rafsanjani and Gorbachev.[46] Iran is also producing its own short-range rockets, such as the Chinese-designed Oghab with a range of 40 kilometers.[47] The United States, at times, has sought to stop Iran's arms purchases from China and North Korea. In March 1992, reports surfaced that the United States was pondering whether or not to board a North Korean ship, which was sailing to the Iranian port of Bandar Abbas, and search it for contraband items.[48] Although the U.S. officers did not board the ship, the incident nevertheless demonstrated the potential for serious U.S.-Iranian conflict on the high seas. The Iranian government even issued a statement calling the threatened U.S. action an act of "international banditry" and a clear violation of the legal norms of international trade and commerce. Irrespective of the current level of Iranian arms purchases, the asymmetrical military balance in the Persian Gulf will continue to compel the Iranian authorities to search for weapons to deter a would-be regional aggressor.

Finally, the end of the Gulf War and the demise of the Soviet Union have provided a unique opportunity for Iran to expand its theater of diplomatic operations to Central Asia and the Caucasus region. These regions have long-standing historical, cultural, and economic ties with Iran. Given the geographic proximity of these areas to Iran, what happens in Central Asia and the Caucasus will have a direct impact on Iran's national security interests. Although many of the Islamic Republic's public statements have been couched in religious terms, it is realpolitik that has guided Tehran's approach to the newly independent neighbors to its north.

Foreign Minister Velayati has been an active player in seeking to resolve the dispute between the republics of Azerbaijan and Armenia over the disputed area of Nagorno-Karabakh. Iran's good offices and mediation efforts between the predominantly Shia Azeris and Christian Armenians are clear indications of the ascendancy of pragmatism over ideology in Iran's new foreign policy posture. Although Iran has been involved in building new mosques in several Central Asian republics and has dispatched clerics to these areas, the Islamic Republic's efforts in this regard are dwarfed by the activities of Saudi Arabia. Building regional cooperation and strengthening economic ties have been the salient characteristics of Iranian foreign policy in Central Asia. Iran was the leading advocate of the expansion of the membership of the Economic Cooperation Organization (ECO), a loose economic union that until recently included only Iran, Turkey, and Pakistan. At Iran's urging, the membership of ECO was expanded in early 1992 to include Azerbaijan and the Central Asian republics of Turkmenistan, Uzbekistan, Tajikistan, and Kyrgyzstan. Similarly, Iran has organized a new organization of the Caspian Sea Users to enhance economic cooperation among the Caspian Sea littoral states.

The expansion and improvement of Iran's relations with its northern neighbors have been viewed with alarm by Washington, which has ignored the pragmatic causes of Iran's foreign policy in this area and has instead chosen to magnify the so-called fundamentalist threat to the region. Former Secretary of State James Baker's official trip to Central Asia and the Caucasus in February 1992 was designed in large part to dissuade the countries of these regions from developing closer ties with Iran.[49] When then President Ayaz Mutalibov of Azerbaijan was asked about the threat of "Iranian fundamentalism," he summarily dismissed the question as "stupid."[50] Similarly, then president Rakhman Nabiyev of Tajikistan dismissed the alarming threat of "Islamic fundamental-ism" in his Farsi-speaking republic by criticizing outsiders, both from the West and the Muslim world, who seek to predetermine the parameters of Tajikistan's foreign policy. As Nabiyev put it: "Those who want to bring us under their influence are badly mistaken. We will go our own way—the way to cooperation with all the peoples of the world—and will learn from the achievements of *both East and West.*"[51] Tajik affinity to Iran is not necessarily for the Islamic Republic but for the cultural ties that have bound Persians and Tajiks together for centuries. The most pervasive ties that are developing between Tajikistan and Iran involve scholars, merchants, and literary figures. To a large extent, this pattern holds true with respect to Iran's relations with the other Central Asian republics and the Caucasus.

In the final analysis, it is too early to offer a definitive assessment of the future development of Iranian foreign policy. However, in most cases pragmatism and the requirements of realpolitik have already brought about noticeable transformations in the Islamic Republic's regional relations. What remains unclear is how Iran's foreign policy toward the United States will evolve. To a large extent, future developments in this area will depend on the role of the "Iran syndrome" in American foreign policy in the Middle East.

NOTES TO CHAPTER 6

1. *Ettela'at,* 23 January 1989, 4.

2. *Tehran Times,* 23 January 1989, 2.

3. Martin Walker, "The U.S. and the Persian Gulf Crisis," *World Policy Journal,* vol. 7, no. 4 (Fall 1990): 796.

4. See Noam Chomsky, "'What We Say Goes': The Middle East in the New World Order," in *Collateral Damage: The New World Order at Home and Abroad,* Cynthia Peters, ed. (Boston: South End Press, 1992), 82–88; John Stockwell, *The Praetorian Guard: The U.S. Role in the New World Order* (Boston: South End Press, 1991), 131–139; and Holy Sklar, "Brave New World Order," in *Collateral Damage: The New World at Home and Abroad,* Cynthia Peters, ed. (Boston: South End Press, 1992), 22–34.

5. Charles Krauthammer, "The Unipolar Moment," *Foreign Affairs (America and the World 1990/91),* vol. 70, no. 1 (1991): 33.

6. *Insight,* 24 December 1990–7 January 1991, 14.

7. *Wall Street Journal,* 18 March 1992, A14.

8. Mark Sommer, "The War Over the Meaning of the Gulf War," *Christian Science Monitor,* 18 March 1991, 18.

9. Fred Halliday, "The Ayatollah Syndrome," *Guardian Weekly,* 23 February 1992, 11.

10. *Iran Times,* 21 September 1990.

11. Said Amir Arjomand, "A Victory for the Pragmatists: The Islamic Fundamentalist Reaction in Iran," in *Islamic Fundamentalism and the Gulf Crisis,* James Piscatori, ed. (Chicago, Ill.: The Fundamentalism Project, American Academy of Arts and Sciences, 1991), 56.

12. *International Herald Tribune,* 21 March 1991, 7.

13. *Iran Times*, 11 January 1991, 15.

14. Norman Friedman, *Desert Victory: The War for Kuwait* (Annapolis, Md.: Naval Institute Press, 1991), 163–164.

15. Amir Arjomand, op. cit., 63.

16. *Kayhan* (Tehran), 9 March 1991, 2.

17. Safa Haeri, "Enemies Again," *Middle East International*, no. 396 (March 22, 1991): 15.

18. *Christian Science Monitor*, 14 March 1991, 2.

19. Mohammad Jafar Mahallati, "The U.S. Should Work Closely with the Iraqi Opposition," *Christian Science Monitor*, 27 March 1991, 19.

20. Hooshang Amirahmadi and Nader Entessar, "Iranian-Arab Relations in Transition," in *Iran and the Arab World*, Hooshang Amirahmadi and Nader Entessar, eds. (New York: St. Martin's Press, 1992), 1–18.

21. "The Today Show," NBC-TV, April 5, 1991.

22. Amirahmadi and Entessar, op. cit., 16.

23. Peter W. Rodam, "Don't Back Down: Humiliate Hussein," *New York Times*, 22 February 1991, A17.

24. Elie Kedourie, "Avoiding a Third Gulf War," *New York Times*, 13 March 1991, A15.

25. Nader Entessar, "Non-Provocative Defence in the Persian Gulf," in *Reconstruction and Regional Diplomacy in the Persian Gulf*, Hooshang Amirahmadi and Nader Entessar, eds. (London and New York: Routledge, 1992), 216–220.

26. Anoushirvan Ehteshami and Gerd Nonneman, *War and Peace in the Gulf: Domestic Politics and Regional Relations into the 1990s* (Reading, United Kingdom: Ithaca Press, 1991), 97–106.

27. *Christian Science Monitor*, 31 March 1992, 1.

28. Shireen Hunter, "The Flaws in U.S. Thinking," *Middle East International*, no. 393 (February 8, 1991): 22.

29. Leon T. Hadar, "Creating a U.S. Policy of Constructive Disengagement in the Middle East," Cato Institute, *Policy Analysis*, no. 125 (December 29, 1989): 1.

30. Earl C. Ravenal, *Designing Defense for a New World Order: The Military Budget in 1992 and Beyond* (Washington, D.C.: Cato Institute, 1991), 13–14.

31. Shireen Hunter, "Iran Through a Distorted Lens," *Christian Science Monitor*, 2 March 1992, 19.

32. International Institute for Strategic Studies, *The Military Balance 1991–1992* (London: Brassey's, 1991), 74–75, 104, 106, and 117.

33. *International Herald Tribune*, 7 February 1991, 3.

34. Richard C. Hottelet, "Iran's Part in Gulf Puzzle," *Christian Science Monitor*, 21 March 1991, 18.

35. For details, see Nader Entessar, "External Involvement in the Persian Gulf Conflict," *Conflict Quarterly*, vol. 4 no. 4 (Fall 1984): 43–44; Joseph A. Kechichian, "The Gulf Cooperation Council: Search for Security," *Third World Quarterly*, vol. 7, no. 4 (October 1985): 853–881; and R. K. Ramazani, *The Gulf Cooperation: Record and Analysis* (Charlottesville, Va.: University Press of Virginia, 1988).

36. Gerald Butt, "Eight Pairs of Eyes on Iraq," *Middle East International*, no. 396 (March 22, 1991): 10.

37. *Iran Times*, 10 January 1992, 15.

38. *Iran Times*, 17 January 1992, 2.

39. David Ignatius, "The West's Next Crusade: Fighting Fundamentalist Islamic Rule," *Washington Post National Weekly Edition*, 16–22 March 1992, 23.

40. *New York Times*, 23 January and 29 March 1992; A4 and *Wall Street Journal*, 18 March 1992, A1.

41. David Albright and Mark Hibbs, "Spotlight Shifts to Iran," *Bulletin of the Atomic Scientists*, vol. 48, no. 2 (March 1992): 9.

42. *NLA Journal* (a publication of the National Liberation Army of Iran) (November 1991): 63.

43. *New York Times*, 13 February 1992, A6.

44. Albright and Hibbs, op. cit., 10.

45. *Iran Times*, 20 March 1992, 2.

46. Norman Friedman, "Russia Stages a Fire Sale," *Proceedings U.S. Naval Institute,* vol. 118, no. 4 (April 1992): 123.

47. For details, see Nader Entessar, "The Challenge of Political Reconstruction in Iran," in *Modern Capitalism and Islamic Ideology in Iran,* Cyrus Bina and Hamid Zangeneh, eds. (New York: St. Martin's Press, 1992), 221; Lora Lumpe, Lisbeth Gronlund, and David C. Wright, "Third World Missiles Fall Short," *Bulletin of the Atomic Scientists,* vol. 48, no. 2 (March 1992): 34; and W. Seth Carus, *Ballistic Missiles in Modern Conflict* (New York: Praeger Publishers, 1991), 20.

48. *New York Times,* 6 March 1992, A6.

49. *New York Times,* 6 and 13 February 1992, A3 and A7.

50. *New York Times,* 13 February 1992, A7.

51. *Iran Times,* 20 March 1992, 15.

7

THE CHANGE OF ECONOMIC AND INDUSTRIAL POLICY IN IRAN: PRESIDENT RAFSANJANI'S PERESTROIKA

Hamid Hosseini

INTRODUCTION

The Iranian Revolution of 1979 was supported by people of all walks of life and of diverse ideological persuasions. In spite of the diversity of the politico-economic goals of these different political factions, the end result, at least in the realms of politics and ideology, was very close to what Ayatollah Khomeini had envisioned in his political work *Velayat-e Faqih.*[1] Ignoring the politico-economic and social goals of secular and more moderate Islamic forces active in the anti-Shah revolution, Khomeini and his associates sought to create a "true" Islamic society. This was justified on the basis of the favorable results of a referendum in which Iranian voters were asked to choose between monarchy and an undefined Islamic republic.[2]

In the name of Islam, the emerging Islamic leadership took very drastic economic measures. These drastic measures made the already important public sector substantially more powerful and provided the government with many new economic roles. It was during this period that banks and insurance companies were nationalized, government came to own and/or control all large manufacturing enterprises, foreign investment was halted, and the government became more involved in direct productive activities. These actions, by reducing the economic role of the private sector, made the public sector the more active component of the economy. Many authors have studied the economic impacts of the Islamic revolution in Iran. These include studies by Katouzian (1989), Behdad (1988), Zangeneh (1992), Valibiegi (1991), Amir Ahmadi (1991), and Hosseini (1988, 1990, 1993).

However, the extent of these drastic economic measures had not been anticipated. There were many reasons for that. For example, Khomeini's politico-religious writings were devoid of economic analysis and, more important, they did not present the economic blueprint of a "true" Islamic society.[3] In addition, these measures, at least partly, were traditionally regarded as un-Islamic.[4]

In essence, the economic structure that emerged after the 1979 revolution, although given an Islamic pretense, resulted from a process of improvisation rooted in the expediency of Iranian Islamic leaders and their deep desire to create an Islamic society/government at any price. In other words, the need to provide a quick response to pressing politico-economic problems, the desire to establish a (Shiite) Islamic government, the absence of specific Islamic economic guidelines for a modern economy, the need to weaken the economic base of the Shah's regime, the need to defuse and discredit the radical demands of Marxist and other radical intellectuals, the desire to consolidate the politico-religious power of Khomeini and his associates, and the need to prevent the further deterioration of the economy made that improvisation necessary and feasible.

The aforementioned drastic economic measures will be discussed first. This will be done by observing the activities of the Islamic regime during the early months of the revolution and by referring to the decrees issued by Ayatollah Khomeini and those issued by the Islamic Revolutionary Council, and by analyzing the 1979 Islamic constitution of Iran, which replaced the relatively secular constitution of 1906. It will be argued that these measures were not necessarily Islamic.

Next the new economic and industrial policies of the Islamic Republic will be discussed. It will be argued that the Islamic government is liberalizing and relaxing many of its formerly drastic economic measures. This can be seen by looking at actual changes taking place and statements made by key leaders of the Islamic government. Obviously, because changes in Iran are new, my discussion of recent changes pertains largely to pronouncements and goals rather than to accomplishments. Examples of these relaxations are privatization of certain industries, the revival of the stock market, and policies dealing with foreign investment. An attempt will also be made to demonstrate the reasons for and causes of these policy changes. As a result of this endeavor, it will be demonstrated that the government of President Rafsanjani is becoming less ideological and more pragmatic.

It is rather tempting to compare Gorbachev's *perestroika* to the one presently taking place in Iran. Undoubtedly, economic changes that took place in the former Soviet Union constituted a departure from Soviet Marxism. After all, privatization of publicly owned enterprises, emphasizing the market mechanism, and introducing the profit motive are not what Lenin and the Bolshevik Party had in mind when they introduced socialism in 1917. Such policies can be called what Marxists often refer to as revisionist. However, such a claim cannot be made with regard to the economic changes in Iran. There is nothing un-Islamic (that is, in opposition to the Islamic economic system) about these liberalization policies. It will be argued that Islam (its economic principles) in no way opposes the new economic changes undertaken by the Islamic government in Iran. In fact, it can (and will) be argued that these policies are more Islamic than the economic measures taken during the early months of the Islamic Revolution. Recent liberalization policies in Iran are more capitalist, and, as demonstrated, Islam is not necessarily anticapitalist. It should be noted that the object is not to show that recent developments in Iran are merely a variant of what has transpired in the former Soviet Union.

CONFISCATIONS AND NATIONALIZATIONS: THE ISLAMIC REPUBLIC'S EMPHASIS ON THE PUBLIC SECTOR

The Case of Confiscations

The postrevolutionary expansion of the public sector in Iran began during the early days of the 1979 revolution. This substantial increase resulted from nationalizations, as well as confiscation, of privately owned firms. These public takeovers were made legal by government and religious decrees as well as by articles of the 1979 constitution. Let's begin with what took place in practice and their legal and religious justifications, then we will discuss their legal base in the constitution.

The properties of many Iranian industrialists were confiscated during the first days of February during the 1979 revolution. These activities, which under normal circumstances could have been viewed as un-

Islamic (and thus sinful), were justified by a decree from Ayatollah Khomeini, who had emerged as the supreme politico-religious leader of Iran.[5] According to Khomeini's March 1, 1979, decree, the Revolutionary Council was instructed to confiscate all the properties of the Pahlavi family (the royal family) and their associates, since they had obtained these assets using illegitimate means. This was done in the name of the "oppressed people of Iran." To manage and control the tremendous amount of wealth created by Khomeini's confiscation decree, an organization known as the Mostazafan Foundation (Foundation for the Oppressed) was created on March 6, 1979. This foundation grew into a gigantic economic entity rather rapidly, which in terms of size and magnitude of economic activity, became second only to the central government. Table 7.1 indicates the extent of the wealth this foundation controlled in 1981. (The items in the third column are those that were decided by Islamic courts established during the revolution.)

TABLE 7.1

Economic Units Owned or Managed by the Mostazafan Foundation by Type of Economic Activity in 1981

Activity	Confiscated	Judgement Pending	Total
Industrial	112	37	149
Mining	24	40	64
Agricultural	465	7	472
Construction	67	34	101
Cultural	13	12	25
Commercial	79	159	238
Real Estate	2786	—	2786

SOURCE: Mostazafan Foundation, *Annual Report in Analysis of Economic Changes After the Revolution,* Central Bank of the Islamic Republic of Iran, 1982.

The extent of this control is also obvious from a statement by the foundation director in 1983. He said, "With the possession of about 200 large factories, 150 thousand large buildings, including palaces, homes, warehouses, and so on, more than 70 percent of the total number of movie theaters, 50 large and small mines, more than 120 construction companies, livestock breeders, and poultry hatcheries, a significant amount of jewelry—some unique in the world—various agrobusiness entities and thousands of acres of agricultural land, the organization is one of the largest economic conglomerates in the world and the largest in Iran."[6]

The Impact of Nationalization Activities on the Public Sector

The purpose of the nationalization activities of the Islamic Republic was different from the purpose of confiscations. Confiscation of properties belonging to the royal family and the close associates of the Shah's regime was a political act aimed at eliminating its economic base and power. Nationalizations, on the other hand, emerged as a result of a debate among Iranian leaders with political, economic, and ideological dimensions. Two examples of this debate were those among various members of the Revolutionary Council and among the various factions of the Assembly of Islamic Experts, who were in charge of framing the new (1979) constitution. The nationalization decision took many by surprise since Islam has traditionally respected the right to private ownership of property (including ownership of the means of production).[7] For different factions of the Islamic leadership nationalization had different motives and reasons. For some, the main reason was the severe crisis of management due to the departure of owners and managers of large enterprises from Iran, who left fearing the unrest before and during the revolution. This crisis had given rise to a low level of productivity. For example, as Bank-e Markazi (Central Bank) data indicate, the large industrial enterprises, before their nationalizations in 1979, were producing at about 59 percent of their capacities. The Revolutionary Council's "legislation number 6738" was originally passed to assign managers to these troubled enterprises.

For others, the main reason for nationalization was to provide a solution to the economic crisis preceding the 1979 revolution. For example, even as early as 1977, the banking system had difficulties, which had resulted from an overextension of credit and very low reserve ratios. This emergency was admitted by a Bank-e Markazi governor in a published report. The crisis was particularly obvious in the case of Bank-e-Iranian, when Citibank reduced its share of the bank from 35 percent to 5 percent.[8]

Still for others the main reason for nationalization was ideological. This was particularly the case among those Hosseini in 1988 had referred to as the "reactive" group.[9] In the name of Islam, many such Islamic leaders were "out-Marxisting" Marxist organizations when it came to ideological issues. This was particularly true when this radicalism was combined with their anti-modern and anti-Western cultural attitudes. For moderate Islamic forces, however, ideology played a very minor role. This is reflected in Prime Minister Bazargan's statement in 1979 that: "We respect private property, but in view of undesirable and unprofitable conditions in the banks, to protect national rights and wealth and to get the wheels of the economy moving, we deemed it necessary to nationalize the banks."[10]

On June 8, 1979, the Revolutionary Council issued a decree in which the Provisional Government of Mehdi Bazargan was instructed to make proper provisions for the management of all 28 private banks (11 with foreign ownership participation), which held 43.9 percent of the total assets of all Iranian banks. Because of the close association of private bankers with the Shah's regime, and also because of Islamic prohibition of usury, the stockholders of these nationalized banks received no compensation. The banking system had already gone through important changes prior to the June 8, 1979, decree. One such change was the emergence of a very stringent foreign exchange market. While Iran had no exchange controls during the last few years of the Shah's regime, the Iranian Revolution brought back more stringent foreign exchange controls. The Islamic regime initially imposed foreign exchange controls to stop the capital flight. But, it did not take much time for foreign exchange controls to become an integral policy imprint of the Islamic government for rationing the existing supply of foreign currency in the face of a widening foreign exchange gap.[11]

Nationalizations went much beyond those of the banking system mentioned earlier. On June 25, 1979, the Islamic government nationalized the entire insurance industry, which, at the time, consisted of some 11 insurance companies. This was followed by a more drastic measure of nationalization on July 5, 1979, when the Islamic government nationalized, without any compensation, the private assets of basic metal industries (steel, copper, and aluminum), the assets of 53 of the largest Iranian industrialists and their immediate families because "they had gained from their illegitimate ties with the Shah's regime," as well as the assets of manufacturing enterprises whose debts to Iranian banks exceeded the value of their assets.

The July 5, 1979, decree and what followed subsequently had the following impact on Iranian industries:

> 1. The oil, gas, petrochemical, steel, electricity, railroads, and
>   a few other industries, which were publicly owned under
>   the Shah, remained government owned and controlled after
>   the revolution. As a result of this act, other strategic industries
>   such as metallurgical, automotive, shipping, and aircraft
>   industries also came under government control and
>   ownership. And, by the summer of 1980, the government

took over the operations of the National Iranian Oil Company's four foreign-operated joint ventures and placed them under the control of the Iranian government's Continental Shell Oil Company.

2. Various types of companies established by associates of the Shah and his relatives, often through illegal means and preferential treatments, were also nationalized.

3. Nationalizations also extended to firms whose liabilities to the banking system exceeded their assets. If a firm's assets exceeded its debts to the banking system, the Islamic government became a shareholder. The shares owned by the government were proportional to the firm's debts to these nationalized banks. As a result of postrevolutionary nationalizations in Iran, the government's share of non-oil manufacturing enterprises went up substantially. For example, in 1976, the government owned and controlled 37.6 percent of manufacturing establishments with 50 to 999 workers and 95.7 percent of those with more than 1,000 workers. This amounted to government control of 3.5 percent of all (small and large) manufacturing enterprises. In contrast, in 1982, the share went up from 3.5 percent to 14.2 percent. These enterprises produced 70.9 percent of the value added in these industries and employed 68.1 percent of workers in the non-oil manufacturing sector. Obviously, by 1982, 100 percent of enterprises that employed 1,000 workers or more were controlled by the public sector, which also includes the Mostazafan Foundation.

THE 1979 CONSTITUTION AND ITS EMPHASIS ON THE PUBLIC SECTOR

As a consequence of the 1979 Islamic Revolution, the relatively secular constitution of 1906 was replaced by an Islamic one. This Islamic constitution, as well as its 1988 amendment, depicts an "Islamic" society in which the public sector plays a very significant role. In this constitution, as is obvious from Article 43, the government is given the responsibilities of bringing about economic independence and eliminating poverty. Specifically, the public sector is given the responsibility to "satisfy fundamental needs for shelter, food, clothing, health care, education, and the requirement of universal preservation of the institution of marriage."[12] In other words, according to the 1979 constitution, it is government and not the individual that has been given the responsibility to achieve these goals. In addition, the framers of the

1979 constitution also gave the Islamic government the responsibility to achieve full employment.

The 1979 Islamic Constitution creates the framework for the Iranian economy. This is obvious from Article 44, where various types of "Islamic" property ownerships are discussed. This article recognizes three forms of property ownerships: public, cooperative, and private, giving the central role to public ownership. This central role for the public sector is obvious from the types of industries that the constitution has designated as government-owned. According to Article 44, "The government sector includes all large enterprises, key (basic) industries, foreign commerce, large mines, banks, insurance companies, electric power industry, dams, large irrigation networks, radio and television networks, the postal service, telegraph and telephone, the airline industry, shipping, the railroad industry, and all similar industries."[13]

Article 45 of the 1979 constitution complements Article 44 by extending public ownership to other areas. The constitution clearly states: "Enfal [assets at the disposal and control of the Prophet and Shiite imams] and public assets such as mavat [unusable land] underdeveloped lands or abandoned lands, mines, seas, lakes, rivers and other public waterways, mountains, valleys, forests, marshes and natural wet lands, unclaimed pastures, unclaimed estates, assets whose owners are not known, and public properties retaken from unlawful owners should all be under the control of the Islamic government."[14]

As is now obvious, the role given to the private sector in the 1979 constitution is only a minor one. In contrast to what is assumed under capitalism, in this constitution the private sector is not the regulator of the entire economy. Rather, it is only a complement of the public sector. This is obvious from Article 44, where it is stated that "the private sector includes those parts of agriculture, animal husbandry, manufacturing, commerce, and services which complement the activities of the public and cooperative sectors."[15]

In the Islamic Constitution of 1979, the government's economic influence far exceeds its large share of ownership of various sectors of the economy. The Islamic government is also given a tremendous amount of regulative power over the private sector. These regulative powers, which have their base in Islamic jurisprudence, can be regarded as very restrictive by the private sector. According to Article 49: "The (Islamic) government is obligated to take away the wealth acquired through usury, usurpation, bribe, extortion, burglary, gambling, the unlawful taking of religious endowments, abuses of government contracts, the sale of mavat and other nonprivate lands, and the wealth acquired through immoral activities and return them to their rightful owners. When rightful owners cannot be found, the (Islamic) government is obligated to add them to public property."[16]

Among the nine sections of Article 43, a few deal with the (Islamic) government's right to regulate the private sector. For example, section five provides the Islamic government with the powers "to prevent: harmful activities committed against others, monopolies, hoarding (of goods), usury, and other religiously unacceptable transactions."[17]

The powers granted to the Islamic government in the 1979 constitution are by no means restricted to the domestic economy; the government is also given the responsibility to regulate and control the external aspects of the Iranian economy. Section eight of Article 43 obligates the government "to prevent the domination of Iran's economy by foreign countries."[18] The framers of the 1979 constitution, perhaps to defuse Marxian critiques, banned foreign investment in various sectors of the Iranian economy. According to Article 81, "Granting foreign nationals permission to establish firms and institutions in the areas of commerce, manufacturing, mining, and services is absolutely forbidden."[19]

Article 82 extends the ban even to the use of foreign consultants by the Islamic government. For it states, "Employing foreign consultants by the [Islamic] government is forbidden. When these services become necessary, the government must seek the parliament's approval."[20]

NEW CHANGES IN ECONOMIC AND INDUSTRIAL POLICY IN IRAN

Eastern Europe and the republics of the former Soviet Union are not the only countries advocating privatization and other forms of economic liberalizations. Many Third World countries (Turkey, Latin America, and others) are also in the process of privatizing their public enterprises. These are inspired by what happened in former socialist countries as well as the change of emphasis of the World Bank and The International Monetary Fund favoring privatization and economic liberalization. The Islamic Republic of Iran is going through a great deal more economic change than other Third World countries. During the last few years, officials of the Islamic Republic have come to realize the enormity of economic problems that Iran faces. Iranian leaders now acknowledge that their policies during the first ten years of the Islamic rule—their severe control of industrial enterprises, and their restrictions of, and interventions in, the activities of the private sector—were not particularly fruitful.[21]

Of course, the Iranian government also has been influenced by the policies of the World Bank and the IMF.

As a result of these changes, the leadership of the Islamic Republic has become less ideological and more economically motivated. To understand the extent of this change, a comparison of a well-publicized statement by Khomeini in 1979 and a statement by Rafsanjani made some ten years later could prove to be useful.

Khomeini said in 1979, "Some persons have come to me and said now that the revolution is over, now we must preserve our economic infrastructure. But our people rose for Islam, not for economic infrastructure. What is this economic infrastructure anyway? Donkeys and camels need hay. That's economic infrastructure. But human beings need Islam."[22]

President Rafsanjani said almost ten years later: "Can we be independent without productivity? Do we always have to get our wheat, meat, industrial parts, machinery, and skilled manpower from others? If so, we have nothing—neither political independence nor economic independence."[23] Since 1989, key Iranian leaders have, rather frankly, talked about liberalizing the Iranian economy by advocating a rather pro-market strategy.

In the last few years, Iran has sought various changes of economic and industrial policy. While some of these changes of economic and industrial policy have already been implemented, others are said to be forthcoming soon, and still others have been discussed by key leaders in Iran. The fact that these changes are even being suggested implies a drastic change of economic-industrial policies, since, up until a few years ago, such change was considered to be taboo. President Rafsanjani and other Iranians who hold key economic positions advocate new (and different) economic-industrial policies. For example, Kayhan Havai on March 11, 1992, reported President Rafsanjani's support for private sector investment in heavy industry.[24] The Rafsanjani administration supports many such changes. For example, in a recent speech given to a group of German business representatives visiting Tehran, an Iranian official made the following remarks: "To further economic growth in Iran, the Iranian government has consistently attempted to increase the efficiency of manufacturing enterprises, to reduce government red tape encountered by businesses, to facilitate commerce, to emphasize and advocate the growth of the private sector, to revive and strengthen the Tehran stock exchange, and to invite back to Iran technocrats who left home during and (immediately) after the revolution."[25]

In fact, various Iranian leaders have invited back exile Iranian industrialists to Iran to take over their expropriated firms. According to these aforementioned remarks, privatization and the revival of the Tehran stock exchange, which is essential for this process, are being emphasized to reflect the new policy of freer trade and less government regulation of the economy. In 1992, M. H. Adeli, the governor of Bank-e Markazi Iran (Central Bank of Iran), who also heads the Iranian Stock and Securities Commission, has advocated various relaxation policies for the Iranian economy, including privatization and the strengthening of the Tehran Stock Exchange.[26] Attending a recent conference in Tehran about securities and stock markets in Iran, he made some very important points that signify significant departures from previous practices of Iranian Islamic leaders. The gist of his speech was as follows: (1) Economic concepts and matters, which are usually politicized in Iran, should be free of politics and ideology and should be taken seriously; (2) At this juncture of Iranian history, economic development and growth are *absolutely necessary*. It is important to realize that a pro-growth economic policy requires that people (private individuals) are taken seriously; (3) A stock exchange is necessary for the achievement of economic growth. Presently, he stated, the pace of its revival is slow. However, with the sale of some of the public enterprises to the private sector and with the replacement of their managers with private ones, the stock market would improve; (4) Inefficient and unprofitable public enterprises must close down. Iran's precious national wealth should not be wasted on the inefficient policy of "domestic production at any price"; (5) Since in Iran capital is a scarce factor, the stock market should be used as an important means of capital formation.[27]

Privatization policies were also advocated by the minister of Economy and Treasury, Mohssen Nourbakhsh.[28] In a recent IMF/World Bank conference held in Thailand, Nourbakhsh advocated privatization of public enterprises and stated that many such enterprises are being sold to the private sector. Privatization policies are also supported by Nezhad Hosseinian, Iran's minister of heavy industry.[29] To him, the private sector must play a significant role in the process of industrialization. Thus, it must be supported by the government. In a recent speech he said, "Private firms must be supported so that they become self-sufficient and dynamic. . . . any entrepreneur interested in investing in heavy industry would have the cooperation of the Ministry of Heavy Industry."[30]

Along the same lines, Hassan Habibi, Iran's first vice-president, has said that the Islamic government would support (financially, and so on) any

entrepreneur with a meaningful implementable industrial project.[31] The
Ministry of Labor and Social Affairs recently announced the procedures
for transferring shares of public enterprises to workers and employees of
those enterprises.[32] There is also discussion of selling the stocks of the
expropriated, and now public, enterprises back to the private sector.[33]
The government has also announced the privatization of more than four
million acres of farmland expropriated from the Pahlavi family during the
revolution.[34] The minister of petroleum has discussed allowing the private
sector to invest in the petrochemical industry. At the end of 1991, the
Iranian government announced an agreement made between the government and the private sector to establish nine petrochemical projects.[35]
However, this unprecedented decision will not be extended to the strategically important oil industry proper. In addition, the Islamic government
has allowed the private sector to invest in mining industry.[36]

As we saw earlier, Article 81 of the 1979 constitution forbids foreign
investment. Ignoring Article 81, or interpreting that article as a ban on
100 percent foreign ownership, or at least as a ban on more than 49 percent, Iranian leaders have consistently advocated the attraction of foreign investment to Iran in recent months. For example, at the IMF–
World Bank conference in Thailand, Mohssen Nourbakhsh, the Iranian
minister of Economy and Treasury, expressed his government's support
for the attraction of foreign investment, particularly in agriculture and
the petrochemical industry. Perhaps to neutralize Rafsanjani's hard-line
critics, he said this decision will not lead to foreign debt, because it
would be in the form of joint ventures.[37]

During the same conference, Bank-e Markazi Governor M. H. Adeli
also stated that the Islamic government is more in favor of the attraction
of foreign investment. He said this would cause a substantial strengthening of Iran's economic infrastructure. Again, to fend off any criticism
from Rafsanjani opponents, he said Iran would be very careful in its
choices of foreign investment—Iran would simply not allow any foreign
company to invest if it is not sure of its positive contributions.[38]

Quoting Adeli and Nourbakhsh, the Center for Iranian Research and
Analysis (CIRA) newsletter reports that foreign investors may own up
to 100 percent of their businesses and will be able to repatriate profits
out of Iran. In fact, the prerevolutionary Law for Promotion and
Production of Foreign Investments has been revived with modifications
to suit the new economic realities of Iran.[39]

According to officials of the Ministry of Economy and Treasury, Iran
is seeking $27.4 billion in foreign investment for its five-year plan, $8.5

billion of which has already been secured.[40] In accordance with its new policy, Iran has sought cooperation in joint ventures with Western Europe, Canada, Japan, Australia, New Zealand, some Arab states in the Persian Gulf, and Iranian businessmen living in those Arab countries. Agreements already made for producing petrochemicals, aluminum, and steel with these partners, automobile production, and joint investments to be made in the Iranian islands of Qeshm and Kish in the Persian Gulf, are testimonies to the change of policy.[41]

Another change of policy that Iran has desired to bring about is in the area of foreign exchange controls. Iran has realized that the type of economic changes it desires requires less stringent exchange controls. Iranian officials seem to be committed to the relaxation of the stringent foreign exchange-rate policy that emerged during the 1979 revolution as a result of the need for foreign exchange during the war with Iraq. Iranian officials, particularly Bank-e-Markazi Governor M. H. Adeli, have spoken about the need to stabilize the Iranian currency (the rial) and its convertibility, and the necessity of a one-rate system.[42] Steps that have already been taken are as follows: according to Bank-e Markazi officials, Iranian rial became convertible in Iranian banks in the Persian Gulf countries beginning in October 23, 1991. At the same time, it was announced that those branches would denominate letters of credit in Iranian rial, rather than in the U.S. dollar or in any other major currency. Another major development has been reducing the several rate system policy of each major currency to a three rate system. For example, for the U.S. dollar, there is a 70 rials to one dollar rate to be used by the government for the purchase of wheat, sugar, and tea from abroad, a rate of 600 rials for every dollar for the purchase of certain essential raw materials and some essential finished goods, and a rate of 1,300 rials for every dollar for the purchase of other items. But, for the rial to be truly convertible, they need to establish a one-rate system. Officials have recently announced that this system would be established in a year or two.[43]

Another new development is changing the restrictive postrevolutionary policy that led to the shortage, and thus the astronomical rise in prices, of automobiles in Iran. The shortage was primarily caused by the almost total ban on the importation of foreign cars, trucks, and buses, and the inability of Iran to come up with sufficient foreign currency to purchase needed parts made in Europe for its auto-producing plants during its eight-year war with Iraq.[44]

Iran's restrictive policy toward the importation of automobiles, trucks, and buses and toward international agreement enhancing domestic production of those vehicles has been changing. The fact that automobile production in Iran has increased substantially, that agreements have been made with British, German, and other foreign car-producing firms, and that car imports have increased show that these changes are real.[45]

Another important development in Iran is a new emphasis on non-oil exports. In fact, Iran's non-oil exports have more than doubled during this past year. This has been partly due to the lifting of some restrictions on the export of Persian rugs, Persian handicrafts, and certain foodstuffs imposed during the 1979 revolution and during Iran's war with Iraq. Iran's aim seems to be gaining more and more foreign exchange from its exports of non-oil products, including manufacturing products.[46] Iran has realized it requires more than oil and gas revenues to embark upon a successful reconstruction effort. This is particularly true since its population is rising tremendously and because oil revenues are too volatile and thus unreliable. Iran seems to be emphasizing an export promotion industrialization strategy that is very different from the sort of import-substitution that it advocated earlier.[47] This is in line with the policies advocated by the World Bank and the IMF.

ARE NEW CHANGES IN IRAN UN-ISLAMIC?

At least the technocrats in the Rafsanjani government have been serious about restructuring and changing the Iranian economy. The Islamic regime openly discusses these new changes, which in many ways seem to be the opposite of what it used to advocate during its first ten years of existence. During Ayatollah Khomeini's tenure, the ultimate goal was the establishment of an Islamic society based on his model discussed in *Velayat-e Faqih,* and at any price. For him, as demonstrated earlier, economic development or growth was not a high priority goal. Somehow he thought he could create his "ideal" society without achieving industrialization. His goal was to transform all social, economic, educational, legal, military, and political institutions to Islamic ones. It can be argued that Khomeini's "social" revolution was really a cultural revolution—an attempt to transform all secular and modern aspects of Iranian culture to "Islamic" ones. He believed this could be achieved if his clique could monopolize the entire educational system, the entire media, the legal system, the legislative branch of the government, the armed forces, the police force, and if it could eliminate the opposition, including other Islamic political forces not subscribing to his notion of the Islamic state. In that type of thinking, economic progress is at best a secondary goal.

Compared to the policies advocated during the first ten years of the Islamic rule, recent changes in economic and industrial policies in Iran and the stated economic goals of the Islamic government—at least as expressed by the regime's technocrats—signify more than mere changes in economic and industrial policy. They demonstrate a change of attitude, and are devoid of Khomeini's simplistic and fanatical notions that belong to past centuries.

This change of attitude has elevated economic goals to a much higher plane, and views industrialization as an important component of the overall goal of building an Islamic society. The Islamic government has become convinced that its religious goals cannot be achieved unless industrialization is a reality. Thus, it has also come to the realization that economic development and industrialization are not possible unless its previous economic-industrial policies are abandoned. In other words, privatization and other changes are seen by the Islamic regime as steps toward achieving their overall goal of creating the "ideal" Islamic society.

Only a change of attitude could explain Rafsanjani's remarks about the need to make Iranian economy competitive internationally, or his emphasis on the importance of quality control for the success of Iranian productive efforts. It is no wonder that rebuilding the infrastructure and the growth of heavy industry are also emphasized, and that modern technology is being sought. Iran's recent five-year plan, the 1371 and 1372 budgets of the Islamic Republic, the many economic agreements with various industrialized countries, and the speeches and remarks made by Rafsanjani in recent months are testimonies to this fact.[48]

Are these changes, which seem to be a reversal of what took place originally, un-Islamic? Should they be opposed by Islamic (or at least by Shiite) theologians? Should they be regarded as un-Islamic? Should they be condemned by Islamic purists? Are they in conflict with the economic principles of Islam stated in the Quran and other sources of Islamic jurisprudence?

The response to such questions should be negative. Hosseini has repeatedly argued that the original Islamic Republic's drastic economic steps, although partly Islamic, were "reactive measures" and in many ways should be regarded as modern and not necessary Islamic.[49] Opposition to foreign investment can be explained more in terms of modern nationalistic theories and/or Lenin's theory of imperialism than Islamic law. Nationalization and confiscations are more in line with modern revolutions than Islamic jurisprudence. The same can be said of the control of foreign trade and exchange controls. By the same token, present economic changes should not be regarded as un-Islamic. This is why they have not been opposed by any Grand Shiite Ayatollah, which could not be said of the original confiscations, which were not appreciated by more conservative ayatollahs.[50]

Why aren't recent economic-industrial policy changes un-Islamic? Specifically, why shouldn't we regard the lifting of restrictions on foreign investment, the relaxation of a stringent foreign exchange policy, the emphasis on exportation, and privatizations as un-Islamic?

Foreign investment, including direct foreign investment, is, relatively speaking, a new phenomenon. Islam, on the other hand, emerged some 14 centuries ago. The Quran and hadith (for all Muslims, the reported words and acts of the Prophet Mohammad and, for Shiites, the reported words and acts of the Prophet and the twelve Imams) as the highest and the second highest sources of Islamic jurisprudence have nothing to say about foreign investment. The same can be said about foreign exchange policy, since exchange rates and their control (or lack of it) are also modern phenomena. But Islam, being a very universal religion, has no reason to oppose these concepts per se.

If early Islamic sources were silent about modern concepts of foreign investment and exchange control, they were by no means silent about trade and privatization (private ownership of the means of production). The Quran and other sources of Islamic jurisprudence have a great deal to say about private property, profit, and trade. In the interest of fairness, there exist various themes in the Quran that suggest social and religious guidance of property and market relations.

Since Prophet Mohammad's occupation prior to receiving revelation was leading trade caravans between his hometown of Mecca in Hijaz and Damascus and Jerusalem, it should not be any wonder that Islam has a great deal of respect for trade. As someone who was so engaged in domestic and international trade, he has been reported as saying that "merchants are friends of God." Since trade, and profits stemming from trade, are so much respected in Islam, it should not be surprising that the Islamic regime in Iran would emphasize trade, including international trade. This claim can be substantiated by referring to Islamic sources.

Several Quranic verses explicitly advocate trade. Verse 198 of the Book of Baqara advocates trade even while on pilgrimage to Mecca. Since pilgrimage to Mecca has always been very international, I believe this verse is a good indication that Islam advocates both domestic and international trade. In Shiite jurisprudence, there exist thousands of hadith in support of legitimate *(halal)* trade. A great source of Shiite hadith is *Vasael-ol-shiah,* which contains 1910 hadith—reported from the Prophet or the Imams—in support of trade. According to one such hadith, the Prophet is reported to have said that "the merchant who is sincere and trustworthy will on the day of judgment be among prophets, the just, and the martyrs."[51]

Privatization, particularly privatization of previously confiscated and nationalized properties, should not be a problem in Islamic jurisprudence. Although Islam also accepts public ownership, in no way should this imply that it is opposed to private ownership of the means of production.[52] Islam, long before the rise of capitalism, respected private property, including the private ownership of the means of production. The "reactive" leaders of the Islamic revolution, being defensive about the respect for private enterprise in Islam, downplayed this respect. Fourteen centuries of Islamic jurisprudence and Islamic practice, the Quran, and thousands of reported hadith did not feel defensive about Islamic respect of private ownership with its Islamic limitations.

Although Islam and the Prophet did not face Marxism and other opponents to private ownership or the means of production or express explicitly Islamic respect for private ownership, there are still explicit references in this respect in the Quran, and particularly in hadith. There are even more indirect references in these two important sources of Islamic jurisprudence. For example, the Quran, in Verse 5 of the Book of Nissa, explicitly supports private ownership. All the Quranic verses that concern inheritance are indicative of this support. These verses recognize the previous ownership of the deceased and the new ownership of the heirs. Examples of these verses are Verses 7, 8, 10, 11, 38, and 175 of the Book of Nissa; Verse 6 of the Book of Ahzab; and Verses 5 and 6 of Maryam. There are a great deal more hadith in support of inheritance as a form of private ownership of property and the means of production. *Vassael-ol shieh* by Hor Amoli contains 705 hadith in support of inheritance, thus, private ownership.

Another indication of the Islamic respect for property is the fact that Islam forbids *Ghasb*—usurpation or confiscation—defined in Islamic jurisprudence as usurping someone's property without his or her agreement and consent. Several Quranic verses forbid *Ghasb*. These verses include Verse 188 of Baqara, 152 of Anaam, 34 of Osara, Verses 2, 9, 10, 29 and 161 of Nissa, 80 of Kahf, and 34 of Tobeh. Thousands of hadith are also indicative of Islamic condemnation of *Ghasb*. There exist other indirect ways that Islam respects property ownership. These include Islamic and Quranic acceptance of the profit motive, the importance of lending and borrowing, respect for obligations made, the importance of contracts and their documentation in Islamic jurisprudence, the right to defend property in Islam, Islamic opposition to trespassing, and the obligation to pay a wealth tax called *Zakat*.

Thus, based on the Quran, hadith, and Islamic jurisprudence, it is possible to argue that new developments are in every respect Islamic. They are, in particular, more Islamic than the practices of the Islamic regime in the first few months of its existence. But will they lead to more economic successes, at least as compared to what happened from 1979 to 1989?

Of course, some improvements can already be seen—the tremendous rise of non-oil exports, the attraction of foreign investment, the tremendous increase of steel production, the increase in domestic automobile production, and the start of certain important industrial projects. There are some reasons to believe that Iran will most probably be more successful than some other countries pursuing liberalization policies. Among these reasons are the abundance of various natural resources in Iran, including the abundance of both oil and gas, and the entrepreneurial ability of the Iranian population. Ironically, the Islamic revolution, because of the difficulties resulting from dislocations caused by the revolution and the war with Iraq, has transformed Iranians into very able entrepreneurs. This could definitely be a tremendous force in causing more economic growth in Iran. A society where everyone, from civil servant to the Bazzari merchant, is seeking some lucrative business venture, particularly when many constraints are lifted, undeniably will witness a great deal of economic progress during the years to come. Of course, only time will tell.

NOTES TO CHAPTER 7
◆

1. Ayatollah Ruhollah Khomeini, *Velayat-e Faqih* (Tehran, 1979), previously published in exile under the title of *Hokoomat-e-Eslami,* 1972.

2. Hamid Hosseini, "From Buchanan to Khomeini: Can Neoclassical Economics Explain the Islamic State of Iran's Ayatollah?" *The American Journal of Economics and Sociology,* vol. 49, no. 2 (April 1990): 167–184.

3. In addition to *Velayat-e-Faqih,* his other "major" politico-religious work was *Kashf-ol-Asrar,* published in the 1940s and also devoid of economic analysis.

4. Hamid Hosseini, "Notions of Private Property in Islamics in Contemporary Iran," *International Journal of Social Economics,* vol. 15, no. 9 (1988): 51–61.

5. Hosseini, "From Buchanan to Khomeini."

6. *Kayhan Havai,* 10 July 1983, 22.

7. Ibid.

8. Mehrdad Valibiegi, " Nationalization and Expansion of the Public Sector in Post-revolutionary Iran," presented to CIRA conference, April 1987.

9. Hosseini, "Notions of Private Property."

10. *Kayhan Havai,* June 1979, 15.

11. Sohrab Behdad, "Foreign Exchange Gap, Structural Constraints, and the Political Economy of Exchange Rate Determination in Iran," *International Journal of Mideast Studies* (1988): 1–21.

12. This is my own translation from the 1979 constitution.

13. Ibid.

14. Ibid.

15. Ibid.

16. Ibid.

17. Ibid.

18. Ibid.

19. Ibid.

20. Ibid.

21. See several issues of *Tadbir,* 1992 (a management journal).

22. Quoted from C. Bina and H. Zangeneh, eds., *Modern Capitalism and Ideology* (New York: St. Martin's Press, 1992).

23. Ibid.

24. *Kayhan Havai,* 11 March 1992, 10.

25. Various issues of *Kayhan Havai* and *Iran Times,* January 1992.

26. Various issues of *Kayhan Havai* and *Iran Times,* January 1992.

27. Various issues of *Kayhan Havai* and *Iran Times,* January 1992.

28. Various issues of *Kayhan Havai* and *Iran Times,* December 1991, January and February 1992.

29. Ibid.

30. *Kayhan Havai,* December 1991 and other issues.

31. Ibid.

32. Ibid.

33. Ibid.

34. Ibid.

35. Ibid.

36. Ibid.

37. Ibid.

38. Ibid.

39. CIRA Newsletter, Summer 1991 (but published much later).

40. *Iran Times* and *Kayhan Havai*, February, 1992.

41. Hamid Hosseini, "Iran Privatizing Public Sector," *Mideast Markets,* 20 January 1992, 7.

42. Hamid Hosseini, "Iran Pins Growth of Foreign Investment," *Mideast Markets,* 9 December 1991, 4.

43. Hamid Hosseini, "Iran Plans to Make Rial Convertible," *Mideast Markets,* 18 November 1991, 3.

44. "Iran Opens up Auto Market," *Mideast Market,* 4 November 1991, 4.

45. Ibid.

46. "Expansion of Non-Oil Exports—A Conversation with the representative of Chamber of Commerce and Industry," *Tadbir,* no. 21, 1992, 18–19.

47. Several issues of *Tadbir,* 1992–93.

48. Hamid Hosseini, in four different issues of *Mideast Markets,* November 1991–January 1992.

49. Ibid.

50. Ibid.

51. It is a well-known Hadith.

52. Ibid.

PRIVATIZATION IN IRAN: ANALYSIS OF THE PROCESS AND METHODS [1]

Hossein Akhavi-Pour

THE ACT OF CABINET OF MINISTERS
*Assembly of Ministers . . . according to articles 134 and 138
of the Constitution of the Islamic Republic of Iran . . .
had approved the policy of transferring assets of state
economic enterprises and organizations.*
—APRIL 25, 1991

ANNOUNCEMENT
*Numbers of electric plants, water plants, |Iran|
Steel Company, |Iran| Airline, |Iran| Railroad, |Iran|
Post and Telegraph, |Iran| National Oil Company . . .
schools, universities, including few ministries and one government
are to be handed to private sector. Interested individuals
should refer to popular newspapers.*
—GOL AGHA
(A PARODY MAGAZINE IN PERSIAN),
NO. 34 (NOVEMBER 1992)

INTRODUCTION

Since the end of the Iran-Iraq War in 1988, and particularly after the death of Ayatollah Khomeini in 1989, the government of Iran has committed itself to a radical reform of the economy, which it has controlled and managed since the 1978–79 revolution.[2] The reform basically involves greater reliance on market forces to determine prices and to allocate production input and finances. The heart of this reform is the privatization of State-owned Economic Enterprises (SEE), or *khoosoosi sazi*. This chapter shows that the top-down approach of the government in the process of privatization is mere denationalization and an inadequate reversal of previous efforts toward nationalization.

BACKGROUND

The Iranian Revolution of 1978–79 marked the turning point for many socioeconomic characteristics of Iran. Before the revolution, the manufacturing industry depended on imports for inputs and machinery. Also, with the U.S. freezing of Iranian assets, a credit crunch developed that highlighted the crisis of dependence, which was exaggerated by foreign banks withdrawing from Iran. The Iran-Iraq War made financial matters worse.[3]

Managing the war forced the Islamic Republic of Iran to compete with the private sector in the labor market, financial markets, foreign exchange markets, and the market for goods and services. In addition, soon after Iraq's initial attack, the war created an expensive refugee problem, which absorbed up to 20 percent of total public expenditures while tax revenues declined at constant prices between 1980 and 1988.[4]

These problems forced further government intervention into the economy, with an important issue being large-scale property ownership of land and industries.[5] Increasing financial debts to the banking system, growing labor strikes, and shortages of parts and raw materials further heightened the crisis.[6]

In August of 1979, the provisional government of Bazargan approved the so-called Law of Protection and Development of National Industries.[7] Under this law, 580 manufacturing establishments were nationalized and the Organization of National Iranian Industries (ONII) was established to control and manage these establishments. In addition, the government nationalized and downsized private banks and insurance companies.[8] The nationalization process made a change in the *ownership and management* of all the nationalized establishments. Nationalization occurred in conjunction with de-Westernization and Islamization of the Iranian economy. In this process, the Iranian economy further *deprivatized.*

NATIONALIZATION AND DEPRIVATIZATION

Nationalization and deprivatization are distinct processes. Nationalization, or state ownership and management of the key businesses, does not necessarily mean loss of economic efficiency. In fact, it may be an optimal solution as in the case of a natural monopoly. The efficiency of the market is due to a marginal cost allocative mechanism of resources rather than property *ownership.* There is no systematic evidence to show that under imperfect market conditions the private sector performs better, in terms of service delivery and cost-effectiveness, than the public sector does. Some SEEs have done very well on standard efficiency criteria when given adequate autonomy and headed by qualified personnel. However, in a market economy, deprivatization destroys the essence of the system, the competition, and the long-term national competitiveness of a nation in a global and regional market. Deprivatization is a state of mind, an attitude, and a culture that manifests itself in an adversarial relationship between the people and the state. In general, it results in the systematic intervention by government in the market economy; in particular, it is seen in the economic life of the domestic private sector. Deprivatization in Iran has created social and economic barriers to private investment and has impeded domestic private entrepreneurial opportunities.

Traditionally in Middle Eastern countries, particularly in Iran, the state or *dawlat* has a great role in economic life and in control of economic wealth as in cultivated lands or *Kha-less-e.* Therefore, the state never was financially dependent on the private sector (people or *mellat),* but rather the reverse was true. Also, the state has never been in support of private business initiatives to accumulate and control physical capital, which means self-imposed limitations on state powers of interference and ownership. As a result, the domestic private sector has not enjoyed complete autonomy in its entrepreneurial decision-making process.[9] Thus, the root of insignificant domestic private investment and growth of domestic private entrepreneurship is not the control of large-scale enterprises by government; it is due to "weakness, discontinuity and insecurity of all forms of private property."[10]

Since the 1978–79 revolution, the private sector's insecurity has manifested itself in economic laws and regulations and in an antibusiness sentiment promoted by some factions of the government.[11] This phenomenon has been observed in other Middle Eastern countries whose governments' claim against businesses was argued to be the impediment to the growth of the private sector and a factor in the failure of privatization.[12]

The creation of many state-owned economic institutions in Iran after the revolution, such as the Foundation of Deprived, or *Bonyad-e Mostazafan,* can be explained by the tradition of public ownership of productive economic assets or *Kha-less-e.*[13] This process is the most convenient way of dominating and controlling the material and economic life of a nation by the state. In Iran, it has been the fundamental reason for the lack of growth of domestic self-seeded capitalism. Historically, such a transfer of assets from private to public sector has not been a major source of economic disturbance and hardship in a system of production where land was the major economic resource. But transferring the ownership and management of large-scale establishments, industries, or services to a state with no management experience proved to be very costly and different from managing land. A large-scale manufacturing or service establishment needs a management team to be able to do coordination, planning, and marketing in a vertical as well as horizontal process, and this has been lacking in Iran, particularly during the postrevolutionary period.

PRIVATIZATION AND MARKET ECONOMY

Privatization is the transfer of a *function* and *activity* from the public to the private sector. In that sense, the most important function to be transferred to the private sector is the regulation of the production and distribution of goods and services in a market. Thus, the success of privatization in market regulation depends on the existing political and economic environments of a nation. Such environments may be measured by the macroeconomic policy framework, the microeconomic incentive structure, and the physical, institutional, and human infrastructures. From this point of view, there are two approaches to privatization: top-down or bottom-up.

A top-down approach to privatization transfers assets of SEEs to the private sector. Because of the lack of adequate infrastructure (financial and nonfinancial) in the Third World, the top-down approach to privatization leads to the control of businesses by financial entrepreneurs with no experience and little interest in production. At best, it creates an environment for monopoly capitalism and accelerates the rate of integration of the economy into the global capitalist system. Such an integration may be in conflict with the elimination of poverty and inequality in the Third World while it reinforces economic vulnerability.[14]

In a bottom-up approach to privatization, governments are in support of the growth of the domestic private sector, particularly with traditional industries. In order to create a strong domestic private sector for job creation, a tax base, and economic stability the state should provide security for property rights and guarantees for popular civil rights. This bottom-up approach to privatization favors establishment of an environment suitable to the development of domestic commerce and industry, as well as promoting the productive use of labor assets in formal and informal sectors of the economy. There is a clear distinction between privatization for the purpose of economic development and the elimination of inequality (a bottom-up approach) and privatization for political gains (a top-down approach).

Third World nations have undertaken privatization since the 1980s, following international pressures from the World Bank and the IMF as a precondition to have access to international financial markets and funds of these institutions.[15] Unfortunately for these institutions, privatization or lack of it are seen as problems of the Third World. The solution to economic stagnation and poverty in these nations will go hand in hand with privatization.

There are three major arguments by economists for and against privatization. The first revolves around the potential improvement in allocative efficiency, reduction in fiscal burden, and elimination of government bureaucracy as the gain. The second states that even if an improvement in efficiency is achieved, it does not necessarily maximize the welfare of a community. The third argument suggests that the question to be addressed is not one of ownership, but rather of what social and economic environments are necessary for the public and private sectors working together to maximize the national welfare and protect the interest of its citizens.[16] It is this third argument that will be most heavily examined.

PRIVATIZATION IN IRAN

The Islamic Republic of Iran (IRI) has not yet spelled out the socioeconomic reasons for privatization, despite the fact that it was mentioned as an objective in the first five-year plan of 1989–93. In this document several goals are outlined: efficiency, job creation, reduction of financial burden, and control of economic systems.[17] The Act of the Assembly of Ministers, number 5285, dated April 25, 1991, reflects the official intention of the IRI in transferring the assets of State Economic Enterprises (SEE) and organizations to the private sector. From this act, it seems that the intention has been "efficiency gain in economic activities and reduction of the role of government in those activities." The act is also included as a general principle in the Plan and Budget Organization draft, but is more articulated in policy. The policy of transferring ownership of SEEs is described by the Organization of National Iranian Industries in the following remarks:

> First, SEE will transfer their ownership to the private sector gradually; second, the stock market has the priority among methods available for doing this transformation; third, the SEE must have a sound fiscal condition to be offered in the stock market; fourth, 33 percent of the stocks must be given to employees of SEE through Financial Organization of Development of Private Ownership of Manufacturing Establishments (or Organization of Development) where priority is given to employee of each SEE. The remaining 67 percent must be offered in the stock market.

It is important to note two pieces of information from this document. First, the stock market receives high marks as the principle vehicle in privatization methods. Second, in this document it is emphasized that employees of each establishment have control over 33 percent of the total stocks.[18] During 1991–92, 225 SEEs participated in the process of getting approval to be offered in the stock market. Seventy-nine of them were accepted.[19] By the end of 1991, according to an internal publication of the Tehran Stock Exchange (TSE), the number of SEEs reached 261 in the stock market with a total of 48,536,393 shares and a nominal value of $358 million, where $1 equals 1,000 rials.

Two results of this policy have been noted. First, the degree of state ownership in many firms considered for privatization declined on the average by 50 percent. Second, the nominal value of stocks offered in the TSE on the average has increased by 42 percent. Considering that in Iran there are no investment firms and there has not been a tradition of financial activities inside a stock market for fulfilling financial needs, such as mutual funds, this activity volume was impressive. One factor with a significant impact on this process is that firms confiscated after the revolution under Title A or *band-e alef* were allowed to register in the stock market, and financial losses of some of the original stockholders were compensated.

However, these activities did not last long. By the middle of fiscal year 1992–93, the stock market seemed to indicate a lack of interest by the public due to many factors. Several of these factors will be discussed.[20]

METHODS OF PRIVATIZATION AND CONSEQUENCES

Two methods of privatization have been used in Iran: the stock market (*boors*) and public offerings through contracted bids (*mozayed-e or mozaker-e*). The latter method seeks buyers who have managerial experience and desire to buy more than 50 percent of the establishment *and* manage it. Following the failed experiences of the stock market, more and more institutions, such as IDRO and the Bank of Mining and Industry, are attracted to this method.[21] However, the dominant method of privatization in Iran, as was recommended by the Assembly of Ministers, has been through the stock market. The following discussion will focus on exploring the reasons for its failure and lessons that can be drawn from it.

1. Lack of education about the behavior of the stock market is widespread. Buyers in general are under the impression that stock prices must continually move upward. This impression was largely conveyed to them by false information from stockbrokers and management of the affected corporations. A downward swing of stock prices creates a panic among public participants in this market.

2. The belief of government organizations is that a management team, particularly the top managers, is not and should not be part of the privatization. Thus, when many SEEs went public and were privatized, they made no change in the management teams, who continued to control and run those businesses as usual.

3. There is a lack of clear goals and explicit reasons for privatization. As a result, there is no overall strategy to guide the process. It seems that the IRI views privatization primarily as a source of additional revenue for the treasury from the sale of state-owned assets. This would be a legitimate goal on its own. However, selling at the best price is not one of the goals in the First Plan enumerated earlier.

4. The dominant state strategy in privatization seems to have
been to quickly sell the SEEs to the private sector so that
favorable socioeconomic conditions for less government
and a more private-dominated economy with sophisticated
financial markets could emerge by itself. This has not
worked because the preconditions for the public to invest
were not present. If this strategy was relatively successful in
Germany, which is referred to as a model, it was because the
West Germans and their economic power base and structures were ready for a swift change. It must be noted that
policies designed for industrialized economies characterized by competition and sophisticated financial markets
cannot be blindly transposed onto economies of the Third
World. These economies are, for a variety of reasons, com-
parable to underdeveloped financial markets.[22]

5. Privatization, as it is understood today, is a new concept
that has been practiced heavily since the early 1980s. Many
countries of the Third World do not have a clear understanding of what is involved. They lack the infrastructure
necessary for successful privatization. It is more so in Iran
where privatization may not be very popular within the
government and religious institutions. As a result, there is
a lack of cooperation and support by government branches
for privatized SEEs. This can be seen in the actions of city
mayors. As soon as the privatization of a SEE was complete and new ownership and management were in place,
the mayors would confiscate the land of the new private
establishment, which on many occasions, was very valuable
in price.

6. The government agencies, such as banks and foundations,
are involved in speculative actions and have a great deal of
interest in keeping stock prices higher than the true market
value. These agencies electronically commit themselves to
sell/buy positions that guarantee a high price and speculative profits.

7. The process of establishing a SEE has a significant impact
on the methods needed for privatization. In Iran, a SEE
could be created by one of the following methods: confiscation, natural monopoly, national security clause, and by
default. The stock market has not proven to be suitable for
all of them and is not a competitive market because the flow
of information is limited. The posted price by brokers is
usually higher than what it should be. There is generally a

lack of available public information on financial perfor-
mances of the SEEs. As a result, the public on many occasions is outside the process of valuation of a company and
not very active in the stock market.

8. The stocks that are up for transaction cannot be liquidated
for some time because of the bureaucratic process involved.
Such delays cause financial losses and lack of effective control of buyers. As of August 1992, any "public corporation" is required by Law of Development to transfer 49
percent of their stocks to the public through the Organization
of Development. By doing so, they can benefit from government support through preferential access to raw materials, foreign exchange currencies, and government
procurement. However, despite these enormous benefits,
the businesses prefer being private corporations in order to
avoid being controlled by government agencies, such as
IDRO.

9. There is no centralized decision-making unit for offering
stocks to the market. A variety of suppliers—such as banks,
the Organization of Development, the Organization of
National Industries, and Bonyads—offer their stocks to the
market. On many occasions they offer a "dead" stock, that
is, stocks of a financially (not legally) bankrupt business. An
example is the action by Bank-e Meli of selling stocks of a
pharmaceutical company. Following deceptive advertising,
stocks were sold at a high price, but Bank-e Meli was forced
to recall those stocks, reprice them more reasonably, and
sell them again.

10. Another problem is a lack of information on the volume of
stocks offered in the market, financial needs, and the
demand for them. Many of the SEEs have huge accumulated debt and bloated payrolls. Therefore, the private sector has no interest in buying those establishments without
explicit permission for reorganization.

11. The laws in Iran, particularly the labor laws, are political
laws not economic laws. The law requires that 33 percent of
each SEE company should be owned by its employees.
Under this condition, the private sector is not willing to
buy a firm that has a concentrated voice from its labor and
does not have the confidence to invest in manufacturing. It
is satisfied with investments in real estate, foreign currency,
and speculative stock markets.

CONCLUSION

The current privatization process in Iran follows a top-down approach that has been practiced in many parts of the Third World during the 1980s. In Iran, the main reason for privatization or denationalization is due to the huge financial costs of running SEEs and international pressure for economic liberalization by the World Bank and the IMF. The dilemma for investors has been that there are no clear-cut boundaries in Islamic laws regarding private or state ownership; this is left wide open. The malleability of law leaves domestic investors insecure and thus affects investment. The failure of true liberalization has made it very difficult for the private sector to get involved in the process of privatization. The bottom-up approach to privatization is a necessary ingredient in the internal growth and development in Iran. The Shah's powerful totalitarian system could not have been overthrown without the active participation of millions of people. There should be no doubt that without the participation of the same people on the social and economic fronts the dilemmas of poverty and economic dependence will not be removed.

NOTES TO CHAPTER 8

1. This paper grew out of field research conducted in Iran between June and August 1992, which was funded by Hamline University. Personal interviews with several government agencies and researchers contributed to the information and analysis contained here. I would like to thank Manoucher Parvin and Hamid Zangeneh for their helpful comments on earlier drafts of this paper.

2. Dates such as "1978–79" refer to the Iranian solar year (1357), which begins with the spring equinox.

3. Manoucher Parvin and Amin Zamani, "Economy of Growth and Destruction: A Statistical Interpretation of Iranian Case," *Iranian Studies* (Winter 1979); Hamid Zanganeh, "Necessary Conditions for Growth and Development for Iran after the Revolution and the War," *Mehregan,* in Persian (Summer 1992): 150–61; Central Bank of the Islamic Republic of Iran, *Iran National Accounts* (Tehran: Office of Economic Accounting, Organization of Printing Currencies, 1991), 191, 245; Office of Economic Accounting, *Iran National Accounts,* in Persian (Tehran: Organization of Printing Currencies, 1983), 159–181; Office of Economic Analysis, *Survey of Economic Affairs of Iran After the Revolution,* written in Persian (Tehran: Iranchap, approx. 1983).

4. Central Bank of the Islamic Republic of Iran, *Iran National Accounts,* written in Persian (Tehran: Office of Economic Accounting, Organization of Printing Currencies, 1991), 245.

5. There were several competing interpretations of private property. None of these had the clear support of the Parliament, the Council of Guardians, the president, or the leader. See Hamid Hosseini, "Notion of Private Property in Islamic Economics in Contemporary Iran: Review of Literatures," *International Journal of Social Economics*, vol. 15, no. 9 (1988): 51–62.

6. To improve and facilitate the renovation of some manufacturing establishments, the Chamber of Mining and Industries provided $2 billion credit in 1979 to industries. However, after a year, only 18 percent of it was used. Central Bank, *Survey of Economic Affairs of Iran After the Revolution,* in Persian (Tehran: Office of Economic Analysis, Iranchap, 1993), 163.

7. This law divided businesses into four major groups by ownership: Title one (*band-e alef*), in addition to the traditional government-owned industries such as oil, gas, electricity, tobacco, utilities, and fisheries, also includes strategic industries of motor vehicles, steel, shipbuilding, and airplane building; title two (*band-e b-e*), those establishments whose owners did illegal activities or had left Iran after the revolution; title three (*band-e jim*), those establishments with financial debts to the banking system of more than value of their assets; title four (*band-e dal*), the last group, includes those establishments that belong to the private sector with "limited and legitimate ownership" that would be protected by the law. Central Bank, *Survey of Economic Affairs of Iran After the Revolution,* in Persian. (Tehran: Office of Economic Analysis, Iranchap, 1983), 165–66.

8. On June 6, 1979, the Revolutionary Council announced that "in order to protect the rights and wealth of its citizens . . . [the Council] will nationalize the domestic banks." The total of 25 commercial banks with $1.3 billion of paid capital were nationalized and later merged into 6 banks. The government-owned noncommercial banks were also merged later that year into three banks. As a result, the 36 banks with 8,275 branches were reduced to 9 banks with 6,851 branches. Central Bank, *Survey of Economic Affairs of Iran After the Revolution,* in Persian. (Tehran: Office of Economic Analysis, Iranchap, 1983), 432–50.

9. See Perry Anderson, *Lineages of Absolutist State* (London: Bookcraft Ltd., 1989), 462–520; in particular, see the "Asiatic Mode of Production," and also Homa Katouzian, *The Political Economy of Modern Iran: Despotism and Pseudo Modernism 1926–1979* (New York: New York University Press, 1981), ch. 1; and "The Arsidolatic Society: A Model of Long-term Social and Economic Development in Iran," *International Journal of Middle East Studies,* (1993): 259–81. For a discussion on contemporary Iran and the role of state see Bizhan Jazani, *Capitalism and Revolution in Iran* (London: Zed Press, 1980), 1–45.

10. Homa Katouzian, op. cit., 264.

11. Hossein Akhavi-Pour, "Barriers to Private Entrepreneurship in Iran," *Critique* (Fall 1992): 54–64.

12. Iliya Harik, in *Privatization and Liberalization in the Middle East,* Iliya Harik and Denis Sullivan, eds. (Bloomington, Ind.: Indiana University Press, 1992), 8.

13. After the revolution of 1978–79, five major socioeconomic foundations were established. These are: (1) *Bonyad-e Mostazafan,* which took control over the Pahlavi dynasty's wealth in Iran and abroad; (2) *Jahad-e Sazandegi,* which has a mission of promotion of economic, social, and cultural life of rural areas; (3) *Bonyad-e Maskan,* for providing and helping the deprived to repair and construct housing units; (4) *Bonyad-e Omoor-e Mohajerin-e Jange,* with the mission of helping dislocated people due to war with Iraq to settle and have a normal life and to reconstruct the regions damaged by the war; (5) *Bonyad-e Shahid,* to help the families of the martyred and handicapped of the Iran-Iraq war. Each institution is an independent government agency, and collectively they own close to 1,500 business establishments. Central Bank, *Survey of Economic Affairs of Iran After the Revolution,* in Persian (Tehran: Office of Economic Analysis, Iranchap, 1983), 268–80.

14. See among others Samir Amin, *Development: Anatomy of a Global Failure* (London: Zed Books Ltd., 1990): 27–74.

15. The minister of Finance and Budget of Iran has acknowledged recently that economic liberalization policies undertaken are seconded by the World Bank and the IMF. However, he denied the allegation that these policies are "dictated" by those institutions. *Iran Times* (Washington D.C.), vol. 23, no. 12, 4 June 1993, 1, 12.

16. For a theoretical discussion and case studies see the following: Paul Cook and Colin Kirkpatrick, eds., *Privatization in Less Developed Countries* (New York: St. Martin's Press, 1988); Gray Cowan, *Privatization in the Developing World* (New York: Greenwood Press, 1990); Iliya Harik and Denis Sullivan, eds., *Privatization and Liberalization in the Middle East* (Bloomington, Ind.: Indiana University Press, 1992); John Heath ed., *Public Enterprise at the Crossroads: Essays in Honor of V. V. Ramanadbam* (London: Routledge, 1990); V. V. Ramanadbam ed., *Privatization in Developing Countries* (New York: Routledge, 1989); and Paul MacAvoy et al., eds., *Privatization and State-Owned Enterprises: Lessons from the United States, Great Britain and Canada* (Boston, Mass.: Kluwer Academi, 1989).

17. Plan and Budget Organization, *A Summary of the First Five Year Economic, Social and Cultural Development Plan of the Islamic Republic of Iran: 1989–1993* (Tehran: PBO Press, 1990), 1–15.

18. The history of selling stocks of large publicly available corporations to employees goes back to 1975, following Principle 13 of *Shah/People's Revolution.* The Financial Organization for Expansion of Private Ownership, known as the Organization of Development, was established to facilitate the transfer of ownership of 40 percent of stocks of these corporations to their employees. A total of 150 establishments were affected by this decision between 1975 and 1978. This trend stopped after the 1978–79 revolution due to a change in ownership of these enterprises. "This information was obtained from internal documents of the Organization of Development."

19. There are 12 steps outlined in the law for a SEE to be eligible to register in the Tehran Stock Exchange Market. These steps may be divided into four categories as follows: First, initial moves by a current manager team of the establishment to apply to be considered for privatization; second, improvement in the financial position of the establishment;

third, the legal steps for transferring the ownership of public assets to private sector; and fourth, the steps required to be taken in the TSE. The common problem is to make an improvement in the fiscal condition of the establishment before applying for stock market procedure.

20. Substance of this and following paragraphs about the privatization and stock market are based on interviews at the Tehran Stock Exchange; Bonyad-e Mostazafan; Industrial Managers Association; The Organization of Development; IDRO; The Bank of Industry and Mining; Office of State Enterprises, Plan and Budget Organization; and The Ministry of Finance.

21. There are significant financial incentives for institutions to use the stock market method to privatization. These incentives include a range of government support from a 10 percent corporate tax reduction to easy access to financial resources.

22. For further discussion and case studies related to this very point see Adam Christopher, et al., *Adjusting Privatization: Case Studies from Developing Countries* (New York: Randle, 1992).

ECONOMIC DEVELOPMENT AND GROWTH IN IRAN[1]

Hamid Zangeneh and Janice M. Moore

R evolution, by its very definition, results in far-reaching and drastic social change. The chaotic atmosphere of the revolutionary
environment promotes mass confusion, shortly replaced by
newly emerging social structures, some of which will prove to be
only temporary while others will become relatively permanent. Much of
the postrevolutionary change occurs by design, having been envisioned,
advocated, and implemented by the triumphant revolutionary forces.

On the other hand, many of the newly emergent social structures
result from other social and political processes that inevitably accom-
pany and follow revolution. The compositions of the social groups who
are active in the revolution and of those who later gain control of the
government apparatus are fluid. The power struggle for prominence,
dominance, or acceptance among the competing groups creates a revolutionary and political environment characterized by continuously shifting goals. Some degree of stability will only be attained when one of the
groups becomes dominant, either by consensus or by forceful elimination of the others.

In general, the composition of revolutionary forces may be divided
into three groups. There are those who participate in the process for
ideological reasons, and therefore expect and demand the establishment of social structures that are ideologically congruent. These are
the groups that would not have been content with simply a reform of the

previous social system. Rather, they demand an overhaul of the entire socioeconomic-political system. Second, there are those who participate in the process because of a real and/or perceived dissatisfaction with the old regime. What is needed to satisfy this group is, at least, the creation of a new regime and/or a new environment. This group will not necessarily demand a particularly new system of government as long as its members perceive the emergent regime as a distinct and separate entity. Finally, there are those who simply go along with the revolutionary movement because it is fashionable and/or because they believe what the revolutionaries have said. This group has no particular agenda or mandate; it will simply follow the tide and move with the wind. That is, members of this group, who probably constitute the majority of the population, will do what they are told by their trusted leaders and/or government officials.

If the leadership of an emergent regime recognizes the existence of these groups, possibly it will not be so quick as to pursue a short-term, popular agenda. Instead, it may seek out ways of improving the welfare of the masses and the future of the country as a whole. On the other hand, if the new leadership does not recognize the true composition of its constituency, it may spend a great deal of time and resources on popular programs and an agenda that, although appeasing the masses in the short run, will lead to a future full of disappointment for all.

We maintain that the government of the Islamic Republic did recognize this breakdown, yet embarked upon short-term, quick-fix solutions for political reasons. As a result, the government inflicted damage upon the economy and failed to address the real economic problems and issues confronting the country. During the initial years following the revolution, the government of the Islamic Republic undertook policies of wasteful "quick fixes" in order to create, appease, and maintain an unreliable power base, the *mostaz'afeen*. Even though the goal of creating and maintaining a power base for the sake of political stability has been achieved, this has occurred at the expense of valuable resources. In order to show the economic failure of the government, in what follows we will provide a brief comparison between pre- and postrevolution achievements and trends.

PREREVOLUTION CONDITIONS

Prior to the revolution, the country had experienced material progress, albeit uneven and lopsided. Although scholars of Iranian affairs traditionally avoided a discussion of the material progress that occurred before the 1979 revolution, there has been a change of attitude in this regard. Today there is little disagreement about the rise in the standard of living that took place before the revolution. During the years preceding the revolution, the traditional yardsticks of economic development, such as infant mortality, life expectancy, road construction, electric generation, and so on, were relatively high and increasing. However, it is recognized that despite the growing economic pie, the gaps between different classes were not closing fast enough to satisfy the masses.[2] In other words the modernization policies of the Pahlavi regime did actually lead to a higher overall gross national income and therefore to a higher standard of living as evidenced by per capita income. However, prosperity did not trickle down to the middle and lower classes.

A growing disparity of incomes was accompanied by repression of the politically active public. This was designed to discourage the masses from engaging in political activities other than those orchestrated by the regime itself. Many millions of people, probably the majority of the population, fell in this category. They chose to be apolitical either to save themselves from the tyranny of the Shah's dictatorship or just because they found politics distasteful. There was a sense of security for these apolitical individuals and for those who did not cross the political line that the Shah's regime drew in the sand.

Nonpolitical crimes elicited varying responses from the legal system. Punitive measures ranged from those that were arbitrary and crude to those that were appropriate and equitable, depending on the case and individuals concerned. Even though the court system was mired in corruption, misuse, and abuse, it was a non-intrusive system of justice in the sense that the public was immune from individual interpretations of the law as long as the political threshold was respected. Reasonable people could disagree about their equity and blind and just applications, but it is an indisputable fact that there was a unified and generally accepted set of legal codes, rules, and regulations.

Socially there was a sense of bewilderment. There was a tug of war between the traditional segment of the society and those in the government who wanted to undertake social engineering and replace the traditional modus operandi with a new imported Western one. Reza Shah used brute force to achieve his modernization objectives while his son, Shah Mohammad Reza Pahlavi (the late last Shah of Iran), used a carrot-and-stick approach. For about three decades, he combined, rather successfully, the brutality of the SAVAK (the repressive secret police) with the promises of the "White Revolution" as vehicles promoting change. Most of his social engineering efforts, such as the women's liberation movement, literacy and medical corps, land reform, and profit-sharing for the working class, appealed to the disenfranchised peasants, women, and laborers.

But given the facade of calm, security, and stability that existed, there were underlying problems that eventually led to the revolution. Even though this chapter is not centered around the theories of revolution in Iran, it would be constructive to provide an explanation, albeit cursory, of some of the speculated causes of the 1979 revolution.

One of the most commonly accepted explanations for the Iranian Revolution is that the country's rapid modernization resulted in the breakdown of the fabric of the society. Due to the tremendous increase in oil prices in the early 1970s, Iran started a series of ambitious economic development programs. In the process, many of the oil revenues were channeled into construction and reconstruction of industries, roads, and other projects. The new economic boom disturbed the social stability and the class relationships that had previously existed. While some Iranians reaped enormous profits from these projects, for most the modernization programs created hardship. The only real beneficiaries of these development projects were the new industrialists, bankers, and large agribusinesses who were less connected to the domestic markets. They were more attuned to the international and multinational corporations than to the domestic system.

These development projects naturally were accompanied by an influx of foreigners whose customs and behaviors did not correspond with the traditional Iranian way of life. The alien cultures became threatening to the existence of the old traditions and culture. Given the less-than-friendly and cooperative relationship that the Shah's regime had with the *ulama* and the rest of the religious community, the intelligentsia, the workers, and other power bases, the regime began to lose legitimacy.

In the 1950s and 1960s, anti-Westernization sentiments grew in prevalence among the intelligentsia and were conveyed through literary works such as those written by Al-e Ahmad[3] and Shari'ati, among others. It was not until the 1970s that these sentiments became popular among average Iranians. Among the intelligentsia, modernization projects were assailed as mechanisms that would drain and channel Iran's resources outside the country rather than as ways of improving everyone's livelihood. They were also viewed as the domination and exploitation of Iranian resources by multinational corporations.[4]

The continuing discontent and malaise due to economic and political factors became widespread during the mid- to late 1970s. The economic "Promised Land" could not be reached, political participation was limited to those events orchestrated by the government, and social and religious traditions were threatened to extinction. By 1977 the country was in turmoil. The Shah's maneuvers to save the monarchy were too little too late in the face of the overwhelming and all-encompassing revolt. As the regime crumbled, a new revolutionary government was established to reverse the "evil trends" that had threatened the existence of the Persian way of life.

Modernization theory, in its many forms and applications, has been accepted, to varying degrees, by many who have sought to explain the revolution. Another theoretical interpretation that has gained some degree of popularity focuses upon class struggle as a primary causative factor. While this second line of thought has much to contribute to our understanding of the Iranian Revolution, its merits, in comparison with those of the modernization theory, have been closely examined by others and will not be debated here.[5]

POSTREVOLUTION REALITIES: AN ASSESSMENT

Although 15 years have passed since the revolution, the new regime has yet to make any headway in ridding the country of its pervasive corruption and economic, social, and legal injustice. In fact, it has delivered little or no relief on any front. Without doubt, all those who have closely followed the unfolding of events in postrevolutionary Iran are aware of the arduous and burdensome load borne by those who live there.

The emergence of problems in the economic, political, and legal spheres as well as excesses within the religious community have been well-documented in a number of scholarly books and journal articles. Economic problems are particularly visible through the pitiful rate of change in the gross national income after the revolution. The real per capita gross national product and real per capita private consumption have been declining due to lower outputs and a higher population growth (see figure 9.1).

It is very easy to attribute the postrevolutionary economic failures of the regime to outside factors such as the antagonistic attitude of the West and the war with Iraq. As with any value-laden judgment, it is very difficult to assign a dollar value to the anti-Iranian campaign of the West. However, in order to estimate the costs born by Iran as the result of its war with Iraq, one has but to review the many estimates of the devastation wreaked by the war. A conservative estimate by the secretary general of the United Nations puts the damage to be just under $100 billion, while Hooshang Amirahmadi,[6] an urban planning professor and Iranian specialist, puts the estimate of direct and indirect damages of the war, up to and including 1987, to about $592 billion. Despite the very important and costly international factors, it is possible for one to identify Iranian government policy decisions, or the lack thereof, which have served to escalate the impact of the war and anti-Iranian Western behavior.

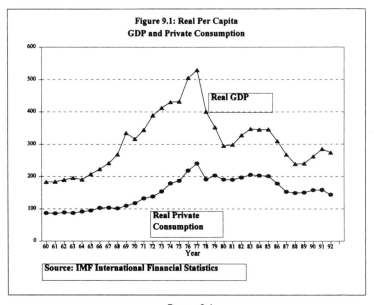

Figure 9.1

PRIVATE PROPERTY RIGHTS AND CAPITAL FORMATION

The first and foremost cause of the Islamic regime's decade of failure is what could be described as the adoption of a "bashful or apologetic Islamic" doctrine by the ruling oligarchy. The direct and indirect impacts of this doctrine have been those of inconsistency in government policy and confusion on the part of the citizenry. In regard to the country's economic condition, it has led to unnecessary bewilderment and complications in Tehran's bazaar as well as in those located in the far corners of Khouzestan, Baluchestan, and elsewhere.

In accordance with this "bashful or apologetic" doctrine, the regime sought to preempt and subdue the religious and Marxist-oriented groups on the left who had constituted a dominant presence within the Iranian intelligentsia before the revolution. In order to accomplish this, the government adopted an unclear position with regard to both property rights and international trade. Rather than espousing the traditional Islamic view, which considers the right to own private property and to engage in trade as acceptable and individual rights to be sacred, the leaders of the new government came close to taking the position that individuals are the guardians of God's property and that there is a still-to-be-defined limit to this guardianship.[7]

Some would argue that there are limits, nonetheless unspecified, to the extent of ownership of private property.[8] However these limits to ownership are not explicit in the Quran and are presumed to be implied from the Quranic pronouncements and the tradition and sayings of the Prophet. It is argued that He created *all* these resources for the benefit and the enjoyment of *all* of His creatures to the extent that it is not considered *israf* (wanton consumption and waste):

> It is He who produceth gardens, with trellises and without, and dates, and tilth with produce of all kinds and olives and pomegranates similar (in kind) and different (in variety) eat of their fruit in their season, but render the dues that are proper on the day that the harvest is gathered. But waste not by excess: for God loveth not the wasters. (Quran VI: 141)

The proponents of the limited ownership of private property argue that limitations to property rights come from the Quranic pronouncements, that "He endowed *all* His creatures with what He has made available" (as in Quran II: 114–116). Also, it is argued, the limited property rights are evident from God's admonishment of the wealthy and of the *mosref* (those who engage in wanton, wasteful consumption) as well as from the desire for social justice as declared by both The Prophet and the first *shia,* Imam Ali. These points are present, both explicitly and implicitly, in the *sharia* and are cited as proof of God's intention for limited and regulated private ownership.

In any case, as of now neither the traditional nor the modified view has been reaffirmed by the Parliament and the Council of Guardians of the Constitution in the Islamic Republic of Iran. The Iranian leadership's ambivalence in regard to the concept of private property has been translated into uncertainty on the part of entrepreneurs and investors. In turn,

this uncertainty has been reflected, dramatically, in private capital formation and investment. Except for a brief period in 1982, the fixed capital formation as a percentage of the gross national product has been
falling, reaching an all-time low in 1987, the last year for which the data
has become available to the public (see figure 9.2). The fall in the rate
of investment as a percentage of GNP has taken place despite the falling
of the GNP itself. Similar damage has been made evident by other economic and political indicators, including those relating to international
trade, the multiple foreign exchange rate system, legal protection of
individuals, and the benign neglect of constitutional matters pertinent to
individual rights.

INTERNATIONAL TRADE

One of the most basic functions of any national government is that per-
taining to the establishment of policies that will promote the social and
economic welfare of its citizenry. The problem confronting national
leaders is that they must choose social and economic policies that, even
though subject to constraints, will be of maximal benefit to the masses.
It is a well-known fact that international trade typically enhances the
economic prosperity of all involved, except under circumstances when
restrictive assumptions apply. For importers and exporters, international trade provides "economic rent." However, such trade opens up
the economy, making it more vulnerable to the influence of foreign cultures and powers.

The leadership of the Islamic Republic wanted to reduce the economic and political dependence upon external powers that had come to
characterize the country during the twentieth century. Therefore, they
had to find a way to avoid the perception that Iran was in any way
dependent upon or in alliance with those who were assumed to be the
root cause of the country's ills—the multinationals. The extra profits
(rent), and foreign influence and domination were considered to be
directly at odds with the social, economic, and political interests of the
country.

Because they were viewed as socially undesirable, it was determined
that these international influences must be eliminated in some fashion.
In the absence of a complete prohibition of international trade, the
Iranian government could remove the rent and foreign control by insti-
tuting regulatory policies, taxation, or nationalization. The framers of
the Iranian Constitution opted for the most extreme solution and called

for nationalization of international trade. Article 44 of the constitution states, "[T]he state sector is to include . . . [the] foreign sector." Therefore, rather than fostering an industrial base in a competitive environment in order to eliminate the perceived and real economic rent, and in an effort to avoid domination, the country's leadership decided in favor of nationalization of international trade. In so doing, the government would collect the rent and prevent "foreign economic domination over the country's economy" (Article 43).

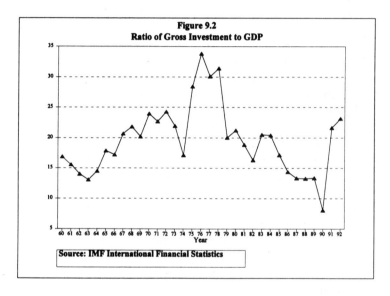

Figure 9.2

In accordance with the mandate of the constitution, a bill was passed by the Parliament to nationalize foreign trade. However, the Council of Guardians of the Constitution vetoed it because it was considered un-Islamic and therefore unlawful. Any bill can be vetoed by this council. A favorable vote by the Parliament and the consent of the president are not sufficient for a bill to become law. Because of the disagreement between the council and the government, foreign trade continues to be another important aspect of the economy that remains in a state of limbo.

HUMAN RIGHTS

On the legal front, more than a decade after the revolution and after more than a decade of continuing domination and control of the country, individual rule rather than rule of law predominates. There is anecdotal published evidence that some kind of *moulook altavaiefy* (an old form of government by tribal chieftains) has reemerged as a governing structure within Iran. In today's Iran, however, tribal chieftains are replaced by *mullahs*. When charged with a crime, determination of one's guilt or innocence depends upon the region in which he/she resides, whether he/she has ties with anyone in power, and upon the ruling *mullah* at the time. Each one of these elements could be a determining factor in the finding of an individual's guilt or innocence.

In spite of the explicit expression of the constitution (as in Article 22), the government has not yet recognized the sanctity of the home and individual rights. Articles published in weekly newspapers such as *Kayhan-e-Havee* (a Tehran-based weekly) and the *Iran Times* (a Washington, D.C.–based weekly) provide evidence of intrusive behavior on the part of the police and other security forces. It is common to read about police raids on homes in search of "un-Islamic conduct," a charge that is open to interpretation. It is fair to say that the brunt of repression has so far been aimed at working and educated women,[9] again, in direct contradiction of the constitution (Articles 20, 21, 28).[10] The governing public discourse in Iran provides no effective protection for dissent or even deviation. The constitution's guarantee of freedom of expression is crippled by exceptions requiring compliance with "the fundamental principles of Islam or the rights of the public."[11]

Somehow right after the revolution when the power struggle was intense among all the religious and nonreligious factions and groups jockeying for power, and when revolutionary fever was still high, some social groups found themselves subject to intense pressure and persecution, again in direct contradiction with the explicit articles of the constitution (26, 27, 32, 33, 37, 38, among others). These social groups were comprised of managers, capitalists, the higher echelon of bureaucrats, and the highly educated.

A great many of these individuals who were subject to the misplaced antagonism of the ruling oligarchy—an estimated three million of them—chose to flee or else were driven out of the country. At the time, the country's leadership was not cognizant of the fact that such a huge "brain drain" in entrepreneurial capacity would cripple the prospect of the nation's economic growth and development for some time to come. The vacuum of educated and trained manpower became acute and problematic as the national leaders tried to execute a deadly war with Iraq and to manage the affairs of the country. Even after a decade of squabbles and debates over this avoidable and reversible mistake, the government has not yet been able to provide a general amnesty to those who are abroad and are uncertain of their situation in Iran. These are the very people who possess the managerial capability and financial resources that are badly needed within Iran in order to foster economic growth and development. These are the very groups that, ostensibly, President Rafsanjani has been trying to lure back into the country. Yet it is somehow against intuition for anyone to expect these people to return to Iran without a blanket and unconditional amnesty. Even so, the parliament, the president, and the leader do not seem to have a common understanding on this issue.

During the first few years after the revolution, a big shift of resources took place by confiscation of property from those who were considered too close to the old regime and transfer of that property to the newly empowered classes. As a result, there was an immediate improvement in income distribution. This situation was short-lived and eventually gave way to even greater disparity among income levels. An immediate explanation for this is that the new management/owners did not improve and maintain their existing capital, and, as the value of capital fell, the wage rate that they could afford to pay lagged behind, therefore widening the gap. Assuming that this explanation is accurate, the problems of poverty and low standard of living could best be ameliorated by following a capital-intensive strategy. As the intensity of capital is increased, the value of the marginal product of labor, and hence wage rates, will increase. This is the best long-term solution to the poverty of disadvantaged classes.

LESSONS FROM THE COLLAPSE OF THE EASTERN BLOC COUNTRIES

The collapse of the Eastern bloc countries provides an experience from which much can be learned by ideologically driven nations such as Iran. First and foremost is the fact that a nation that cannot feed its people cannot survive, even though it might possess top technological know-how and might have the best industrial blueprint for manufacturing. While a huge smelting plant or a sophisticated automobile-producing plant might be truly awesome, the obvious truism remains—these plants require people to run them and these people need food.

In years past, it appeared that a popular approach to development supported rapid industrialization at the expense of agriculture. Iran itself has witnessed and felt the detrimental effects that can result from such a policy. During the Shah's regime, a policy was pursued that focused on development and industrialization. As all resources were devoted to this goal, agricultural production began to fail. Eventually food costs rose, and it became increasingly difficult for average citizens to afford the costs of a balanced diet.

A second point which can be learned, particularly from the experience of the Soviet bloc, is that industrial plants that are large in size are not necessarily better. Even though economy of scale considerations are important in the choice of a plant's size, largeness might prove to be a handicap because of the associated resource requirements. A good example of this point is the existence of numerous inefficient plants throughout the Eastern bloc countries that are not operational because the necessary raw materials and manpower are lacking.

The alternative policy, that is, introducing new technology in smaller units, might prove to be more successful for several reasons. Thinking in terms of small, manageable, malleable, and adaptable technology has the advantage of limiting the inevitable cultural intrusion that a new technology will eventually have upon the country. In the first place, the ability to master the technology and adapt, retain, maintain, and indigenize it to the local environment might prove to be easier if the technology is kept at a level that is manageable. This policy probably has a higher chance of creating forward and backward linkage with the traditional domestic industries, whereas a large and sophisticated industry might not develop linkages with these industries and, as a result, it would necessitate the need for an ongoing, permanent dependence upon the source that has provided the technology. Technological interdependence would be stymied. Iran has experienced this process time and again. One prime example pertains to the automobile industry. Mostly composed of assembly factories, the industry did not promote the creation of other down- or upstream production facilities. Consequently, opportunities for further ancillary industrial development were lost.

A third point is that nationalization of industries does not necessarily mean an undertaking for the good of the masses. A nationalized nonoperational factory is only good as an ugly environmental hazard. Although nationalization might provide a sense of security at the time it is being introduced, in the long run, it will neither feed nor clothe the public if, as has usually been the case, the government proves to be an inefficient manager. It would be to the benefit of the masses if the government denationalized (privatized) its viable units as a damage control step. It would save the government vast amounts of resources that could be used to improve the infrastructure of the country.

SYNTHESIS

To achieve meaningful and balanced economic growth and development, a country first must formulate a long-range vision of development that is tailored to its needs, endowments, and ideological constraints. The lack of any long-term vision for the country's future well-being is probably the most dangerous source of disruption and the greatest contributor to worsening economic conditions. Without this vision, declining conditions will most likely be met with wasteful economic "quick fix" mindsets and programs. Second, the country must systematically reinvest in both its infrastructure and its human resources. Constant attention must be paid to transportation, communication, and educational systems as part of an effort to promote general welfare within the society. Each of these systems is a necessary ingredient of industrialization, without which development will not materialize. Accomplishment of this goal requires that the leadership arrive at some degree of consensus in regard to the strategy that will be followed in an effort to acquire the technology needed for both the upgrade and maintenance of the infrastructure, as well as the technology needed to produce consumer and investment goods.

Third, an understanding of economic interdependence is a necessary condition for any country that is embarking upon a path toward economic development in today's world. During the 1960s, and probably during the 1970s, there were only a few sources of new technologies. The Western industrialized world held an oligopolistic control over the "know-how." Now, in the 1990s, this is no longer the case. There has been a definite breakdown in Western dominance and control of technology because of the activities of multinational or transnational corporations, which do not confine themselves to any particular political boundary. These corporations will go wherever they feel they are *safe,* and where they believe the potential for profit is higher. In the case of Iran, if the multinational or transnational corporations who possess the needed technologies are to be enticed to invest in the country, the government must come to a definite consensus and must clearly enunciate its position with regard to these key issues. A clear stance must be taken in regard to property rights and to due process for individuals involved in the court system, and it is imperative that government leaders clearly express their commitment to a process that will allow and encourage full and open debate around the type of society Iranians might envisage for the nation as it prepares for the twenty-first century.

Presently, a country need not be entirely dependent upon foreign technology. Attaining a degree of national self-sufficiency is especially important as the country unavoidably enters into the international system of technological interdependence. The country could identify and build upon its own indigenous technologies based upon local needs and capabilities. When importation is necessary, this provides an opportunity for the importing country to study the new technology and to further refine and improve upon it. The former Soviet Union, Japan, South Korea, Taiwan, and many other countries have been recognized for their ability to improve upon and eventually re-market technologies that have originated elsewhere.

It is important to note that there is no one particular way of adapting to a new technology. Nor is there any one technology that is useful and adaptable to all environments. Each country has first to consider its ability to receive and apply each new form of technology, along with all the "baggage" that comes with it. As evidenced worldwide, any imported technology brings with it unique demands upon the sociopolitical-economic structures and upon the culture of the receiving country. If the receiving environment is not ready to accept and meet the requirements of the new technology (that is, new management, ability to market, necessary human and capital resources, culture, and so on), its implementation will fail, and all the resources that were expended in the process will be wasted.

If the economic and cultural environments are not adequately prepared for the introduction of new technology, the all-important linkage to the rest of the community will not be made. The imported technology will not develop forward and backward linkages with other segments of the economic system. Therefore, it will not contribute to an overall balanced growth of the economy. A good example of this has to do with the introduction of new technology that enabled the extraction of large quantities of oil in Iran. Because the oil industry never developed necessary linkages with other economic and social sectors, it therefore did not function as a propellant for the whole economy. Its development did not lead to the development of other indigenous support groups.

In their pursuit of economic and political stability, the leadership of Iran must focus their attention upon a number of issues that, heretofore, have been ignored. The government must understand that technoeconomic ability is no longer monopolized by either the East or the West. Also, it must come to understand that there is much to be learned from the experiences of other nations. The collapse of the Eastern bloc and the failure of many Third World countries to achieve a higher standard of living for their citizens provide ample evidence that there is no shortcut to economic development. It is a tedious, long-term, and slow process. In order for this process to succeed, the government must provide an economic and cultural environment and an infrastructure that are conducive to economic development. Essential to this is the assurance that there is security for individuals, and for property as well, through the enforcement of human rights and property rights.

It remains to be seen whether or not, for the sake of its collective well-being, the ideologically based government of the Islamic Republic of Iran can compromise or modify the blend of ideology, nationalism, and religion that it has constructed and purveyed over the past decade.

NOTES TO CHAPTER 9

1. The authors would like to thank Akbar Mahdi, Bernard Reilly, and Charles Waldauer for their comments. However, they alone remain responsible for any remaining errors. A version of this paper was presented at the tenth annual CIRA conference in Austin, Texas, in April 1992.

2. M. H. Pesaran, "Income Distribution and its Major Determinants in Iran," in *Iran: Past, Present, and the Future,* J. W. Jacqs, ed. (Aspen, Colo.: Aspen Institute for Humanistic Studies, 1976); Sohrab Behdad, "Winners and Losers of the Iranian Revolution: A Study in Income Distribution," *International Journal of Middle East Studies,* vol. 20 (1988): 327–58.

3. Jalal Al-e Ahmad, *Gharbzadegi* (Westoxication), 2nd ed. (Tehran, Iran: Entesharat-e Rav'aq, 1956).

4. Abol Hassan Banisadr, "The Present Economic System Spells Ruins for the Future," in *Iran Erupts,* Ali-Reza Nobari, ed. (Stanford, Calif.: Iran-American Documentation Group, Stanford University, 1978), 117–40.

5. Janice M. Moore, "The Iranian Revolution Revisited," in *Modern Capitalism and Islamic Ideology in Iran,* Cyrus Bina and Hamid Zangeneh, eds. (New York: St.

Martin's Press, 1992); Said Amir Arjomand, *The Turban for the Crown: The Islamic Revolution in Iran* (New York: Oxford University Press, 1988); Said Amir Arjomand, "Theories of Revolution and the Contemporary Revolutions in Iran, Eastern Europe, and Central Asia," in Persian, *Mehregan, An Iranian Journal of Culture and Politics,* vol. 2, no. 1 (Spring 1993): 37–50.

6. Hooshang Amiahmadi, *Revolution and Economic Transition: The Iranian Experience* (Albany: State University of New York Press, 1992). Also, Hooshang Amirahmadi, "Economic Cost of the War and Reconstruction in Iran," in *Modern Capitalism and Islamic Ideology in Iran,* Cyrus Bina and Hamid Zangeneh, eds. (New York: St. Martin's Press, 1992), 257–81.

7. H. Piedar, *Ownership, Work and Capital* (Muslim Student Association, 1988); Mahmood Taleqani, *Islam and Ownership,* Ahmad Jabbari and Farhang Rajaee, trans. (Mazda, 1983); M. H. Beheshti, *Islamic Economic* (Teheran, 1368); Hamid Hosseini, "Notions of Private Property in Islamic Economics in Contemporary Iran: A Review of Literature," *International Journal of Social Economics,* vol. 15, no. 9 (1988): 51–61.

8. Piedar, op. cit.; Taleqani, op. cit.; Beheshti, op. cit.

9. See, for example, Nayereh Tohidi, "The Women Question and National Development in Iran," paper presented at the International Conference on Social and Economic Development in Pre- and Post-Revolutionary Iran, Queen's University, Kingston, Ontario, Canada, April 8–10, 1991; Nayereh Tohidi, "Women and Revolution in Iran: Lessons to Be Learned," Educational Resources Information Center, ERIC, *Viewprints* 120 (1986).

10. Hamid Algar, trans. *Constitution of the Islamic Republic of Iran* (Berkeley, Calif.: Mizan Press, 1980).

11. Human Rights Watch, *Guardians of Thought: Limits on Freedom of Expression in Iran* (New York: Human Rights Watch, August 1993), 11.

S·E·L·E·C·T B·I·B·L·I·O·G·R·A·P·H·Y

Abrahamian, Ervand. *Khomenism: Essays on the Islamic Republic.* Berkeley, Calif.: University of California Press, 1993.

——. *The Iranian Mojahedin.* New Haven, Conn.: Yale University Press, 1989.

——. *Iran Between Two Revolutions.* Princeton, N.J.: Princeton University Press, 1982.

Afkhami, Glolam R. *The Iranian Revolution: Thanatos on a National Scale.* Washington, D.C.: The Middle East Institute, 1985.

Aghajanian, Akbar. "Ethnic Inequality in Iran: An Overview." *International Journal of Middle East Studies,* vol. 15 (May 1983): 211–24.

Ahmadu, Fuambai, Neil Bascomb, Joseph Heiman, and Aline Van Duyn. "Middle East." *Euromoney* (September 1992): 105–19.

——. "The Summoning: 'But They Said, We Will Not Hearken.'—Jeremiah." *Foreign Affairs,* vol. 72 (September/October 1993): 2–19.

Ajami, Fouad. "Iran: The Impossible Revolution." *Foreign Affairs,* vol. 67 (Winter 1988–1989): 135–55.

Akhavi, Shahrough. "Reflections on a Decade of Scholarship On The Iranian Revolution: Background to Two Recent Perspectives in the Literature." *The Middle East Journal,* vol. 43 (Spring 1989): 289–95.

——. *Religion and Politics in Contemporary Iran: Clergy- State Relations in the Pahlavi Period.* Albany, N.Y.: State University of New York Press, 1980.

Alam, Asadollah. *The Shah and I: The Confidential Diary of Iran's Royal Court, 1969–1977.* Edited and introduced by Alinaghi Alikhani. London: I. B. Tauris, 1992.

——. "The New Iranian Left." *Middle East Journal,* vol. 41 (Spring 1987): 218–33.

Alaolmolki, Nozar. "The New Iranian Left." *The Middle East Journal,* vol. 41 (Summer 1993): 409–28.

Algar Hamid. *Islam and Revolution: Writings and Declarations of Imam Khomeini.* Berkeley, Calif.: Mizan Press, 1981.

Ali, Salamat. "From Bazaar To Bloc: Teheran Signals Improved Economic Ties." *Far Eastern Economic Review,* vol. 153 (September 5, 1991): 26–27.

——. "Iran: Friends and Foes." *Far Eastern Economic Review,* vol. 149 (July 5, 1990): 23–25.

Alnasrawi, Abbas. "Iraq: Economic Consequences of the 1991 Gulf War and Future Outlook." *Third World Quarterly,* vol. 13, no. 2 (1992): 335–52.

——. "Oil Dimensions of the Gulf Crisis." In *The Gulf Crisis: Background and Consequences,* Ibrahim Ibrahim, ed. Washington, D.C.: Georgetown University, 1992, 38–75.

——. *Arab Nationalism, Oil and the Political Economy of Dependency.* Westport, Conn.: Greenwood Press, 1991.

——. "Emergence and Growth of Public Sector in the Arab World" (in Arabic). In *Public Sector and Private Sector in the Arab World,* Nader Furgani, ed. Beirut: Center for Arab Unity Studies, 1990, 23–37.

——. "On Collective Reliance in the Arab World" (in Arabic). In *Interdependence and Economic Integration in the Arab World: Theoretical Approximation*, Ismail Sabic Abdalla, ed. Beirut: Center for Arab Unity Studies, 1990, 331–42.

——. "Economic Integration: A Missing Dimension of Arab Nationalism." In *Arab Americans: Continuity and Change*, Baha Abu-Labor and Michael W. Suleiman, eds. Belmont, Mass.: AAUG Press, 287–302.

——. "U.S. Foreign Policy in the Middle East." *Arab Studies Quarterly*, vol. 11, no. 1 (winter 1989): 55–83.

——. "The Arab Economies: Twenty Years of Change and Dependency." *Arab Studies Quarterly*, vol. 9, no 4 (Fall 1987): 357–82.

——. *OPEC in a Changing World Economy*. Baltimore, Md.: The Johns Hopkins University Press, 1985.

——. *Arab Oil and United States Energy Requirements*. Belmont, Mass.: AAUG Press, 1982.

——. *Financing Economic Development in Iraq: The Role of Oil in Middle Eastern Economy*. New York: Praeger, 1967.

Amid, Mohammad Javad. *Agriculture, Poverty and Reform in Iran*. New York: Routledge, 1990.

Amin, S. H. "Commission Agreements In Iran And Qatar." *Middle East Executive Reports*, vol. 13 (June 1990): 11, 21–23.

Amir Arjomand, Said. *The Turban for the Crown: The Islamic Revolution in Iran*. New York: Oxford University Press, 1988.

——. *The Shadow of God and the Hidden Imam*. Chicago, Ill.: University of Chicago Press, 1984.

Amirahmadi, Hooshang, ed. *The United States and the Middle East: A Search for New Perspectives*. Albany, N.Y.: State University of New York Press, 1993.

Amirahmadi, Hooshang. "Economic Costs of the War and the Reconstruction in Iran." In *Modern Capitalism and Islamic Ideology in Iran*, Cyrus Bina and Hamid Zangeneh, eds. New York: St. Martin Press, 1992.

——. *United States and the Middle East: A Search for New Perspectives*. Albany, N.Y.: State University of New York Press, 1992.

——. "Global Restructuring, Persian Gulf War and the U.S. Quest." *Executive Report*, vol. 12, no. 7 (July 1992): 9–17.

——. "Toward a Multi-Gap Approach to Medium-Term Economic Growth in Iran." *Orient*, vol. 33, no. 1 (January 1992): 97–117.

——. *Revolution and Economic Transition: The Iranian Experience*. Albany, N.Y.: State University of New York Press, 1990.

——. "Economic Reconstruction of Iran: Costing the War Damage." *Third World Quarterly*, vol. 12, no. 1 (January 1990): 26–47.

——. "Popular Movements, Incidental Factors, and the State's Measure for Regional Development in the Islamic Republic of Iran." *The Review of Urban and Regional Development Studies*, vol. 1, no. 1 (December 1988): 47–64.

———. "The State and Territorial Social Justice in Post- Revolutionary Iran." *International Journal of Urban and Regional Research,* vol. 13, no. 1 (March): 92–120. An expanded and modified version was reprinted in *The Iranian Journal of International Affairs.* vol. 1, no. 273 (Summer–Fall 1989): 225–58.

———. "A Theory of Ethnic Collective Movements and Its Application to Iran." *Ethnic and Racial Studies,* vol. 10, no. 4 (October 1987): 363–91.

——— (with F. Atash). "Dynamics of Provincial Development and Disparity in Iran: 1956–84." *Third World Planning Review,* vol. 9, no. 2 (May 1987): 155–85.

———. "Regional Planning in Iran: A Survey of Problems and Policies." *The Journal of Developing Areas,* vol. 20, no. 4 (July 1986): 501–30.

Amirahmadi, H., and James A. Bill. "The Clinton Administration and the Future of U.S.-Iran Relations." *Middle East Insight* (1993).

Amirahmadi, Hooshang, and Nader Entessar, eds. *Iran and the Arab World.* New York: St. Martin's Press, 1993.

———. *Reconstruction and Regional Diplomacy in the Persian Gulf.* London: Routledge, 1992.

Amirahmadi, Hooshang, and Eric Hoogland. *US-Iran Relations: Areas of Mutual Interest.* Washington, D.C.: The Middle East Institute, 1994.

Amirahmadi, Hooshang, and A. Kiafar. "Tehran: Growth and Contradiction." *Journal of Planning Education and Research,* vol. 6, no. 3 (Spring 1987): 167–77.

Amirahmadi, Hooshang, and Manoucher Parvin, eds. *Post Revolutionary Iran.* Boulder, Colo.: Westview Press, 1988.

Amjad, Mohammed. *Iran: From Royal Dictatorship to Theocracy.* New York: Greenwood Press, 1989.

Amuzegar, Jahangir. *Iran's Economy Under the Islamic Republic.* London: I.B. Tauris, 1993.

———. "Oil and a Changing OPEC." *Finance & Development,* vol. 27 (September 1990): 43–45.

———. *Dynamics of the Iranian Revolution: The Pahlavi's Triumph and Tragedy.* Albany, N.Y.: State University of New York Press, 1991.

Anonymous. "Through the Qeshm Window." *Banker,* vol. 143 (September 1993): 48.

———. "Iran: Back to Basics." *Banker,* vol. 142 (February 1992): 27–33.

Avanessian, Aida. "Iran: Establishing A Presence in the Islamic Republic." *Middle East Executive Reports,* vol. 15 (July 1992): 9, 11–13.

Bahmani-oskooee, Mohsen. "Black Market Exchange Rates Versus Official Exchange Rates In Testing Purchasing Power Parity: An Examination Of The Iranian Rial." *Applied Economics,* vol. 25 (April 1993): 465–72.

Bakhash, Shaul. *The Reign of the Ayatollahs: Iran and the Islamic Revolution.* New York: Basic Books, 1984.

———. *The Politics of Oil and Revolution in Iran.* Washington, D.C.: Brookings Institution, 1982.

Bakhash, Shaul, and K. Mofid. "After the Gulf War." *The World Today,* vol. 45 (March 1989): 46–49.

Bani-Sadr, Abol Hassan. *My Turn to Speak: Iran, the Revolution and Secret Deals with the U.S.* London: Brassey's, 1991.

Banuazizi, Ali, and Myron Weiner, eds. *The State, Religion and Ethnic Politics: Afghanistan, Iran, and Pakistan.* Syracuse, N.Y.: Syracuse University Press, 1986.

Bayat, Assef. *Workers and Revolution in Iran.* London: Zed Press, 1987.

Behdad, Sohrab. "Islamic Economics: A Utopian-scholastic-neoclassical-Keynesian Synthesis!" *Research in the History of Economic Thought and Methodology,* vol. 9 (1992).

———. "Property Rights in the Contemporary Islamic Economic Thought: A Critical Perspective." *Review of Social Economy,* vol. 47, no. 2 (Summer 1989): 185–211.

———. "Winners and Losers of the Iranian Revolution: A Study in Income Distribution." *International Journal Of Middle East Studies,* vol. 21, no. 3 (August 1989): 357–58.

———. "Foreign Exchange Gap, Structural Constraints and the Political Economy of Exchange Rate Determination In Iran." *International Journal Of Middle East Studies,* vol. 20, no. 1 (February 1988): 1–21.

———. "Political Economy of Islamic Planning in Iran." In *Post-Revolutionary Iran,* H. Amirahmadi and M. Parvin, eds. Boulder, Colo.: Westview Press, 1988, 107–25.

Behnam, M. Reza. *Cultural Foundations of Iranian Politics.* Salt Lake City, Utah: University of Utah Press, 1986.

Behrooz, Maziar. "Factionalism in Iran under Khomeini." *Middle Eastern Studies,* vol. 27 (October 1991): 597–614.

Benard, Cheryl, and Zalmay Khalilzad. *"The Government of God": Iran's Islamic Republic.* New York: Columbia University Press, 1984.

Bennigsen, Alexandre. "Mullahs, Mujahidin and Soviet Muslims." *Problems Of Communism,* vol. 33 (November–December 1984): 28–44.

Bill, James A. *The Eagle and the Lion: The Tragedy of American-Iranian Relations.* New Haven, Conn.: Yale University Press, 1988.

———. *The Politics of Iran: Groups, Classes and Modernization.* Merrill, 1972.

Bina, Cyrus. "Towards a New World Order: U.S. Hegemony, Client-States and Islamic Alternative." In *Islam, Muslims and the Modern State,* H. Mutalib and T. Hashemi, eds. London: Macmillan, forthcoming.

———. "Oil, Japan, and Globalization," *Challenge,* vol. 37, no. 3 (May-June 1994): 41-48.

———. "The Foreign Crisis and the Fragility of the Iranian Economy," *Mehregan,* vol. 2, no. 4 (Winter 1994): 117-31 (in Persian, with English Abstract).

———. "Mossadegh and British Plots to Abort the Oil Negotiations," *Mehregan,* vol. 2, no. 3 (Fall 1993): 119-134 (in Persian, with English Abstract).

———. "The Rhetoric of Oil, and the Dilemma of War and American Hegemony." *Arab Studies Quarterly,* vol. 15. no. 3 (Summer 1993): 1–20.

———. "Global Oil and Unviability of Pax Americana." *Economic and Political Weekly,* vol. 37, no. 28 (July 11, 1992).

———. "A Prelude to the Internationalization of Post-War Economy." *Journal of Economic Democracy,* vol. 2, no. 2 (January–March 1992).

———. "War over Access to Cheap Oil or the Reassertion of U.S. Global Hegemony." In *Mobilizing Democracy: Changing the US Role in the Middle East,* Greg Bates, ed. Monroe, Maine: Common Courage Press, 1991, 71–81.

———. "The Political Economy of Global Oil." *The World and I,* special issue on the Middle East (December 1990).

———. "Limits of OPEC Pricing: OPEC Profits and the Nature of Global Oil Accumulation," *OPEC Review,* vol. 14, no. 1 (Spring 1990): 55-73.

———. "Some Controversies in the Development of Rent Theory: the Nature of Oil Rent," *Capital and Class,* no. 39 (Winter 1989): 82-112

———. "Price Formation, Control and Competition in the International Energy Industry." *Energy Economics,* vol. 11, no. 3 (July 1989).

———. "Internationalization of the Oil Industry: Simple Oil Shocks or Structural Crisis." *Journal of Fernard Braudel Center,* vol. 11, no. 3 (Summer 1988): 329–70.

———. *The Economics of the Oil Crisis.* New York: St. Martin's Press, 1985.

Bina, Cyrus, and Check Davis. "Transnationalization of Capital, the Global Labor Process, and the International Labor Movement." In *The Labor Process and Control of Labor: The Changing Nature of Work Relations in the Late Twentieth Century,* B. Berberoglu, ed. New York: Praeger Publishers, 1993.

Bina, Cyrus, and Behzad Yaghmaian. "Post-War Global Accumulation and the Transnationalization of Capital." *Capital and Class,* special issue: *Beyond the Nation-State,* no. 43 (Spring 1994): 43–64.

Bina, Cyrus, and Hamid Zangeneh, eds. *Modern Capitalism and Islamic Ideology in Iran.* New York: St. Martin's Press, 1992.

Boroujerdi, Mehrzad. *Iranian Intellectuals and the West: A Study in Orientalism in Reverse.* Albany, N.Y.: State University of New York Press, forthcoming.

——— (with Ali Mirsepassi). *Modernity and Authenticity: Dilemmas of Iranian Print Culture.* Austin: Center for Middle Eastern Studies, The University of Texas, forthcoming.

———. "The Encounter of Post-revolutionary Thought in Iran with Hegel, Heidegger and Popper." In *Cultural Transitions: The Articulation of Religious and Secular Discourses in the Middle East,* Serif Mardin, ed. Leiden: E. J. Brill, forthcoming.

———. "Can Islam be Secularized?" In *In Transition: Essays on Culture and Identity in Middle Eastern Societies,* M. R. Ghanoonparvar, ed. Laredo, Tex.: Laredo State University Press, forthcoming.

———. "Gharbzadegi: The Dominant Intellectual Discourse of Pre- and Post-revolutionary Iran." In *Iran: Political Culture in the Islamic Republic,* Samih K. Farsoun and Mehrdad Mashayekhi, eds. London and New York: Routledge, 1992, 30–56.

———. "Hizbullah (The Party of God)." *Encyclopedia of the Modern Islamic World.* New York: Oxford University Press, forthcoming.

———. "Iranian Cultural Identity: A Dissenter's Tableau." *Iranian Studies* (forthcoming).

——— (with Ali Mirsepassi). "Rethinking Third Worldism." *International Third World Studies Journal and Review* (forthcoming).

———. "Prospects for Civil Society and Secularism in Iran" (in Persian). *Kankash* 8 (Spring 1992): 13–44.

———. "Westoxication and Orientalism in Reverse" (in Russian). *Iran Nameh*, vol. 8, no. 3 (Summer 1990): 375–390.

———. "The Distinctive Features of the Iranian Revolution" (in Persian). *Kankash*, vol. 5 (Fall 1989): 19–49.

———. "Iranian Intellectuals and the Enigma of Westernization" (in Persian). *Kankash*, vols. 2 and 3 (Spring 1988): 11–47.

———. Translation of Nicos Poulantzas's "Is There a Crisis of Marxism?" *Journal of the Hellenic Diaspora VI*, vol. 3 (Fall 1979); *Kankash*, vol. 1 (Summer 1987): 62–74.

Bozorgmehr, Mehdi, and Georges Sabagh. "High Status Immigrants: A Statistical Profile of Iranians in the United States." *Iranian Studies*, vol. 21 (October 1988): 5–36.

Buffington, Milton P. "Rebuilding Iran's Economy: Qeshm Free Trade Zone." *Middle East Executive Reports*, vol. 14 (October 1991): 9–11.

Burrell, R. M. "Ruler and Subject in Iran." *Middle Eastern Studies*, vol. 25 (April 1989): 253–61.

———. "Iran: Revolution, Illusion—and Reality?" *Middle Eastern Studies*, vol. 20 (April 1984): 232–37.

Chehabi, H. E. *Iranian Politics and Religious Modernism: The Liberation Movement of Iran Under the Shah and Khomeini*. Ithaca, N.Y.: Cornell University Press, 1990.

Chubin, Chahram, and Charles Tripp. *Iran and Iraq at War*. Boulder, Colo.: Westview Press, 1988.

Clad, James. "Teheran's Asian Links: Pragmatism Prevails." *Far Eastern Economic Review*, vol. 129 (July 4, 1985): 26–28.

———. "Iran Woos Peking." *Far Eastern Economic Review*, vol. 128 (June 13, 1985): 44–45.

Clawson, Patrick, and C. A. Kupchan. "Iran After Khomeini." *Orbis*, vol. 34 (Spring 1990): 241–51.

Clawson, Patrick. "Islamic Iran's Economic Politics and Prospects." *The Middle East Journal*, vol. 42 (Summer 1988): 371–88.

Clawson, Patrick, and Cyrus Sassanpour. "Adjustment To A Foreign Exchange Shock: Iran, 1951–1953." *International Journal of Middle East Studies*, vol. 19 (February 1987): 1–22.

Cooley, John K. *Payback: America's Long War in the Middle East*. Washington, D.C.: Brassey's, 1991.

Cordesman, Anthony H., and Abraham R. Wagner. *The Lessons of Modern War*, vol. 2: *The Iran-Iraq War*. Boulder, Colo.: Westview Press, 1990.

———. *The Iran-Iraq War and Western Security 1984–87: Strategic Implications and Policy Options*. London: Jane's Publishing Company, 1987.

Cottam, Richard W. "Inside Revolutionary Iran." *The Middle East Journal*, vol. 43 (Spring 1989): 168–85.

———. *Iran and the United States: A Cold War Case Study*. Pittsburgh, Penn.: University of Pittsburgh Press, 1988.

———. *Khomeini, the Future, and U.S. Options*. Muscatine, Iowa: 1987.

Dabashi, Hamid. *Theology of Discontent: The Ideological Foundations of the Islamic Revolution in Iran*. New York: New York University Press, 1992.

———. *Expectation of the Millennium: Shi'ism in History.* Albany, N.Y.: SUNY Press, 1989.

Dabashi, Hamid, Seyyed Hossein Nasr, and Seyyed Vali Reza Nasr, eds. *Shi'ism: Doctrines, Thoughts, and Spirituality.* Albany, N.Y.: SUNY Press, 1988.

Darvish, Tikva. "Inter-industry Mobility After Migration: Theory and Application." *Economic Development and Cultural Change,* vol. 38 (April 1990): 611–23.

Dorraj, M. *Political Culture in the Middle East.* London: Routledge Publishing House, forthcoming.

———. "Privatization, Democratization and Development in the Third World: Lessons of a Turbulent Decade." *Journal of Developing Societies,* vol. 10, no. 2 (Spring 1994).

———. "Will OPEC Survive?" *Arab Studies Quarterly,* vol. 15, no. 4 (Fall 1993).

———. "The Change in International Political Economy and the Third World" (in Persian). *Mehrgan: An Iranian Journal of Culture and Politics,* a publication of Teachers Association of Iran, vol. 2, no. 2 (Fall 1993).

———. "Populism and Corporation in Post-revolutionary Iranian Political Culture." In *Iran: Political Culture In The Islamic Republic,* S. Farsoun and M. Mashayekhi, eds. London: Routledge Publishing House, 1992.

———. "The Political Sociology of Sect and Sectarianism in Iranian Politics: 1960–79." *The International Journal of Comparative Religion,* vol. 1, no. 3 (October 1992).

———. "The Revival of Islam and Politics of Counter-culture Mobilization in the Middle East." In *Multinational Culture: Social Impacts of a Global Economy,* C. Lehman and R. Moore, eds. New York: Greenwood Press, 1992.

———. *From Zarathustra to Khomeini: Populism and Dissent in Iran.* Boulder, Colo.: Lynne Rienner, 1990.

———. "The Religion-political Proclivities of the Iranian Mind: The Pre-Islamic Roots." *Central Asian Survey,* vol. 5, no. 1 (Summer 1986): 49–57.

Dorraj, M., and M. Vanderlaan. "Third World Foreign Policies in Post-revolutionary Era." *Journal of Third Word Studies,* vol. 8, no. 2 (Fall 1991).

Dyer, Geoff. "Iran Reins In Reform." *Euromoney* (October 1992): 81–85.

Ehteshami, Anoushiravan. "After Khomeini: The Structure of Power in the Iranian Second Republic." *Political Studies,* vol. 39 (March 1991): 148–57.

Ehteshamin, Anoushiravan, and Manshour Varasteh, eds. *Iran and the International Community.* London: Routledge, 1991.

Elm, Mostafa. *Oil, Power, and Principle: Iran's Oil Nationalization and its Aftermath.* Syracuse, N.Y.: Syracuse University Press, 1992.

Elrahman, Ossama Iran. "Urbanization And Regional Disparities In Post-revolutionary Iran." *Journal of Developing Areas,* vol. 27, (April 1993): 435–36.

Enayat, Hamid. *Modern Islamic Political Thought.* Austin, Tex.: University of Texas Press, 1983.

Entessar, Nadar. "Azeri Nationalism in the Former Soviet Union and Iran." In *The Rising Tide of Cultural Pluralism: The Nation-State at Bay?* Crawford Young, ed. Madison, Wisc.: University of Wisconsin Press, 1993, 116–37.

———. *Kurdish Ethnonationalism.* Boulder, Colo.: Lynne Rienner, 1992.

———. "The Downfall of a Client: The United States and the Shah of Iran." *Journal of Third World Studies*, vol. 8 (Fall 1991): 324–32.

———. "Dilemmas of Revolutionary Participation in Revolutionary Iran." *Journal of South Asian and Middle Eastern Studies*, vol. 12 (Summer 1989): 75–90.

———. "Criminal Law and the Legal System in Revolutionary Iran." *Boston College Third World Law Journal*, vol. 8 (Winter 1988): 92–102.

———. "Superpowers and Persian Gulf Security: The Iranian Perspective." *Third World Quarterly*, vol. 10 (October 1988): 1427–51.

———. "Educational Reforms in Iran: Cultural Revolution or Anti-Intellectualism?" *Journal of South Asian and Middle Eastern Studies*, vol. 8 (Fall 1984): 47–63.

———. "The Kurds in Post-Revolutionary Iran and Iraq." *Third World Quarterly*, vol. 6 (October 1984): 341–58.

———. "External Involvement in the Persian Gulf Conflict." *Conflict Quarterly*, vol. 4 (Fall 1984): 41–45.

———. "Changing Pattern of Iranian-Arab Relations." *Journal of Social, Political and Economic Studies*, vol. 9 (Fall 1984): 341–358.

Esposito, John L., ed. *The Iranian Revolution: Its Global Impact.* Miami, Fla.: International University Press, 1990.

Farazmand, Ali. "Bureaucracy, Development, and Regime-Politics: The Case of Iran." *International Journal of Public Administration*, vol. 12 (January 1989): 79–111.

Farsoun, Samih K., and Mehrdad Mashayekhi, eds. *Iran: Political Culture in the Islamic Republic.* London: Routledge, 1993.

Fathi, Asghar, ed. *Iranian Refugees and Exiles Since Khomeini.* Costa Mesa, Calif.: Mazda Publishers, 1991.

Fathi, Farideh. *States and Urban-Based Revolutions: Iran and Nicaragua.* Urbana, Ill.: University of Illinois Press, 1990.

Foran, John. *Fragile Resistance: Social Transformation in Iran from 1500 to the Revolution.* Boulder, Colo.: Westview Press, 1993.

Forum on American-Iranian Relations. "Iranian Rearmament: Myth or Reality?" FAIR Foundation Policy Paper, April 1993.

Forum on American-Iranian Relations. "The Evolution of Clinton's Policy Towards Iran." FAIR Foundation Policy Paper, September 1993.

Frank, Lawerce P. "Two Responses To The Oil Boom: Iranian And Nigerian Politics After 1973." *Comparative Politics*, vol. 16 (April 1984): 295–314.

Fuller, Graham E. *The Center of the Universe: The Geopolitics of Iran.* Boulder, Colo.: Westview Press, 1991.

Gasiorowski, Mark J. *U.S. Foreign Policy and the Shah: Building a Client State in Iran.* Ithaca, N.Y.: Cornell University Press, 1991.

———. "The 1953 Coup d'etat In Iran." *International Journal of Middle East Studies*, vol. 19 (August 1987): 261–86.

Ghasimi, M. R. "The Iranian Economy After the Revolution: An Economic Appraisal of the Five-year Plan." *International Journal of Middle East Studies*, vol. 24 (November 1992): 599–614.

Ghods, M. Reza. *Iran in the Twentieth Century: A Political History*. Boulder, Colo.: Lynne Rienner, 1989.

Gillespie, Kate. "U.S. Corporations and Iran at the Hague." *Middle East Journal*, vol. 44 (Winter 1990): 18–36.

Graham, Robert. *Iran: The Illusion of Power*. New York: St. Martin's Press, 1980.

Green, Jerrold D. "Countermobilization As a Revolutionary Form." *Comparative Politics*, vol. 16 (January 1984): 153–69.

Grummon, Stephen R. *The Iran-Iraq War: Islam Embattled*. Washington, D.C.: Center for Strategic and International Studies, Georgetown University; New York: Praeger, 1982.

Halliday, Fred. "West Is West But East Is East." *New Statesman and Society*, vol. 4 (November 29, 1991): 16–17.

———. *Iran: Dictatorship and Development*. New York: Penguin Books, 1979.

Harney, Desmond. "The Iranian Revolution Ten Years On." *Asian Affairs*, vol. 20 (June 1989): 153–64.

Hashmi, Zia H. "The Dynamics of Contemporary Regional Integration: The Growth of Regionalism among Iran, Pakistan, and Turkey." Ph.D diss., University of South Carolina, 1970.

Hickman, William F. *Ravaged and Reborn: The Iranian Army*. Washington, D.C.: Brookings Institution, 1982.

Hiro, Dilip. *The Longest War: The Iran-Iraq Military Conflict*. London: Routledge, 1991.

———. *Iran Under the Ayatollahs*. London: Routledge, 1985.

Holloway, Nigel, and Mark Clifford. "The Profits of Peace: Japan and South Korea See Business Gains in War's End." *Far Eastern Economic Review*, vol. 141 (September 8, 1988): 36–37.

Hooglund, Eric J. "Iranian Populism and Political Change in the Gulf." *Middle East Report*, vol. 22 (January–February 1992): 19–21.

———. *Land and Revolution in Iran, 1960–1980*. Austin, Tex.: University of Texas Press, 1982.

Hunter, Shireen T. *Iran after Khomeini*. New York: Praeger Publishers, 1992.

———. *Iran and the World: Continuity in a Revolutionary Decade*. Bloomington, Ind.: Indiana University Press, 1990.

———. "Post-Khomeini Iran." *Foreign Affairs*, vol. 68 (Winter 1989–1990): 133–49.

———. "After the Ayatollah." *Foreign Policy*, vol. 66 (Spring 1987): 77–97.

Huyser, Gen. Robert E. *Mission to Tehran*. New York: Harper and Row, 1986.

Irfani, Suroosh. *Revolutionary Islam in Iran: Popular Liberation or Religious Dictatorship?* London: Zed Press, 1983.

Izady, Mehrdad R. *The Kurds: A Concise Handbook*. Washington, D.C.: Crane Russak, 1992.

Joyner, Christopher C. *The Persian Gulf War: Lessons for Strategy, Law And Diplomacy*. New York: Greenwood Press, 1990.

Kamrava, Mehran. *The Political History of Modern Iran: From Tribalism to Theocracy.* New York: Praeger Publishers, 1992.

———. *Revolution in Iran: The Roots of Turmoil.* London: Routledge, 1990.

Karimi-Hakkak, Ahmad. "Revolution Posturing: Iranian Writers And The Iranian Revolution of 1979." *International Journal of Middle East Studies,* vol. 23 (November 1991): 507–31.

Karshenas, Massoud. *Oil, State and Industrialization in Iran.* New York: Cambridge University Press, 1990.

Katouzian, Homa. *Musaddiq and the Struggle for Power in Iran.* London: I. B. Tauris, 1991.

———. "The Political Economy of Iran Since The Revolution: A Macro-historical Analysis." *Comparative Economic Studies,* vol. 31 (Fall 1989): 55–66.

———. *The Political Economy of Modern Iran: Despotism and Pseudo-Modernism 1926–1979.* New York: New York University Press, 1981.

Katzman, Kenneth. *The Warriors of Islam: Iran's Revolutionary Guard.* Boulder, Colo.: Westview Press, 1993.

Kazemi, Farhad. *Poverty and Revolution in Iran.* New York: New York University Press, 1980.

Keddie, Nikki R. *Neither East nor West: Iran, the Soviet Union, and the United States.* New Haven, Conn.: Yale University Press, 1990.

———. *Religion and Politics in Iran: Shi'ism from Quietism to Revolution.* New Haven, Conn.: Yale University Press, 1983.

———. *Roots of Revolution: An Interpretive History of Modern Iran.* New Haven, Conn.: Yale University Press, 1981.

Kelly, Ron, Jonathan Friedlander, and Anita Colby, eds. *Irangeles: Iranians in Los Angeles.* Berkeley, Calif.: University of California Press, 1993.

Kennedy, Charles R. "Multinational Corporations And Political Risk in the Persian Gulf." *International Journal of Middle East Studies,* vol. 16 (August 1984): 391–403.

Khan, Mohsin S., and Abbas Mirakhor. "Islamic Banking: Experiences In The Islamic Republic of Iran and in Pakistan." *Economic Development and Cultural Change,* vol. 38 (January 1990): 353–75.

Khavari, Ali. "Those Who Find Peace Deadlier Than Poison." *World Marxist Review,* vol. 31 (October 1988): 11–16.

Khomeini, Ruhollah. *Islam and Revolution: Writings and Declarations of Imam Khomeini.* Berkeley, Calif.: Mizan Press, 1981.

Kianuri, Nureddish. "The Arduous Path Of The Iranian Revolution." *World Marxist Review,* vol. 26 (March 1983): 30–36.

L'Estrange Fawcett, Louise. *Iran and the Cold War: The Azerbaijan Crisis of 1946.* New York: Cambridge University Press, 1992.

Ladjevardi, Habib. *Labor Unions and Autocracy in Iran.* Syracuse, N.Y.: Syracuse University Press, 1985.

———. "The Origins of U.S. Support for an Autocratic Iran." *International Journal Of Middle East Studies,* vol. 15 (May 1983): 225–39.

Limbert, John W. *Iran: At War with History.* Boulder, Colo.: Westview Press, 1987.

Loeffler, Reinhold. *Islam in Practice: Religious Beliefs in a Persian Village*. Albany, N.Y.: State University of New York Press, 1988.

Looney, Robert E. "Human Capital Development in the Analysis of Budgetary Conflicts in an Era of Relative Austerity." *Public Budgeting and Financial Management* (1993): 573–96.

———. "Government Planning in a Small Oil Economy: Factors Limiting Industrial Diversification Efforts of Qatar." *Industry and Development*, vol. 32 (1993).

———. "Budgetary Priorities in a Crisis State: Shifts in Iranian Government Allocations." *Crossroads*, vol. 32 (1992): 68–75.

———. "Guns Versus Butter in the Middle East: Paradoxes Surrounding the Economic Impact of Defense Expenditures." *Japanese Journal of Middle Eastern Studies (Jime)*, no. 15 (1992): 57–73.

———. "Factors Affecting Employment in the Arabian Gulf Region, 1975-85." *International Journal of Social Economics* (1992): 43–59.

———. "War, Revolution, and the Maintenance of Human Capital: An Analysis of Iranian Budgetary Priorities." *Journal of South Asian and Middle Eastern Studies* (Fall 1991): 1–17.

———. "Patterns of Economic Divergence in the Middle East: The Case of Labor Importers and Exporters." *Scandinavian Journal of Development Alternatives* (1991): 207–31.

———. "Mobilizing Human Resources in the Gulf States: Key Issues for the 1990's." *Fururics* (1990): 2–5.

———. "The Role of Military Expenditures in Pre-Revolutionary Iran's Economic Decline." *Iranian Studies* (1988): 52–83.

———. "The Iranian Economy in the 1970s: Examination of the Nugent Thesis." *Middle Eastern Studies* (October 1988): 490–94.

———. "Origins of Pre-Revolutionary Iranian Economic Cycles and Policy Response." *Middle Eastern Studies* (January 1987): 83–94.

———. "Origins of Pre-Revolutionary Iran's Development Strategy." *Middle Eastern Studies*, vol. 22 (January 1986): 104–19.

———. "The Impact of Oil Revenues on the Pre-Revolutionary Iranian Economy." *Middle Eastern Studies*, vol. 21 (January 1985): 61–71.

———. *Economic Origins of the Iranian Revolution*. New York: Pergamon, 1982.

McDaniel, Tim. *Autocracy, Modernization, and Revolution in Russia and Iran*. Princeton, N.J.: Princeton University Press, 1991.

Mcfarland, Stephen L. "Anatomy of an Iranian Political Crowd: The Tehran Bread Riot of Dec. 1942." *International Journal of Middle East Studies*, vol. 17 (February 1985): 51–65.

Mackinnon, Colin. "Financing Trade With Iran: How the Deals Work." *Middle East Executive Reports*, vol. 15 (May 1992): 9–11.

Mahar, Maggie. "Santa Satan?: A More Pragmatic Iran May Gradually Change its View of the U.S." *Barron's*, vol. 69 (January 16, 1989): 10–11, 17–21.

Maleka, M. H. "The Impact of Iran's Islamic Revolution on Health Personal Policy." *World Development*, vol. 19 (August 1991): 1045–54.

———. "Capitalism in 19th-Century Iran." *Middle Eastern Studies*, vol. 27 (January 1991): 67–78.

———. "Elite Factionalism in the Post-Revolutionary Iran." *Journal of Contemporary Asia*, vol. 19 (1989): 435–60.

Mangan, David. "Downstream Investment: Major Threat to OPEC." *Middle East Executive Reports*, vol. 12 (January 1989): 11, 22–25.

Marr, Phoebe. "Iraq in The 90s: Its Role in Regional Politics." *Middle East Executive Reports*, vol. 13 (July 1990): 9, 14–17.

Martin, Josh. "Trade Beckons in the Middle East Bazaar." *International Business*, vol. 5 (June 1992): 54–63.

Mayer, Ann Elizabeth. *Islam and Human Rights: Tradition and Politics*. Boulder, Colo.: Westview Press, 1991.

Menashari, David. *Education and the Making of Modern Iran*. Ithaca, N.Y.: Cornell University Press, 1992.

———. *Iran: A Decade of War and Revolution*. New York: Holmes & Meier, 1990.

———, ed. *The Iranian Revolution and the Muslim World*. Boulder, Colo.: Westview Press, 1990.

Metz, Helen Chapin. *Iran: A Country Study*. Washington, D.C.: Headquarters, Dept. of the Army, 1989.

Meyer-reumann, Rolf. "United Arab Emirates: Jebel Ali Free Zone." *Middle East Executive Reports*, vol. 14 (October 1991): 21–24.

Middle East Watch. *Guardians of Thought: Limits on Freedom of Expression in Iran*. New York: Human Rights Watch, 1993.

Milani, Mohsen M. "Harvest of Shame: Tudeh and the Bazargan Government." *Middle Eastern Studies*, vol. 29 (April 1993): 307–29.

———. *From Rebellion to Revolution: The Politics of Social Change in Modern Iran*. Boulder, Colo.: Westview Press, 1988.

———. *The Making of Iran's Islamic Revolution: from Monarchy to Islamic Republic*. Boulder, Colo.: Westview Press, 1988.

Ming He. "Chronology of The Iran-Iraq War." *Beijing Review*, vol. 31 (September 5, 1988): 14.

Moaddel, Mansoor. *Class, Politics, and Ideology in the Iranian Revolution*. New York: Columbia University Press, 1992.

———. "Ideology as Episodic Discourse: The Case of the Iranian Revolution." *American Sociological Review*, vol. 57 (June 1992): 353–79.

———. "Class Struggle in Post-Revolutionary Iran." *International Journal Of Middle East Studies*, vol. 23 (August 1991): 317–43.

Moens, Alexander. "President Carter's Advisers and The Fall of the Shah." *Political Science Quarterly*, vol. 106 (Summer 1991): 211–37.

Mofid, Kamran. *The Economic Consequences of the Gulf War*. New York: Routledge, 1990.

Moghadam, Fatemeh E. "An Historical Interpretation of the Iranian Revolution." *Cambridge Journal of Economics*, vol. 12 (December 1988): 401–18.

Moghadam, Valentine. *Modernizing Women: Gender and Social Change in the Middle East*. Boulder, Colo.: Lynne Rienner, 1993.

Mottahedeh, Roy. *The Mantle of the Prophet: Religion and Politics in Iran.* New York: Simon & Schuster, 1985.

Motter, Thomas, and Hubbard Vail. *The Persian Corridor and Aid to Russia.* Washington, D.C.. Office of the Chief of Military History,

Mukerjee, Dilip. "The Gulf War Lesson: Most Third World Conflicts Have Become Unwinnable." *Far Eastern Economic Review,* vol. 141 (September 8, 1988): 38.

Nahas, Maridi. "State-Systems and Revolutionary Challenge: Nasser, Khomeini, and The Middle East." *International Journal of Middle East Studies,* vol. 17 (November 1985): 507–27.

Najmabadi, Afsaneh. *Land Reform and Social Change in Iran.* Salt Lake City, Utah: University of Utah Press, 1987.

Nasri, Fareen. "Iranian Studies and the Iranian Revolution." *World Politics,* vol. 35 (July 1983): 607–30.

Navabpour, Reza. *Iran.* Oxford: Clio Press, 1988.

Nazmi, Nader. "Economic Growth and Underdevelopment in Iran: 1951–78." *Comparative Economic Studies,* vol. 31 (Fall 1989): 33–54.

Orme, John. "Dismounting The Tiger: Lessons From Four Liberalizations." *Political Science Quarterly,* vol. 103 (Summer 1988): 245–65.

Ostock, Frances. " Oil, State and Industrialization in Iran." *Business History Review,* vol. 66 (Spring 1992): 244–45.

Pahlavi, Mohammad Reza. *Answer to History.* New York: Stein and Day, 1980.

Parsa, Misagh. *Social Origins of the Iranian Revolution.* New Brunswick, N.J.: Rutgers University Press, 1989.

Parsons, Anthony. *The Price and the Fall: Iran 1974–1979.* London: Jonathan Cape, 1984.

Parvin, Manoucher, and Ruzbeh Parvin. "Intellectuals, the State, Morality and Economics: A Fuzzy Discourse." *Critique* (Spring 1993): 64–78.

Parvin, Manoucher, and Mostafa Vazuru. "Shi'ism and the State in the Constitution of the Islamic Republic of Iran." In *Iran: Political Culture in the Islamic Republic,* Samih K. Farsoun and Mehrdad Mashayekhi, eds. London and New York: Routledge, 1992, 116–32.

Parvin, Manoucher, and Hashem Dezbakhsh. "Trade, Technology Transfer, and Hyper-Dutch Disease in OPEC: Theory and Evidence." *International Journal of Middle East Studies* (August 1988): 469–77.

Parvin, Manoucher, and Majid Taghavi. "A Comparison of Land Tenure in Iran Under Monarchy and the Islamic Republic." In *Post Revolutionary Iran,* Manoucher Parvin and Hooshang Amirahmadi, eds. Boulder, Colo.: Westview Press, 1988, 168–182.

Parvin, Manoucher, and M. Sommer. "'Dar Al-Islam': The Evolution of Muslim Territoriality and its Implication for Conflict Resolution in the Middle East." *International Journal of Middle East Studies* (February 1980): 1–21.

Parvin, Manoucher. "On the Synergism of Gender and Class Exploitation Theory and Practice Under Islamic Rule." *Review of Social Economy,* vol. 11 (Summer 1993): 201–16.

———. "The Political Economy of Divine Unity: A Critique of Islamic Theory and Practice." In *The Economic Dimensions of Middle Eastern History: Essays in Honor of Charles Issawi.* Pennington, N.J.: Darwin Press, 1990: 215–37.

————. "Islamic Rule, Economics, Woman and Man: An Overview of Ideology and Reality." *Comparative Economic Studies* (Fall 1989): 85–102.

Parvin, M. "Political Economy of Soviet-Iranian Trade: An Overview of Theory and Practice." *The Middle East Journal,* vol. 31, no. 1 (Winter 1977): 31–43.

————. "Economic Development with a Modicum of Fossil Fuel and Foreign Exchange Resources." *The Journal of Energy and Development.* vol. 8, no. 1 (August 1982): 127–45.

Parvin, M., and Amir N. Zamani. "Political Economy of Growth and Destruction: A Statistical Interpretation of the Iranian Case." *Iranian Studies.* vol. 7, nos. 1–2 (Winter 1979): 43–47.

Pelletiere, Stephen C. *The Iran-Iraq War: Chaos in a Vacuum.* New York: Praeger Publishers, 1992.

Pesaran, M. H. "The System Of Dependent Capitalism In Pre- And Post-revolutionary Iran." *International Journal of Middle East Studies,* vol. 14 (November 1982): 501–22.

Pipes, Daniel, and Patrick Clawson. "Ambitious Iran, Troubled Neighbors." *Foreign Affairs,* vol. 72 (1993): 124–41.

Poya, Maryam. "Iran: Background to the Gulf War." *Capital and Class,* vol. 33 (Winter 1987): 21–27.

Prasad, K. N., A. A. Banouei, and A. M. Swaminathan. "Weather-induced Instability In Agricultural Produce with Respect to Buffer Stocks in India and Iran: An Integrated Optimization and Dynamic Input-output Model." *International Journal of Production Economics,* vol. 26 (February 1992): 89–97.

Precht, Henry. "Ayatollah Realpolitik." *Foreign Policy,* vol. 70 (Spring 1988): 109–28.

Rahnema, Ali, and Farhad Nomani. *The Secular Miracle: Religion and Politics in Iran.* London: Zed Books, 1991.

Rajaee, Farhand, ed. *The Iran-Iraq War: The Politics of Aggression.* Gainesville, Fla.. University Press of Florida, 1933.

Ram, Haggay. "Islamic 'Newspeak': Language and Change in Revolutionary Iran." *Middle Eastern Studies,* vol. 29 (April 1993): 198–219.

————. "Crushing the Opposition: Adversaries of the Islamic Republic of Iran." *Middle East Journal,* vol. 46 (Summer 1992): 426–39.

Ramazani, Nesta. "Women in Iran: The Revolutionary Ebb and Flow." *Middle East Journal,* vol. 47 (Summer 1993): 409–28.

Ramazani, R. K. "Iran's Foreign Policy: Both North and South." *Middle East Journal,* vol. 46 (Summer 1992): 393–412

————, ed. *Iran's Revolution: The Search for Consensus.* Bloomington, Ind.: Indiana University Press, 1990.

————. "Iran's Foreign Policy: Contending Orientations." *The Middle East Journal,* vol. 43 (Spring 1989): 202–17.

————. *Revolutionary Iran: Challenge and Response in the Middle East.* Baltimore, Md.: Johns Hopkins University Press, 1986.

————. "Iran: Burying The Hatchet." *Foreign Policy,* vol. 60 (Fall 1985): 52–74.

————. *The United States and Iran: The Patterns of Influence.* New York: Praeger Publishers, 1982.

Ramin, Taghi. "A Regression Analysis of Migration to Urban Areas of a Less-developed Country: The Case of Iran." *American Economist,* vol. 32 (Fall 1988): 26–34.

Rashid, Ahmed. "Central Asia: Point of Conflict." *Far Eastern Economic Review,* vol. 156 (June 3, 1993): 24–25.

———. "Central Asia: Linking Up for Trade." *Far Eastern Economic Review,* vol. 156 (February 25, 1993): 19–20.

Razi, G. Hossein. "An Alternative Paradigm to State Rationality in Foreign Policy: The Iran-Iraq War." *The Western Political Quarterly,* vol. 41 (December 1988): 689–723.

———. "The Nexus of Legitimacy and Performance: The Lessons of the Iranian Revolution." *Comparative Politics,* vol. 19 (July 1987): 453–69.

Reed, Stanley, and Sarah Gauch. "Could Egypt Be The Next Iran?" *Business Week* (July 12, 1993): 48–50.

Refsanjani, Hashemi, and Jubin Goodarzi. "Address by Ali Hashemi-Rafsanjani, President of the Islamic Republic of Iran." *The Middle East Journal,* vol. 44 (Summer 1990): 459–66.

Rejali, Darius M. *Torture and Modernity: Self, Society, and State in Modern Iran.* Boulder, Colo.: Lynne Reinner, 1993.

Rezun, Miron. "Iran and Afghanistan; With Specific Reference to Their Asian Policies and Practices." *Journal of Asian and African Studies,* vol. 25 (January–April 1990): 9–26.

Rezun, Miron, ed. *Iran at the Crossroads: Global Relations in a Turbulent Decade.* Boulder, Colo.: Westview Press, 1990.

Riesebrodt, Martin. *Pious Passion: The Emergence of Modern Fundamentalism in the United States and Iran,* Don Reneau, trans. Berkeley, Calif.: University of California Press, 1993.

Roosevelt, Kermit. *Countercoup: The Struggle for the Control of Iran.* New York: McGraw-Hill, 1979.

Roshandel, Jalil, and Saideh Lotfian. "Horizontal Nuclear Proliferation: Is Iran a Nuclear-Capable State?" *Iranian Journal of International Affairs,* vol. 5 (Spring 1993): 208–28.

Rubin, Barry M. *Paved with Good Intentions: The American Experience and Iran.* New York: Oxford University Press, 1980.

Saikal, Amin. *The Rise and Fall of the Shah.* Princeton, N.J.: Princeton University Press, 1980.

Salehi-Isfahani, Djavad. "Population Pressure, Intensification of Agriculture, and Rural-urban Migration." *Journal of Development Economics,* vol. 40 (April 1993): 371–84.

Salinger, Pierre. *American Held Hostage: The Secret Negotiations.* Garden City, N.Y.: Doubleday, 1981.

Samii, Kuross A. *Involvement by Invitation: American Strategies of Containment in Iran.* University Park, Penn.: Pennsylvania State University Press, 1987.

Sanchez, James. *Index to Iran-Contra Hearings Summary Report.* Jefferson, N.C.: McFarland, 1988.

Sareen, Rajendra. "Picking Up the Pieces: War-ravaged Iran Moves to Rebuild Foreign Economic and Political Ties." *Far Eastern Economic Review,* vol. 141 (September 8, 1988): 35–36.

———. "Pragmatists and Radicals: Factions Among the Clergy Fight for Supremacy after Cease-fire." *Far Eastern Economic Review,* vol. 141 (September 8, 1988): 36–37.

Saunders, Harold. "Iran: A View From The State Department." *World Affairs,* vol. 149 (Spring 1987): 219–23.

Scoville, James G. "The Labor Market in Pre-Revolutionary Iran." *Economic Development and Cultural Change,* vol. 34 (October 1985): 143–55.

Sharabatoghlie, Ahmad. *Urbanization and Regional Disparities in Post-Revolutionary Iran.* Boulder, Colo.: Westview Press, 1991.

Shipman, Alan. "Turkmenistan: Oil And Gas Exports Earn 'Best Risk' Rating." *International Management,* vol. 48 (July–August 1993): 13–14.

Siavoshi, Sussan. *Liberal Nationalism in Iran: The Failure of a Movement.* Boulder, Colo.: Westview Press, 1990.

Sick, Gary. "Iran's Quest for Superpower Status." *Foreign Affairs,* vol. 65 (Spring 1987): 697–715.

———. "Iran: A View from the White House." *World Affairs,* vol. 149 (Spring 1987): 209–13.

———. *All Fall Down: America's Tragic Encounter with Iran.* New York: Random House, 1985.

Sobhani, Sohrab. *The Pragmatic Entente: Israeli-Iranian Relations, 1948–1988.* New York: Praeger Publishers, 1989.

Stork, Joe. "October Reprise: A Critical Review of the 'October Surprise' Scenario and Its Critics." *The Middle East Journal,* vol. 47 (Summer 1993): 509–17.

Swearingen, Willd. "Geopolitical Origins of the Iran-Iraq War." *The Geographical Review,* vol. 78 (October 1988): 405–16.

Tabarestani, Cirus. "Fundamental Contradictions of the Islamic Republic of Iran: An Iranian View." *Capital & Class,* no. 49 (Spring 1993): 19–35.

Taheri, Amir. *Nest of Spies: America's Journey to Disaster in Iran.* New York: Pantheon Books, 1989.

Thuermer, Karen E. "Iran: Yesterday's Enemy, Tomorrow's Customer?" *Global Trade,* vol. 112 (February 1992): 19–20.

Timewell, Stephen. "Iran: Waking up from a Nightmare." *Banker,* vol. 143 (September 1993): 43–45.

———. "Iran: Back To The Future." *Banker,* vol. 142 (February 1992): 24–27.

———. "Iran: Forging A New Revolution." *Banker,* vol. 141 (February 1991): 33, 35.

Tippee, Bob. "Iran Rebuilding Petroleum Industry, Output Capacity." *Oil and Gas Journal,* vol. 89 (December 2, 1991): 45–48.

United States Congress. *IRANSCAM: The Official Senate Intelligence Committee Report on the Iran Arms Sale.* DIANA Pub. Co., 1987.

United States Congress House Select Committee to Investigate Covert Arms Transactions with Iran. *Report of the Congressional Committees Investigating the Iran-Contra Affairs: With Supplemental, Minority, and Additional Views.* Washington, D.C.: U.S. Government Printing Office, 1987.

United States Joint Economic Committee. *Economic Consequences of the Revolution in Iran: A Compendium of Papers.* Washington, D.C.: U.S. Government Printing Office, 1980.

United States President's Special Review Board. *Report of the President's Special Review Board.* Washington, D.C.: U.S. Government Printing Office, 1987.

United States President's Special Review Board. *The Tower Commission Report: The Full Text of the President's Special Review Board.* New York: Bantam Books, 1987.

Valibeigi, Mehrdad. "Islamic Economics and Economy Policy Formation In Post-revolutionary Iran: A Critique." *Journal of Economic Issues,* vol. 27 (September 1993): 793–812.

Vaziri, Mostafa. *Iran as Imagined Nation: The Construction of National Identity.* New York: Paragon House, 1993.

Vreeland, Herbert Harold. *Iran.* New Haven, Conn.: Human Relations Area Files, 1957.

Weiner, Myron, and Ali Banuazzi, eds. *The Politics of Social Transformations in Afghanistan, Iran, and Pakistan.* Syracuse, N.Y.: Syracuse University Press, 1993.

Wright, Robin. *In the Name of God: The Khomeini Decade.* New York: Simon and Schuster, 1989.

Yar-Shater, Ehsan. *Encyclopedia Iranica.* Boston, Mass.: Routledge & Kegan Paul, 1985.

Yodfat, Ariyeh Y. *The Soviet Union and the Iranian Revolution.* New York: St. Martin's Press, 1983.

Yousefi, Mahmood. "Dimensions of the Iranian Revolution: A Review Essay." *The Western Political Quarterly,* vol. 37 (June 1984): 343–52.

Zabih, Sepher. *The Iranian Military in War and Revolution.* London: Routledge, 1988.

———. *Iran Since the Revolution.* Baltimore, Md.: Johns Hopkins University Press, 1982.

———. *The Communist Movement in Iran.* Berkeley, Calif.: University of California Press, 1966.

———. *The Left in Contemporary Iran.* London: Croom Helm, 1986.

Zangeneh, Hamid. "Islamic Republic of Iran and International Trade." *Mehregan,* Summer 1994, forthcoming (in Persian).

———. "Conditions for Economic Growth and Development in Iran" (in Persian). *Mehregan* (September 1992).

———. "Third World Debt and Oil Prices." In *Oil in 1980s: A Decade of Decline,* Siamack Shojai and Bernard Katz, eds. New York: Praeger Publishers, 1992, 153–60.

———. "Islamic Banking: Theory and Practice in Iran." *Comparative Economic Studies,* vol. 31 (Fall 1989): 67–84.

Zangeneh, Hamid, and Cyrus Bina, eds. *Modern Capitalism and Islamic Ideology in Iran.* New York: St. Martin's Press, 1992.

Zangeneh, Hamid, and Bernard Reilly. "Islamic Economic Value System and Other Optimal Economic Systems: A Critical Comparative Analysis." *International Journal of Social Economy,* vol. 17, no. 11 (November 1990): 21–35.

Zangeneh, Hamid, and Ahmad Salam. "Central Banking in an Interest Free Banking System." *Journal of Research in Islamic Economics, Center for Research in Islamic Economics,* King Abulaziz University, forthcoming.

———. "Analytical Model of Islamic Banking Firm." In *Modern Capitalism and Islamic Ideology in Iran,* Cyrus Bina and Hamid Zangeneh, eds. New York: St. Martin's Press, 1992.

Zirinsky, Michael P. "Blood, Power, and Hypocrisy: The Murder of Robert Imbrie and American Relations with Pahlavi Iran." *International Journal Of Middle East Studies*, vol. 18 (August 1986): 275–92.

Zonis, Marvin. *Majestic Failure: The Fall of the Shah*. Chicago, Ill.: University of Chicago Press, 1991.

———. "Iran: A Theory of Revolution from Accounts of the Revolution." *World Politics*, vol. 35 (July 1983): 586–606.

INDEX

A

B

R

Rafsanjani, Ali Akbar Hashemi 7, 54, 125, 127, 135, 139, 141, 143-144, 150, 152, 160-161, 169, 176, 178, 181, 211
Ravenal, Earl 156
Reagan, Ronald 48, 80, 146
Revolutionary Council 168, 170-171
Revolutionary Guard 141, 159
Rida, Rashid 49
Romania 31
Rosenfeld, Stephen 90
al-Rubaie, M. 152
Rushdie, Salman 88, 117
Russia 99-100, 120, 147
Russian Revolution 41

S

Sanders, Jerry 16
Saudi Arabia 15, 25, 56-57, 61, 81, 83-85, 88, 100, 103-104, 113, 117, 120, 126, 128, 157
    1987 Hajj massacre 102-103, 122
    anti-Iranian policies 106, 116, 155
    arms buildup 6, 32, 106, 108-109, 126, 154, 156
    role in Iraqi revolts 153
SAVAK 203-204
Shabib, Talib 153
Shah, the (Shah Mohammed Reza Pahlavi) 49, 89, 171-172, 196
    policies of 9, 52, 98-99, 104, 106, 111-112, 202-203, 212
Shari'at-Madari, Seyyed Kazem 51
Shari'ati, Ali 49
Shatt al-Arab dispute 103, 149
Shiism 102, 104, 127, 152, 182-183
Singapore 31, 34, 84
Slovakia 31
Somalia 18, 90, 137
South Korea 26, 31, 34, 84, 116, 214
Soviet Union 2, 18-26, 34-35, 46, 81, 98-99, 136, 214
    dissolution of 3, 5, 8, 13-14, 29, 31, 41-42, 46-48, 76, 85, 113, 135, 158
    foreign policy under Gorbachev 24-26
    successor states 82, 175
    weapons sales 32-33, 154, 161
Stalin, Josef 13, 20-21
State-owned Economic Enterprises (SEE) 10, 188-196
Sudan 55-56, 62, 90, 113
Sunnism 102
Supreme Assembly of the Islamic Revolution in Iraq 152
Syria 87, 109, 123, 150, 157-158

T